Expressive
Details

Expressive Details

Materials, Selection, Use

DUO DICKINSON

McGraw-Hill

New York   San Francisco   Washington, D.C.   Auckland   Bogotá
Caracas   Lisbon   London   Madrid   Mexico City   Milan
Montreal   New Delhi   San Juan   Singapore
Sydney   Tokyo   Toronto

Library of Congress Cataloging-in-Publication Data

Dickinson, Duo.
    Expressive details : materials, selection, use / Duo Dickinson.
        p.   cm.
    Includes index.
    ISBN 0-07-016833-4 (hardcover)
    1. Architecture—Details.   2. Building materials.   I. Title.
NA2840.D53   1996
721—dc20   96-12959
                                                          CIP

McGraw-Hill

A Division of The **McGraw·Hill** *Companies*

1 2 3 4 5 6 7 8 9 0   KGP/KGP   9 0 1 0 9 8 7 6

ISBN 0-07-016833-4

The sponsoring editor for this book was Wendy Lochner, the editing
supervisor was Paul R. Sobel, and the production supervisor
was Donald F. Schmidt. Preliminary layout by Duo Dickinson.
Design and composition by Silvers Design.

Printed and bound by Quebecor/Kingsport Press.

McGraw-Hill books are available at special quantity discounts to use as premiums
and sales promotions, or for use in corporate training programs. For more information,
please write to the Director of Special Sales, McGraw-Hill, 11 West 19th Street,
New York, NY 10011. Or contact your local bookstore.

This book is printed on acid-free paper.

To Louis Mackall, the finest craftsman I know
and the father of my choice of craft

CONTENTS

Movement

Millwork/Minutiae

Systems/Mechanical

PREFACE

This book is the fifth in a series of books I have written about aspects of residential architecture. Although not all the details in this book come from single family residences, almost all the scale and spirit represented is definitively personal and often overtly domestic in sensibility. It can be said that the act of creating architecture is the material manifestation of our hearts and minds. Not unlike many of the details depicted, this book is itself the product of a long process and had its final form shaped by the experience of gathering all the data depicted.

Selection Methodology and Criteria

Over a period of three years, three separate mailings were sent out to all state and local chapters of the American Institute of Architects and all accredited schools of architecture throughout the United States. Secondarily, having written four books over the last decade about architecture, I have a long list of contributors to those previous books, and thus well over one hundred individual architects received personalized solicitation for detail work. Lastly, the last five years of every professional and popular American magazine focusing on architectural design was reviewed to discover new professionals to solicit work from

The results of this multi-year/multi source search were mixed. Despite the fact that I tried to make it clear that the details in question were to be impressively innovative and *expressive*, many of the hundreds of details I received were inappropriate for two reasons.

A large number of submitted details were simply "invisible." Seemlessly unseen, these details revelled in the fact that "ignorance is bliss" when it comes to expressing how materials connect with each other when they are assembled. Most of these details could be categorized as having a Modernist aesthetic—conspiring to make monolithic materiality out of a multiplicity of parts. But that is also the rule for almost all spec built light frame wood "traditional" homes built in America today. Given the fact that the bias of this book is that, where possible, detailing should be *expressive*, and not disingenuous, such details were rejected out of hand. The problematic aspect of gloss-over detailing is that over time, almost all such detailing has a propensity to evidence its inherent dishonesty. Materials have different expansion coefficients, they accept or reject water to varying degrees, some materials propagate organic or biological infestations while others preempt them, and oxidation and galvanic action are always waiting patiently to undo the best laid plans an architect can come up with. Rather than age gracefully, most of these examples are inevitably fated to lose their battle with the elements and time far more rapidly than those who *express* both materiality and *use* the knowledge of weatherability as a design criteria rather than subordinated "baggage." Detailing based in denial advocates an anorectic "elegance" born of an artificial attitude of unnatural distillation.

The second group of projects that were deemed to be inappropriate for this book had to do with the polar opposite bias to the "less is more" school of thought described above. A fair number of projects were received which were simply decoration. Although ornament is one of the great under-utilized aspects of architectural design, (and one that, hopefully, is finding a modest resurgence amid the obvious failures of so many stoic attempts at transcending time, material, and native cultures), this book does not focus on the decorative arts without an *expressed* overlay of utility or craftsmanship. Thus the painterly arts, trim treatments that were artful, but without a functional or craftsmanly focus, or details where the effective use of color or material change is used solely to highlight different aesthetic possibilities were generally rejected.

There are a few examples included where the craftsmanship or techniques employed were extraordinary even though there was little or no functional overlay to the design criteria. There are also one or two projects which are relatively invisible, but accommodate an idiosyncratic condition. Even though a great many subject projects were rejected for inclusion in this book, I am sure some readers will find some areas which are underrepresented by the examples shown. Rather than select projects by their use, with every possible building component represented (6 railings, 3 light fixtures, 2 windows, etc., etc.) this book deals only with those details that evidence the most inspirational combination of art, technology, and craftsmanship to effect small scale virtuosity regardless of function. Despite some functional underrepresentations, hopefully the examples offered convey aesthetic vision and rigorous intellectual application. Although diversity was sought, there was no maximum number of acceptable projects from any given designer, so several designers (including this author) have multiple examples presented.

Cost was not a criteria for selection, so there are some details in this book which are extraordinarily expensive to execute. But many of the most successful details included in this collection represent the invigorating mindset of creative cost control via the use of standard materials or semi-pre-fabricated components that are artfully combined to solve (almost literally) nuts and bolts questions.

Presentation

Projects are, by and large, presented in two ways—photos and drawings. In the use of graphics, this book also tows a middle line, this time between an abstracted presentation of the details depicted and one that is perversely technical. Many books focusing on detailing use Swiss art pieces of ink rendering—preciously self conscious and ultimately pseudo-scientific as they strive more for graphic luster than to convey the inherent properties of the materials or the techniques of fabrication employed. While appearing to be coolly mechanistic and scientifically unbiased, these drawings are, in fact, thoroughly manipulated for graphic zest, drawn by those with little or no understanding of what's being represented (architecture students or graphic artists). Hence, these renderings can be paper thin and disingenuous communications oblivious to the latent properties of the details depicted.

Conversely, many technical journals opt to present details in such a way that they are almost opaque to the viewer—simple cross sectional views that are awkwardly labeled and often without graphic representations of materiality. This book tries to overcome both of those unfortunate rendering techniques by the presentation of the actual drawings that were used to effect the fabrication of the details depicted. Often I have found that the *way* a project is represented for construction bespeaks more about the mindset of the designer than can be seen in the finished product. A few projects had *no* drawings, they were simply worked out in the field. Others had only seminal design sketches. One project's working drawing technique was a significant criteria for inclusion.

The commentary that is provided in the book often utilizes the statements of the architects themselves as seen in the gray boxed text, as well as my own musings as to why this detail is inherently innovative or expressive—as set in the context of the knowledge I have gained in the practice of architecture over the last fifteen years as well as in the review of so many hundreds of specific approaches to detailing, and in the production of my previous books.

Thus the presentation is only coordinated by format and approach, not by graphic technique nor by rigorous cross referential analysis of the technologies employed.

As said, creating an absolutely "complete" categorical review was secondary to the presentation of the most expressive and innovative qualities of the individual details depicted. The book's organization follows a semi-hierarchial organization, which *generally* allows for bigger details to come first, smaller later. The categories of Structure, Skin, Openings, Movement, Millwork, and Systems are easy for the reader to reference, but several projects either straddled categories or seemed to have only a tentative connection to any of them. Internally, these categories have their details organized by analogous problems addressed (stair, fireplace, etc.), and then by designer.

In Gratitude

I would like to start my list of "thank yous" with Joel Stein, an editor who was both encouraging and realistic, and Wendy Lochner, who followed the book through to its publication. The copy editing by Marsha Scott, and book execution were undertaken by Silvers Design, Don Schmidt, and Paul Sobel. Four administrative assistants have been invaluable in their aid in compiling this book. Sara Gannon, Carla Lesh, Cheryl Alison, and Barbara Cook have worked long hours (often at odd times of the day and week) to see this book into reality. And, as with all my endeavors, my wife Liz and my sons, Will and Sam, are the source of my strength and, unfortunately, often bear the brunt of my overcommitment in undertaking tasks like this, and my loving thanks go out to them.

Duo Dickinson

FOREWORD
The Nature of Detail

Peter Bohlin

(All photos courtesy of the architect)

Some people say "Don't bother me with the details," or "It's only a detail," but it is the details and their myriad and wonderful possibilities that make the practice and experience of architecture so rich.

Details have the ability to speak at various levels from practical necessity to elusive reference. They can reveal and celebrate the nature of circumstance and touch subconscious sensibilities. Using both intellect and intuition, the architect selects the potent position, how to begin and end, what truths to tell and not tell, ways of doing more than one thing at once and whether to employ simple or complex means.

How we chose to reveal truths or not to reveal them is fascinating. At the Hanover Bank we cut a hole in the drywall ceiling that note only opens to a clear square skylight, but reveals the rinky dink nature of steel open web joists—we chose not to edit. The yellow edged hole is Harp-like, or is it a cloud negative?

Many details tell us of their circumstance and remind us subconsciously of other quite unrelated things. Our House in the Adirondacks has peeled white cedar columns—legs that sit on stone. They are flashed with lead that is fit into a sawn reglet and pounded to the shape of the wood, revealing the rich forms of the trunks. But—are they also socks or strange feet?

Details may exaggerate or selectively lie to reveal their circumstance. At our House in the Catoctin Mountains, columns that sit on the stone ledge have wedged feet—their weight and attachment is clear. But, of course, they have pipes hidden below that extend through the ledge to actual concrete foundations. Where columns meet wood floors they visually slip through down to unseen beams below; metal recesses separate columns from the wood floor plane. Apparent truths prevail.

Accommodation, doing this *and* that, rather than this *or* that, can make some of the most satisfying architecture. We could have positioned my parents' summer house to miss the boulder at its south corner, or we might have moved the boulder. But we carved the edge of the deck to the shape of the boulder, making both more poignant, speaking of the forest's nature and building in its midst.

Doing more than one thing at once can be resonant and moving. At Shelly Ridge the stepped brick stage is simultaneously a hearth and seating for children. Is its Aalto-like shape also a topographic model or the planes of a stream stepping down through a Pennsylvania forest?

Most details have to do with what we must do, but that doesn't mean there's just one way. Without seeming to try too hard, details can calm, comfort, titillate, amuse, mask, speak of modesty or wealth, and remind us of intimate or historic experience. Details are all around us, in our circumstance and the places we make, and I believe that being alive to their infinite possibilities is at the heart of exceptional architecture.

INTRODUCTION

Context

When the word *detail* is used, most architects cringe. For most architects, working on the details of a building is akin to spending time as a slave on a Roman galley, blindly pulling on an oar in a battle that you never see, gripped by the fear of the unknown, and attempting to survive great emotional and physical stress by flailing effort. There is a simple reason for architects' anxiety: Architecture schools, despite their best academic attempts at providing abstract knowledge of materiality and environmental forces, are simply incapable of conveying anything but generic examples of standardized detailing. The schools can teach only stock answers for problems that are inherently idiosyncratic.

Contributing to this professional blind spot are the details presented in design and theory courses, as well as those dealt with in more technical classes. Many architects who used detailing as a seminal part of their practice, such as Alvar Aalto, Greene and Greene, Louis Sullivan, and even Frank Lloyd Wright, are grossly underrepresented as underpinnings for architectural education. It is harder to teach about buildings utilizing a multiplicity of materiality and creative application of technique because you need a viable knowledge base born of experience. It is hard to teach that which you do not know. It is easy to teach that which can be abstracted to the point where it can be intellectually understood by academics and editors versus appreciated by practitioners. Too often, detailing is thought to be a means to an end allowing overarching aesthetic concepts to be effected with a minimum amount of attention to "taking care of business"—structurally, environmentally, or, in the basic moral/ethical world of affordability, either up-front or long-term. The reality is that most professors who teach architectural design, theory, or technology have engaged in only a limited amount of professional practice, and only a few have actually seen the quanity of construction over a long period that enables one to develop a second sense about how to detail buildings ways which are neither mute nor silly. In truth, it is only through a renaissance of apprenticeship that a young architect can fully engage in the sort of intimate exposure to a wide variety of materials and learn about their inherent qualities. I left Cornell University with absolutely no knowledge of anything other than the qualities of a 2 x 4 and a 10d nail. I had engaged in some masonry construction and a modest amount of finish work, but it took a nine-year association with Louis Mackall, one of the most experienced and innovative practitioners of architectural detailing we have, to give me hands-on experience in some of the most basic elements of construction.

Since my experience is rare and the academic experience almost universal, the terrorism of technological ignorance washes over the entire field of architecture, and the vast majority of practitioners simply replicate details they find in a book or attempt details that are simply impossible to execute.

Standard architect humor calls *Architectural Graphic Standards* (a compendium of tens of thousands of standardized—and thus unthinking—details) "the Bible." It is to be followed by rote via ignorantly worshipful relication. Some of the great anecdotal architectural disasters of our time have to do with architects' lack of understanding of the inherent properties of materials interreacting with natural forces and the structural implications of specific use patterns to which particular parts of buildings are subjected. In other words, many buildings of great cost and consequence ultimately fail to be useful, efficient, or cost effective because architects are often in intellectual denial when it comes to aggressively addressing the gnarly nitty gritty of detail design.

The problem with expressive and innovative detailing is that it requires a great deal of knowledge on a wide variety of fronts, many of which are simply not accessible to most architects without a career's worth of experience. So it is a very strange occurrence in the field of architecture when the least experienced practitioners (interns) are trusted with the act of detailing some of the most significant structures that are build in our culture. It was only when Ludwig Mies van der Rohe elevated the role of detail to something to be worshiped—"God is in the details"—that Modernist architects paid lip service to the potential of details to be transforming, lively, and innovative. This sound bite gained punch simply because it went against the grain of the overwhelming preconception of so many of van der Rohe's contemporaries. One might say that his idea of detailing was limited to structural abstraction, where materiality was only incidentally embraced given the limited palette of materials he utilized. Most architects engage in a fearful worshipfulness born of ignorance which pervades a profession more concerned with affectations of fine art than the rich rewards of craftsmanship. Either you take on the scary unknown, or you treat it with a mystical hands-off reverence. If you write your own rule book for success, and the rules simply don't deal with technicalities, then it is easy to ignore the reality that buildings deal with the natural world and idiosyncratic use.

In truth, the Xeroxing of a standard solution may be safer than attempting to find an untested answer to a question which perhaps should never have been asked in the first place. Faulty details are typically what cause a building to become terminally dysfunctional, and successful expressive details are often the elements that make people feel that their buildings give their lives meaning.

How often do you touch a doorknob that "feels right" in your hand? How often can you actually sense the *way* something was put together simply by the way it looks? These are relatively intangible concepts that are very hard to quantify, let alone teach.

In this context, there seem to be two types of books dealing with architectural detailing: books offering up dry distillation where exquisitely inked abstracted axonometric projections and layered cut away cross-sections stand in artful silence on a shiny cold page or books intended for the hands-on practitioner (usually builders) who may eschew artfulness to the point of having the appeal of an assembly manual for a small appliance. The unfortunate reality is that the gap between these two presentations is a metaphor for the gap that exists in the minds of most architects as they attempt to detail the projects that they have already designed on the macro level.

Focusing on the field of microdesign as if it were simply a different level of esthetic exploration is seldom, if ever, dealt with in academia or in the world of professional practice. There are two reasons for this. The first has already been stated—namely, that ignorance breeds fear and the rush to replicate "safe" details. The second is the practical difficulty that most expressive or innovative detailing usually equates to "busting the budget." Such budgetary commitment is hard to justify for elements which are often viewed as an afterthought to the overall design.

The extremes of mindless replication of standardized detailing and a "budget busting" obsession with microdesign are evidence that in architectural detailing, it is easier to put all the eggs of your aesthetic exploration in one of two baskets—either "think big" or "small is beautiful." In other books I have written about house design, I have stated that residential design is often threatening to architects simply because it introduces the scary realm of personal communication (with clients) and the acceptance of the validity of the absolute knowledge that clients have about their lifestyle. Hence, homes are often viewed as stepping stones to "more important" commissions or as opportunities to evidence preconceived notions that effectively rob the home design of the ability to mesh with its context or embrace its occupants. Architect self-interest can be seen in the "Big" vs. "Small" mind sets as well. Either an overarching aesthetic concept is executed in a way which mandates that the detailing be inarticulate, unexpressive, and often simply inappropriate, or conversely, a preconceived detail can lie dormant in an architect's mind until an avenue is found for its expression—often creating something which is excruciatingly costly, environmentally dubious, and misapplied either in terms of scale or usefulness.

It is easier for people to deal with the self-serving easy answers of prejudicial preconception. Often, the sweep and distillation of large, scaleless Modernist buildings gloss over any potential for articulate interfaces between components or the expression of subordinate parts. Alternatively, useless and frivolous decoration is often tacked onto buildings with myopic ignorance of their context. Hopefully, this book attempts to span the gap between the historically recognized importance of those who define a building's essential design approach via a tiny "parti" sketch, and the vast "underground" of disgruntled practitioners who have been forced by those who draw the "parti" sketch to focus upon the smallest scale of design as if it were the dirty work of the profession.

The best products of architectural design evidence the widest range of answered opportunities. Architectural detailing *is* one of the most undervalued opportunities present in the profession. Although it is true that design is traditionally taught from the "top down," voices such as Kent Bloomer of Yale University advocate the arts and crafts sensibility that architecture can (and perhaps should be) designed from the bottom up. This book provides evidence that cross-pollination can occur when the Small and the Big not only meet but fertilize each other and allow for a tertiary reality where the visual clarity and power of the Big can dance with and be celebratory of the glistening poignance and intimate relevance of the Small.

So it is up to architects to look at the work in this book and not simply cubbyhole its contents as the product of trivial pursuits. Rather, the intention of almost all the work in this book is to have buildings sustain interest and extend usefulness to the point where their occupants feel an intimacy with the structures that surround them. Designing innovative architectural detailing should not be scary, and it needn't be costly. There is only one way to remove fear and reduce cost, and that is the conveyance of the fruits of the years of experience that these small projects evidence. So it is hoped that this book will help the architectural profession see that, although expressive detailing can be time consuming, fraught with risk, and potentially frustrating, it affords a powerful potential for enrichment.

Means and Methods

Architectural detailing is really about materials. Materials often fail within hostile environments involving the intrusion of water, extreme temperatures, and corrosion by acidic elements or simply oxygen. In addition, details accommodate movement (doors and windows). Details allow for light and sound to be transmitted (natural and human-made). Detailing can provide for iconic references which have personal or cultural resonance within the mind of the beholder.

Even though usefulness is perhaps the paramount concern of the architectural detailer, usefulness often becomes secondary to affordability—without the ability to *build* it, a costly detail is simply the tree that falls in the woods when no one is listening. Inappropriate, and hence unbuilt, detailing has been the bane of many architects' quests for credibility.

Whether it was Frank Lloyd Wright's assumption in his Usonian houses that a construction of many pieces of cheap wood were cheaper than fewer pieces of more expensive wood (even though the time involved in assembling the cheap pieces of wood sent the budget over the top) or Corbusier's metaphoric use of "industrial" components (which were in fact as custom fabricated as any fine Swiss watch and thus excruciatingly costly), architects are often prisoners of their own mental constructs—constructs which often leave the designer impotent when it comes to the capacity to fabricate good ideas due to a blind budgetary eye.

The most typical answer to this fiscal dilemma is the use of catalog components. But just as Mr. Wright vainly sought affordability by lowering the cost of materials, the preponderant cost of expressive architectural details is in the time-consuming handiwork required to actually create the detail itself. The quantities involved are usually so small that even extraordinarily expensive materials (such as teak, stainless steel, or stone) represent a small fraction of the overall cost. Similarly, in the mind of an architect, the *idea* of usefulness often does not equate to practical utility once the project is built. The concept that even though water flows downhill it can be *contained* in the top of a building rather than be shed by allowing water to flow freely *away* from a building has created some of the most massively damaging testimony of architectural incompetence in the eyes of those who judge us, our clients. When it leaks, you lose. In reality, focusing on the inappropriateness of so many architects' attempts at detailing is a cheap shot. The attempt to do that which has not been done before, that which is *not* in *Architectural Graphic Standards*, is an effort worth undertaking, and the only way to perfect the knowledge base needed to create useful, affordable, *and* artful details is via thoughtful resolution of unprecedented problems while picking up on undeniable opportunities for expression. Few precedents are available for study, so the opportunity for failure is ever present.

In truth, because building expressive detailing often demands a greater level of skill, some of the truly thoughtful and innovative (and even practical) ideas of designers can fall prey to incompetent execution. Even if all has been correctly conceived, designed, and rendered, the best detailing can fall prey to minds closed to all but the standard. Flashing which doesn't extend to a designated point in a detail drawing, or the absence of specified steel reinforcement within a cast concrete assembly, or even the omission of a gasket between two materials that can evidence galvanic decay, can render an architect's brilliance irrelevant.

This book showcases *successful* details on a case-study basis. Beyond the conceptual means and methods of fabrication and design, this book presents the actual working and shop drawings for most projects—illustrating graphic techniques employed to communicate those ideas to those who would fabricate the constructions on display.

For many projects, the method of graphic communication is quite crude, and often details are defined in the field far beyond that which can be graphically depicted. Often, models are the only way that certain elements can be depicted for fabrication. All these methods will be related to the reader in the text and captions provided and often by the words of the designers themselves as seen in quotations boxed in gray tone.

Beyond the means and methods for the successful application of a broad knowledge base, all the details that are presented demonstrate the invigorating spirit of a design progressing-beyond shape and space and spiraling into the realms of joinery, materiality, and human contact. The multiplicity of projects presented and problems solved will give the reader a sense of the potential present in *any* design project, no matter how big or small.

Practitioners Versus Product

Details offer insights into their designer's soul. More than a building's formal presence or the psychological manipulations of its spaces, the details of a building can often convey the underlying mindset of its designer. Whether intended to be appreciated by the human senses of touch, sight, hearing, perhaps even smell, to evoke memories via stylistic iconography, or to illustrate the latent materiality of the elements employed, details have the capacity to communicate philosophical values and/or emotional underpinnings.

Is it any wonder that Albert Speer's doorknobs were set at eye level? Is it surprising that Corbusier would attempt to fuse the variety of structural and infill components of so many of his projects under a thin veneer of stucco? That Charles Moore would use his own visage as humorous ornament in his work? Whether architecture is intended to intimidate, distill reality, or make you laugh, the vehicles for these intentions are often made manifest by the details employed by individual designers.

Large buildings are often the product of a team. Details are often simply the act of one mind dealing with one problem, or the individual designer's fascination with a material or an act. How do you open a door? How do you filter light? What happens when wood expands or contracts? Where does water go when it rains? How do you capture the sounds of the ocean? These micromanaged elements can either be ignored in deference to the "big picture," they can be wished away with standardized plug-in components, or they can be addressed with innovative creativity.

Innumerable hard edges are available to evaluate the success or failure of architectural details. Does the detail answer the specific problems it should have addressed or are they ignored? Is it affordable or so custom-crafted that it remains a fantasy? Will it survive its context or will nature's variations and the abuse of use render it useless or, worse yet, a liability to the parent building? When so many hoops must be jumped through, the judgment of architectural details is merciless. As with architectural design at any scale, attempts at a heightened level of innovation exponentially increase the potential for failure, and it is inevitable that in the individual projects cited in this book, readers will discover what is to them inappropriate or questionable applications of material, technique, or even esthetics.

There *can* be absolute knowledge of an architectural detail. A detail's academically abstracted meaning can be problematic as incidental or unintended interpretations or allusions can obscure the true intentions of the designer. In this book, "symbolic" details which are merely the logo for a building's preexisting sensibility (the tacked-on I-beam of the Seagram building by Mies van der Rohe, for example), and the application of tongue-in-cheek inside jokes told by architects to each other (such as the never-ending application of brightly painted sliced-and-diced trim in post-modern architecture) are both eschewed in favor of details that deal with specific problems in ways that evidence the designer's creativity and inspire the observer's exploration of both the creator's intent and of the specific problem tackled.

More so than any other aspect of architectural design, the detail is a personal communiqué on several levels. Perhaps originating as a small psalm to architectural design, the small-scale built product can celebrate materiality, evidence the kinesthetic potential of use, and measure the passage of time via weathering or seasonal adjustment.

A mountain is made of these many little molehills. The sum of the work presented is a statement that the attention lavished on the smallest parts of our built environment is not inherently autoerotic or anal compulsive. The formal and spatial obsession evidenced by most building design conveys a perspective that overwhelms intimate scale. But for some architects, there is an abiding fascination with truly innovative details that conveys a depth of commitment and intensity that often is the result of a long history of intimate connection with the craft and materials employed. "Cheap thrills" architecture and truly innovative details seldom coexist in the same structure as they are an anathema to one another. Although expressively innovative detailing is not necessarily part of large-scale architectural genius, it is clearly true that large-scale architectural incompetence is seldom graced by small-scale architectural genius.

Thus architectural detailing can be said to be symptomatic, and often overtly symbolic, but this book shows that it is exquisitely human and, when successful, evidences all the best aspects of our desire to enrich our lives while adapting to our environment. Would that all architectural scales had the same mantle of ethical invigoration.

Expressive
Details

Structure

The most essential requirement for any building is that it stand up against gravity and acts of God. Providing shelter simply means there is something over your head and under your feet of sufficient size and strength to keep the elements at bay and support whatever you wish to keep separate from the natural world. If all we needed was safety, then our structures would be far different from what we have grown to expect and cherish. In all architecture, but especially in residential construction, it is the human touch in our buildings that holds our hearts and energizes our minds. Perhaps the most essential role that architectural detailing can play in the articulation of the intentions present in any building is when the presence of structural support gains expression via the use of creative architectural detailing. The following examples convey a variety of "takes" on the expressive resolution of structural forces that are dealt with in the buildings within which these details reside. First, the common denominator for all these constructions is that they celebrate their role. Second, the materialities involved are never obscured; rather, they are boldly manifest. Whether in the form of a column, a truss, or a rafter tail, these details speak to the core of what it means to boldly build good ideas.

STRUCTURE

Bohlin Cywinski Jackson, Architects

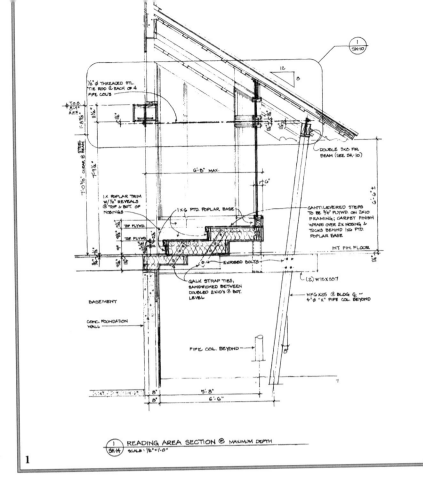

Details are often seen to be the "icing on the cake"—unnecessary embellishments that are extraordinarily costly and inherently idiosyncratic and quirky. In a project that cost under $70 per square foot, Bohlin Cywinski Jackson, Architects, has taken the most generic of materials and simply arrayed them for extraordinary contrast, providing a vigorous expression that completely defies the project's budgetary limitations. Virtually all the products used are generic, and none of their interfaces/connections are problematic to build. Rather than focus on a singular detail, here we focus on an approach used by architects Bohlin Cywinski Jackson to create a building which is both affordable and exhilarating in its approach. Often, it is the detailing and material selections which provide ultimate affordability for buildings rather than intricate ingenuity. In this particular case, however, there is ample evidence of both.

This project, the most simple of building shapes—simply a large shed—has infill that is visually intricate and yet made mostly of stock parts. Standard prefab trusses essentially support the largest part of the roof and intermediate structural supports incorporate post-and-beam wood members, steel I-beams, tree-trunk columns, standard light-frame wood construction, as well as tubular steel columns, steel flitch plates, and a wide variety of trim and window manipulations that simply evolve standard components in interesting and innovative ways.

This catalogue of parts is extraordinary simply because it displays the best spirit of *expression* of materials and details, versus hiding them under

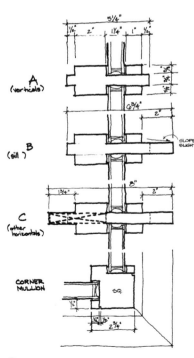

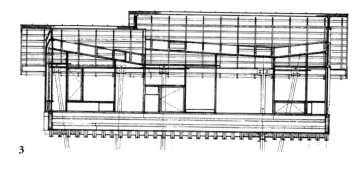

3

Figure 1 *The cross section of the shed reading area demonstrates many of the reasons that this building has had a great deal of impact despite its modest budget. Steel structure (lower right) is allowed to express itself via extension of the beam end and the canting of its columnar support. Note also that different types of steel columns are employed as well, enhancing contrast. In addition, the wood floor framing is also allowed to evidence its latent properties by the stepping action of the bay's bottom side. The extraordinarily simple and yet highly animated glazing is used as simple direct infill between the shed roof (similarly formed by standard rigid insulation with board and batten finishing) and the stepped floor noted earlier. A steel beam that spans the gap in the wall formed by the bay is allowed to have its bottom edge expressed (a cheap connection as well). Rafter tails are continually celebrated. Angling the glass wall underneath an angled shed forms a variety of glass shapes in the transom areas.*

Figure 2 *Glass wall mullions. These quick softline drawings depict a system that utilized ⁵/₈" and ³/₄" standard dimension clear wood (and an occasional custom corner post). The architects manipulate the dimension of the center mullion piece to either extend or retract, thus providing more or less shadow play and more or less stiffness.*

Figure 3 *Bay longitudinal section. Looking out from the interior of the building, the variety of structural components can be seen in blissful contradistinction to each other. Note the overarching steel structure that supports the entire leading edge of the shed roof and its occasionally angled columnar supports. Note also the gapped, paired dimensional lumber for support, and the unrelenting presence of the 2-ft module of shed roof rafters coursing through the angled glass wall. In addition, note the use of an occasional (and somewhat pricey) glass transom that is set between these rafters. The patterning of the glass allows for the insinuation of operable windows as well as the easy accommodation of breaks in the beveling surface. Cantilevers are consistently employed both for rafter tails and the beam that supports them, as well as the floor joists themselves, and the layers and the organization of the structure has an implicit rhythm and meter that is defined by the 2-ft structural bay with an occasional and resonant coordination between the two providing stiffness and interlocking the various materials used. This is a straightforward kit of parts arrayed in an innovative and fresh, invigorated fashion—the sort of work that can be effectively executed only with adequate experience and innovative thought.*

Figure 4(a) and (b) *Column and truss. Note the utilization of absolutely standard size prefabricated 2 x wood trusses that have their orientations centered on a post-and-beam system that utilizes a double column with large scale expressed bolt connections that in turn is stiffened by a standard steel section flitch plate which both connects the columns and is painted to contrast the wood's expressive graining. In and around all these expressed structural components is the standard sheetrock construction which prototypically marks buildings of this type, but note that everything has been manipulated to be child friendly and reflective of childlike innocence. Cubbies become benches, trim becomes support for coat pegs, windows are set low for child use and are patterned as a grid, as focal perforations, or as wonderfully angular top-lighting dormers. Even stock smoke detectors and egress lighting fixtures become part of this wonderful dance of components.*

(Courtesy of Karl A. Backus.)

4 (a)

4 (b)

sheetrock or above a dropped ceiling. Every visible element is allowed to be articulated by paint, orientation, and material distinction. For example, the saddlebag tack-on that forms a glazed seating area allows standard steel supports to be blissfully attenuated or angled. Its extended standing seam aluminum roof projects out to create a heavy shadow line, and its glazing, as mentioned, is artfully manipulated. There is nonstructural expressionism too, best seen in marvelously animated lattice work that uses stock 1 x 4 wood sheathing to create a pattern that is then voided by ellipsoidal, free-line openings providing direct view access out from a glazed wall which rests behind this lattice work. Or, more whimsically, the most standard of prefabricated trusses is supported by heavy timber construction which is in turn reinforced by steel which in turn often stands proud of standard sheetrock construction. Standard windows are often put in skewed orientations. In short, this building is a manual for how to use standard components in invigorated and expressive ways to provide something which is both affordable and catches the imagination of the children who use the building on a daily basis.

6

5

Figure 5 Sitting area. Debarked tree trunk columns become the focal point of a thoroughly permutated mullion pattern involving stock operable windows and custom fixed glass units where paint articulates both structure and infill. Steps become lightly animated and interface with each other, and the overarching structural system of standard trusses is also present. Beyond these windows is a thoroughly expressive array of steel superstructure supporting wood beams and standard dimensional lumber shed roof overhang. (Courtesy of Karl A. Backus.)

Figure 6 Exterior view. The simplest of roof forms overhangs to create shadows and seems to facilitate the mounding of earth as well—and has sheds tacked onto it. Each item expresses its structure with great clarity, and each item involved, including windows, is part of some symbolic and/or systemic interface. (Courtesy of Karl A. Backus.)

Figure 7 Shed extension. Simple cantilevers of structure. Both dimensional lumber and heavy timber have their end points articulated to support a large steel beam. (Courtesy of Karl A. Backus.)

"The Children's Pavilion at Silver Bay in the Adirondacks was done on an exceptionally tight budget. Yet it was to have a variety of indoor and outdoor spaces for young children. As an overall strategy, we've made a rather simple rectangular pavilion whose gabled roof is framed by economical residential wood trusses. The roof trusses are supported by an edge beam that rings the building and a wood and steel composite beam extending through its center. This visually rich roof framing is revealed at the heart of the pavilion, leading one from its entry to a gathering/reading/skit area that projects from the pavilion's face toward the lake and early morning sun. The plan can be freely shaped to the children's varied needs beneath this simple roof.

"A rich variety of columns supports the pavilion. The porches of the entry face are marked by a series of round tapered wood columns ordered from a catalogue. Simplified through the removal of usual bases and capitols, they speak of the past and allude to older historic buildings nearby. The pavilion's roof edge at another play porch is supported by economical 4 inch by 4 inch wood columns that also provide the framework for a whimsical lattice. The morning sun casts animated shadows along this porch. At the light filled gathering/reading space, the perimeter beam is supported by a pair of peeled tree trunks from Silver Bay's forest. These natural columns inhabit the story telling space like people. The roof sheds of this space are supported by playfully tilted slender steel pipe columns that the children look past toward the lake. The central beam is supported by a line of paired milled timber columns that are visually married to the beam and mark the pavilion's center. One pair is doubled to encourage a child's view through its crack.

"There is much pleasure in making rich buildings with such simple means."

BRACKETS/ BEAMS

James Cutler, Architect

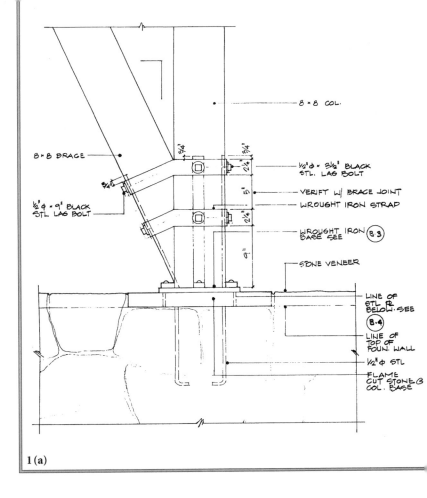

1 (a)

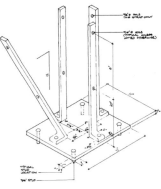

1 (b)

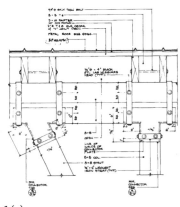

1 (c)

What makes a detail special? One might say that what separates architectural detailing from decoration is the detail's capacity to physically communicate its function. There are many ways to do this, but material distinction and stylistic contrast between the elements employed are the most essential tools with which architects can manifest their desire to express a specific condition's properties and potentials. The desire to *express* the fundamental properties of building components versus hiding their potential under a bushel basket of faux simplicity is inherently honest. Feigning poignance via an architectonic veneer glossed over a lot of structural and mechanical rationalizations is fundamentally disingenuous. In the best tradition of architectural honesty, Washington State architect James Cutler has designed a simple evocation of structural support for a new building using post-and-beam wood superstructure connected with cast-iron brackets. Whereas it is clear that these brackets are starkly structural, using wrought iron and steel bolts set into the context of the large-scale wood framework, it is also clear that the materials used are exquisite and the detailing employed articulate, subtle, and yet expressive. First, the wood is of exceptional quality, almost dead clear, remarkable for such large timbers (typically 8 x 8s), and the edges, surfaces, and cross-cuts of the wood have been marvelously sanded to an almost perfect finish. The brackets themselves, using simple wrought iron, are formed of two separate systems—brackets that are often let into the wood itself creating a flush condition and tethering straps, often custom-cut to accommodate the

Figure 1(a), (b), and (c) These crisp, hand wrought drawings evidence a clarity of the understanding of the details involved. Note the use of a three-dimensional isometric projection of the base plate and tie down detail. Note the corners of these units were rendered to be more bent than cast but in the final form became much beefier (and stiffer).

Figure 2 Bracket and beam. Beams, brackets, and even a diagonal strut are tied via expressive wrought iron banding, bracing, bracketing.
(Courtesy of the architect.)

2

large-scale angled bracing of some of the vertical members. Although the "rules" are played with a bit, the essential truth is that brackets and straps do not align, and square bolt heads are always finally twisted to orient to the orthogonal or angular geometries employed by the wood framing's orientation. There are virtually no unconsidered joints. At angled connections, where a diagonal strut stiffens or supports a horizontal member, the somewhat acute angle of the diagonal is mitigated by the angling of the line of the bracket verticals that supports the horizontal member. A square joint would have been easier, but the very slight cant employed is extraordinarily effective in lightly integrating the two orientations. Where the straps are cut to orient themselves to the diagonals employed, their break lines relate directly to the joint between the wood members. At the bottom of the vertical, diagonal column assembly, the bracket base plate extends beyond the perimeter of the combination column to accommodate a flared base to the strapping, which serves as a built-in stiffener to a condition which cannot afford to rack out of plumb. Although these are not inexpensive details, they are extraordinarily efficient and absolutely honest, and, although they are not to be found in any catalogue (save the bolts and their washers), they are made with a sort of elegant simplicity that allows almost any competent metalsmith to fabricate them. Thoughtfulness, material contrast, micromanagement of detail and geometry, and finally, aesthetic invention are realized within the context of an absolutely functionalist response to a hard-edged structural problem. All these principles of successful architectural detailing are employed by these brackets, and their power is clearly evident.

Figure 3 Context. *A roof structure clearly extends beyond a glass wall and masonry firebox, and while the perimeter plinth organizes the beaming and roof edge, a subordinate (and nonbearing) inner wall floats. Note the incised quality of the steel brackets set in contrast to the laid over quality of the strapping employed to hold them in place (and to hold the end conditions of the solid, unlaminated wood together).*
(Courtesy of the architect.)

"The connectors at the Bloedel Reserve Building are designed to structurally stiffen the timber frame to support the roof, while reflecting the serene elegance of the whole of the arboretum where it is sited."

3

COLUMN/BEAM CONNECTION

*Arne Bystrom,
Architect*

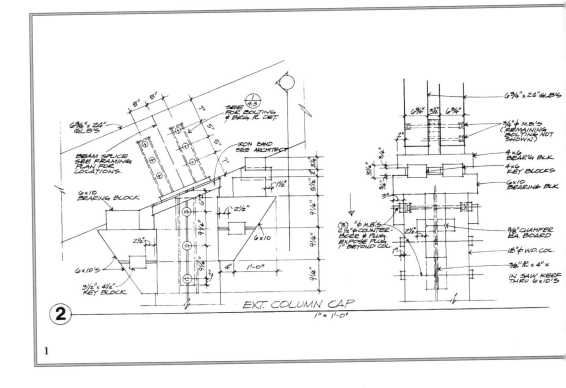

(2) EXT. COLUMN CAP
1" = 1'-0"

1

Perhaps the simplest structural detail is the post and lintel framing bay. The lintel, a beam over an opening, redirects the loads along its length down into posts. This simple act of spanning is, in one way or another, the way the vast majority of loads are dealt with in buildings of any size or type. Rather than leave well enough alone and follow a well worn path, architects have found great delight in articulating this connection, often to the point of obscuring its structural reality. Either by applied ornament, or by disingenuous surfacing of all components in a homogeneous material, this most basic structural feature is often rendered to give no real visual clue as to the realities dealt with. Rather than deal dishonestly with details such as this, Arne Bystrom revels in their reality and articulates his interpretation of this simple transfer of load into miniature sculptures that display both craftsmanly skill and structural understanding. Perhaps the most expressive and yet ethical detail one can imagine in this genre is this detail where Bystrom not only takes care of the vertical loads imposed, but allows for the splicing together of a discontinuous roof-beam while accommodating the diagonal forces of a classic roof-bearing situation. Rather than distilling this connection down to a simple piece of steel, or a series of hidden gussets, or even with simple triangulating struts, Bystrom chooses to create an ensemble of parts that are

Figure 1 Careful dimensions and cogent notes do not convey the sculptural and craftsmanly appeal of this unique detail, but do note the variety of overlaps, interfaces, and the insinuative presence of steel brackets that facilitate attachment between the massive column below and the spliced beam above while diagonal braces support objectified blocking that meets, bird's mouth style, into the bottom edge of the beam.

Figure 2 (a) and (b) View of column capital (see cover photo for an additional view). This view allows the full sculptural presence and nascent organic quality of this heavily articulated intersection to be fully appreciated.
(Courtesy of the architect.)

Figure 3 A series of ascending column capitals make the transition from diagonal to horizontal and stability is provided not only by the column capital detail represented in this section but also by large-scale diagonal struts which are set to intermediate levels, treelike, that allow a massive roof to be stable despite the vagaries of wind and earth movement.

2(a)

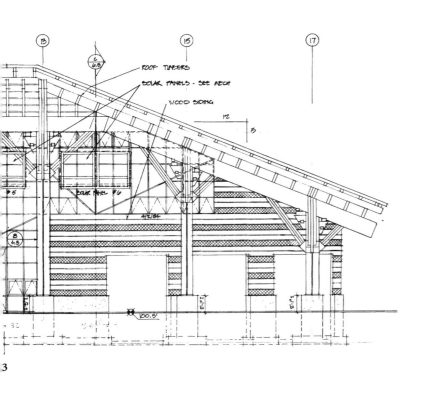

3

2(b)

expressive of their individual characteristics while providing a diagram of structural needs that have been met. First and foremost in the creation of this connection is an 18-in-diameter solid redwood column composed of a material which accommodates a wide variety of fastening potential (solid wood)—in this case, through bolting is used both to stabilize the end grain of this particular piece and to facilitate the direct attachment between the microlam beams and the solid wood column. To hold the wood together, resisting the organic material's tendency to split under the influences of moisture-content-related movement, an iron band is applied around the column's head. To prevent rotation or unwanted shifting from the column's dead plumb orientation, solid wood blocks are utilized that project off of the sides of this column top reaching up to the beam above. Braces have blocks laid upon them to meet the underside of the beam, the blocks being accepted by a bird's mouth connection let into the beam itself.

Each of these moves is formed with a sense of integrity and purpose that is remarkable. The compressive realities of the varying conditions are almost intuitively expressed by using the chunky blocks of solid wood at the corners of the detail. The triangulating stiffeners express their identity by the heavy beveling sides of the solid wood pieces employed. The "pieces and parts" construction of these braces is beautifully articulated via the lapped, mortised joinery employed. These pieces of wood are literally stacked one upon each other while being held together by their interlocking forms. The presence of buried steel through bolting is evidenced in all the expressed wood plugs projecting off the surface of the assembly. The variety of materials is also clearly expressed by clear coating of all the elements employed. Although this is a very large-scale detail involving an 18-in-diameter column and 24-in-deep glu-lam beams, the final product seems to be virtually scaleless—it could be half its size or perhaps two times as large without losing its sense of proportion.

Often, rudimentary concerns can evoke extraordinary responses. The simple need to support a roof and collect loads can either be handled blindly, as in the buried steel frame of a skyscraper, or handled expressively, as with this connection. Expressive connection no doubt costs more in terms of time, and often in terms of the materials employed, but the final product is something which not only grabs attention but sustains it, not only evokes a sense of panache and innovation but conveys the power of the natural forces dealt with. It is one thing to be structurally honest, it is another thing to be structurally eloquent. Honesty is always the best policy, but if the reality of natural forces can be conveyed in an aesthetically inspirational way, not only are problems solved but opportunities are joined, and the artfulness which is implicitly within every construction can be made manifest.

Figure 4 Straight-run connection. In transition from the diagonal capitals discussed and drawn in this chapter, this more symmetrical and centered column capital occurs at the middle of the roof lines where double hipping of the eave line allows for a straight run. Note the consistent use of the specific elements employed to its angled counterpart. (Courtesy of the architect.)

"This connection shows how to pose a structural function in a decorative way. It holds up the roof, spreading the loads, and adding stiffness to the column connection."

4

MICROLAM ARCH/BEAM

Arne Bystrom, Architect

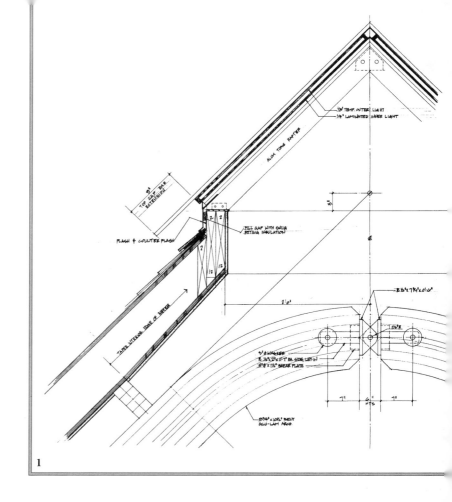

1

Often the most memorable architectural detailing has to do with the act of connection between materials. Arne Bystrom is an architect who is fascinated by connections, and perhaps one of his finest can be seen where two 8-3/4-in x 10-1/2-in microlams meet. What makes this connection so special is its artfulness, involving an eighth-radius turn of two microlam beams to meet each other while they are in the act of supporting a roof. When these two beams bend-to-connect, their joint is structurally critical, and Bystrom renders it to be aesthetically provocative. This joint is articulated by means of a simple chamfered bevel cut of the extreme wood members at the top and bottom of the end of each glu-lam and by letting into the ends of each of these two beams a large shear plate and three pins, one within each beam and one connecting the two beams together via two lapped 1/2-in-thick steel plates. Through the use of some large-scale washers and some careful radiusing of steel work, the overall effect is one of conspired coordination versus rude support. The net product of this connection is that the two beams take on the sensibility of an arch, and this arch, rather than being buried within the context of the building's skin, is actually celebrated by having the roof plane held off these beams by microlam spacers which in turn support rafters. In a subtle but powerful move, these rafters have a 1-1/2-in taper set over the last 2 feet of their run prior to supporting a ridged skylight made of aluminum tubing. The overall effect is a combination of something which is fully expressive and simultaneously honest. As such, it represents some of the finest motivations in

2

Figure 1 *The overall context of this detail is an extraordinary construction built into a hillside where glu-lam beams are used to articulate the aspirational aspects of the entire construction. Note the multiple bearing points and transitional uses of redundant construction, all set in a conspiratorial effort to provide for an energized transition from the lower level to the upper.*

Figure 2 *A ridge skylight hovers above the shamelessly expressive connection below where two glu-lam beams have their endpoints turned to touch at a steel hinged connection, providing the stability of an arch while facilitating the easy buildability of a gable formed roof. Note the taper of the rafter from the spring point of the solid laminated wood blocking which supports the final layer of roof. Note also the minimal qualities of the ridged skylight employed—using a simple thermapane glazing with "chop and channel" tubular aluminum support which gains presence via extension of the mullion system employed.* (Courtesy of the architect.)

3

Figure 3 *Quartet. At the double-hipped return of the roof, glu-lams that form the beams supporting the hips join with those ending the long gable form of the roof itself, creating an extraordinary coincidence of wood and steel. Note also the double-hipped skylight above reinforcing the power of these pieces.* (Courtesy of the architect.)

Figure 4 *Taken during construction, one can see the extraordinarily simple overall layout of this building structure and the inherent focal quality of the detail depicted. Given the size and scale of the space, this one detail carries the maximum bang for the buck.* (Courtesy of the architect.)

architectural detailing, taking care of necessary elements of structure and weatherability while at the same time celebrating the materiality and the techniques of construction. Practical and pragmatic concerns are given life by the reinvention of the elements employed. In Bystrom's case this means an animation of line and overtness of connection, resulting in manipulations which create an animated if not animistic quality to his detailing.

> *This detail "emulates three-hinge connection. To define upper space in an exciting way with a curved lam 3-in arch connecting under the skylight. Arches allow for free open space under an entire roof span."*

4

Structure 17

ARCED TRUSS

Duo Dickinson, Architect

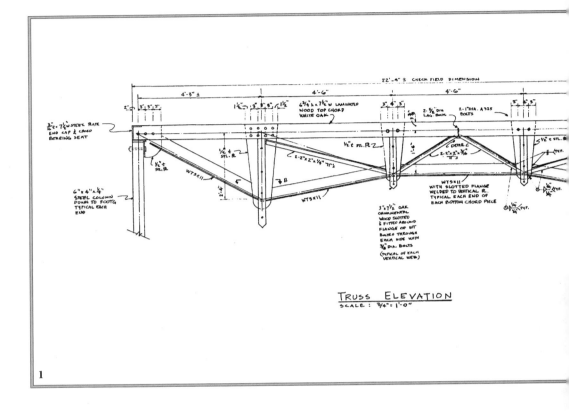

TRUSS ELEVATION
SCALE : 3/4" = 1'-0"

1

Figure 1 *Truss. Triangulating steel elements become more frequent and of heavier gauge toward the center of this arced truss. Formed of cut steel plate and stock steel channel (both "T" and "L" shaped), this truss relies on significant compressive reinforcement of two 3-in x 6-3/4-in solid laminated oak members across its upper cord. The four verticals shown here are purely ornamental, and their shape was greatly modified during the construction.*

Typically, the interiors of urban rowhouses have two consistent aspects—namely, that the short ends of their rectilinear perimeter accept light and, frequently, a center bearing line between the two long bearing walls. This center line is almost always supported by a continuous interior wall whose line of support is unbroken throughout the entire house interior save for openings set to provide access to rooms. Typically, this center bearing wall is located closer to one common wall than the other, with the narrow bay being used predominately for circulation and the wider bay being used for habitable spaces. Often this wall disappears at the back side of the house facing the yard, and the framing can change direction or an intermediate beam can support the floor and roof framing. In this particular townhouse, the structural bays were of very normal size—a little over 6 ft on one side and 14 ft on the other. The owner's request was a radical one—namely to void the entire bearing wall condition for almost one-half the length of the townhouse. This bearing wall supported 50 percent of the live and dead load for the roof and second and third floors of the house. Those loads had to be translated down through the cellar and basement floors below the "common" or "public" middle floor of this classic Park Slope Brooklyn brownstone. It would have been a relatively mindless exercise to simply go to the steel manual, find an I-beam

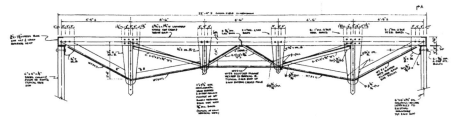

Truss Elevation
Scale: ¾" = 1'-0"

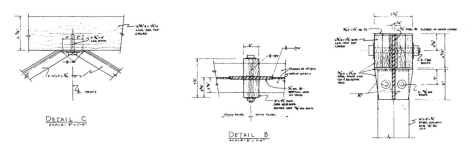

Detail C
Scale: 3" = 1'-0"

Detail B
Scale: 3" = 1'-0"

Figure 2 Details. *These drawings by Martin Gehner, structural engineer, define virtually every component of the truss fabricated. All joints are explicitly called out with orientations and welding specifications critical to the overall success of the project.*

Figure 3 Stair-bound view. *The triangulating lines of the diagonal stiffeners seem to radiate from the arced underside of the middle three bays. Note how the far bay (right) is pulled back up to the support condition. The top horizontal cord of wood is used by the truss for compressive reinforcement, whereas the verticals that splay to match their steel counterparts and taper to provide a three-dimensional "kick" to the overall form are purely ornamental.*
(Courtesy of Justin van Soest.)

2

3

whose weight-to-depth ratio was relatively efficient and whose web depth was acceptable. These owners had a different outlook. They wanted to transform a potential structural nightmare into an artful use of material and technology to create a focal point within the context of their visually expanded living space.

But there was an inner conflict present. One owner devoutly wished the intervening structural accommodation of this new open space to be in the form of an arched opening, while the other owner was a devotee of expressive steel trusses. One owner was in love with wood's viscerally evocative presence, while the other owner favored brightly painted steel as an allusive icon of the bygone Industrial era so much a part of Brooklyn's past. The resulting design fuses all these concerns while "taking care of business" structurally. Rather than relying on the Statics textbook exemplars of truss design, the structural engineer involved, Martin Gehner, saw the cross-purposes of arch/truss and wood/steel as being complementary rather than contradictory. The overall design for this hybrid created an ever-deepening dimension as the truss progressed toward its support conditions, while, archlike, providing a minimum depth at the middle of the span—completely contradictory of a truss's desire to be deepest at its center point. Aggressive diagonal reinforcement of the center of the truss with added steel members provided the needed strength that was geometrically obviated by reduced available depth. To provide efficiency of installation and to express the nature of this construction, the truss's connections to the walls gather back up the steel web to a single bearing point (rather than a deep line of bearing which would be set along the side of the wall). Whereas the quantity of steel members and their thicknesses are increased at the center of the truss to compensate for its reduced depth, wood is employed in two consistent ways. Solid oak horizontals are used heavily at the top edge of the truss to best use the relatively high compressive strength of wood. Further emphasizing the archlike dimensions of the bottom half of the truss, ornamental solid oak verticals are set upon tapered steel verticals. The shape of these appliques is bevelled in three dimensions, lightly reflecting the relative plasticity of wood. The shape of the vertical steel members employed also expresses the necessary structural properties as all verticals splay to provide more "meat" at the top edge of their condition and less at the bottom where less rigidity and stiffness is required. Large high-strength bolts were used to fasten steel to steel and wood to steel, and these bolt ends were painted to match the truss itself providing a three-dimensional "read" as the interlacing steel and wood virtually intertwine to create a viable support for a large-scale loading condition. Easy answers are not the hallmark of enriching detailing, and the fact that this truss can be seen from all levels as it sidles up against the main stair that connects the public spaces with the bedrooms above meant that every angle of its realized form would be visually accessible—up close and personal. Because of this, the care and attention paid to virtually every joint and condition is greatly appreciated by all who encounter it, and yet its large-scale sweep and scope—utilizing the ascending and centering "archway" sensibility—is fully appreciated upon immediate passage through the front door as the truss fully frames the view of the living room and the kitchen and dining spaces beyond. To attempt innovation on a variety of levels of technological design and fabrication, while embracing craftsmanly detailing and expressing materiality, is in the best traditions of any thoughtful construction. Absent an innovative mindset, either a harsh industrial form would slice through a newly unified space with an unrepenting hard edge, or a mute or buried visual obviation of the rather significant structural rerouting employed would enigmatically strive

Figure 4 The removed bearing wall (left) facilitated a new stair and a great sense of openness in a formerly subdivided living area. Note the resonant curves present throughout this entire renovated floor, including balusters, treads, hearth, mantel, and plaster cornice.
(Courtesy of Justin van Soest.)

4

to deny its own presence. Or in the worst of both worlds, an artificial piece of false work, wood trim or otherwise, would create the illusion of a true arch with supporting buttresses creating a form which does not allow for the full unification of the two spaces once divided by the central bearing wall.

Obviously, there are large-scale steel columns buried at either end of this truss which redirect the loading down through to the basement into the newly reinforced existing line of central bearing, but the overpowering message of this particular detail is that structural honesty *can* coexist with expressive geometry and artful combinations of materials.

COLUMN CAPITAL

Kent Bloomer, Designer
Paul Bierman-Lytle, Builder
Kimo Griggs, Artisan

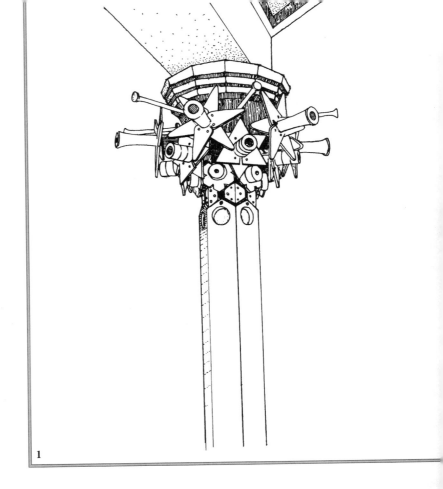

1

Column capitals have been the recipient of a great deal of architectural detailing. Often, they were used symbolically to allude to ancient construction techniques of bundling smaller members together to create a single stiff support. They have been rendered to figuratively or literally anthropomorphize their shape. Or, more recently, they have been overtly used as iconic references to what a given culture held dear (most often in civic architecture). But in small-scale residential design, applied whimsy can often serve to "depontificate" any element of architectural detailing. So it is with this simple column which serves as the ultimate focal point of the entry to a house in Guilford, Connecticut.

Kent Bloomer served as the fundamental designer of this column with direct input from Paul Bierman-Lytle, the codesigner and builder of the home, and the detail itself was fabricated and finetuned by Kimo Griggs, who provided much of the microarticulation seen here. You will note that there are no working drawings for this column, as it was built piece by piece and bit by bit in a "design as you go" mode, often associated with the best traditions of folk art. Suffice it to say, the hexagonal and triangular petal motif, and conical bloom projection of the daffodil served as the basic aesthetic generator for components employed. This unapologetic botanical sensibility was made fresh via the considered coincidence of the various components, involving bandsawing cedar into simple interlocking shapes that mesh with stock doweling to bring to life the aesthetics of progression, in this case from bud to bloom

2

Figure 1 In truth, a retroactive representation, more for PR purposes than for detail determination, this freeline sketch conveys the "pieces and parts" aspect of a thoroughly enriched treatment of a column capital.

Figure 2 Made of a multiplicity of parts choreographed to coincide with the polygonalizations of a dimensional lumber column, many pieces progressively project, animate, and evolve. (Courtesy of the architect.)

and finally the abstraction of the bloom in a trumpeting "stamen." If this were simply art for its own sake, the detail would lose the potential for the impact that it has, but given that it is slipped into the context of a stark corner entry, it serves as the "jewel in the crown" for an entire entry prospect, one that ultimately defeats the large-scale presence of one of our culture's more omnipresent elements—the garage door set as the "front door" of most homes. Given the fact that the topography mandated that this home's front door be set at a full level above the grade used to access the site, this column needed to be beckoning. Given that it is so close to the front door itself, its ability to sustain interest for those who are awaiting entrance was also critical. Finally, as with most residential details, it needed to be affordable. Thus the simplest of woodworking techniques were unapologetically used, making it both delightful and craftsmanly.

This blissfully ornamental column capital slips over the support column itself and has its form married to that column through the hexagonal application of a mitered wood sleeve (with appropriate circular cutouts at its top). Playing off of the generic eave detail that it supports, this particular piece of ornament is effervescently expressive, yet because of its rigorous use of a carefully composed radial geometry, the progressive definition of the shapes employed, and the generic detailing, fastening systems employed, its sensibility is anything but frivolous and is, in fact, absolutely integral to the appreciation of the entire house. As with many details, this construction proves that often it is the smallest elements employed that provide the greatest rewards.

3

"To add visibility and ceremony upon the entrance to a country retreat, the clients specified the daffodil as a flower that held specific significance in their lives and work. To provide a capital crowning to a corner post in front of the main entrance door, we developed a design that conformed to the traditional shape and location of a classical capital. It incorporated the six-fold geometry of daffodil petals. Those shapes increased in size and transformed from bottom to top from the simplicity of a hexagonal post to the effervescence of trumpet-like protrusions from the center of the flower form. The trumpets added a note of welcome. The pieces were assembled like machine parts cut from stock wood and bolted together, detailed and fabricated by Kimo Griggs. This is an example of a single capital or ornament, rather than the traditional aedicular double capital, fixed at the corner rather than centered upon an elevation."

Figure 3 Context. *A grade level change was mandated by the surrounding terrain and garage doors (unseen to the right) had the potential for a depressing distraction. So the detail in question served to both beckon those encountering the site and reward their ascendance to the level of entry with a hyperarticulated confection supporting a thoroughly normative roof.* (Courtesy of the architect.)

Figure 4 Pieces and parts. *The literal "before" picture to the "after" product.* (Courtesy of the architect.)

4

EGG COLUMNS

Kimo Griggs,
James Volney Righter, Architects

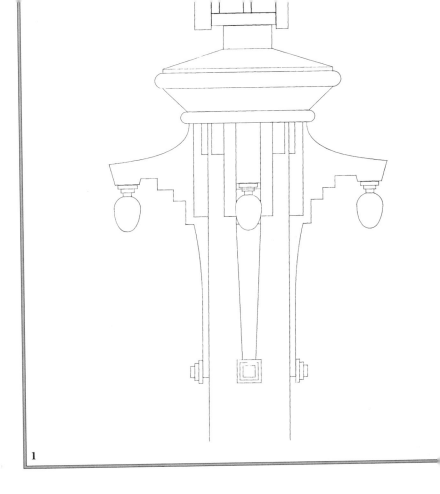

1

Columns are perhaps the most direct structural expression possible. Simply put, they hold things up and are the bottom line when it comes to dealing with gravity. In the oxymoronic tradition of Modernist architecture, columns were treated as abstract distillations of a universal approach to dealing with gravity. *Pilotis* was a term coined to remove any potential historicist or decorative association from the word *column*. In reality, by their very nature as vertical supports, columns inherently reference many elements found in nature, to such an extent that those who are unjaded by architectural theory can literally see the forest for the trees when viewing columnar support. Typically, because they are by definition isolated elements set amid a sea of space and, more often than not, serve as funnels for human passage, creating columns that are without an added layer of craftsmanly expression or aesthetic "attitude" begs their potential for visual sustenance. To reward those who inevitably encounter columns with enriching detail, the world of the Small must be dealt with—the world of architectural details.

Does it really matter whether an abstracted Modernist column is 10 ft in diameter and 400 ft high, or whether its plain cylindrical shaft is 2 in. high and has a diameter of ¹/₈ in? To James Kimo Griggs (at the time a young architectural intern in the office of James Volney Righter, Architects, in Boston) the Small was and is *the* obsession. The Small is what we touch, see most clearly, and can most directly reference into our day-to-day lives and memories. So it is with Mr. Griggs's aggressive embrace of the columns seen

Figure 1 *This preliminary drawing evidences the way details evolve once fabricated by human hands. As Griggs fabricated his design, the eggs became demountable, three or four more layers were applied to the column shaft, and the nature of the stepped bracketing from which the eggs dangle changed with the entire construction gaining a sense of depth and presence a drawing simply does not have.*

Figure 2 *Column capital. A column composed of crenelating layers spawns brackets from which dangle turned eggs. Atop it all, a turned cap piece is set to catch light and thus help make the final connection to the dropped beam supporting the porch roof above (a blank block of wood) disappear.*

(Courtesy of the architect.)

2

in this vacation house on Fisher's Island, New York. Rather than look at them as stylistic replications of the shingle style architecture that is often so gracefully a product of Righter's office, Griggs saw the latent ornamental possibilities present amidst the need for simple structural support. Set at the point of entry of a cranking covered terrace-deck, these half columns (supported by beveling and shingled low walls) are uniquely ambiguous. They are at once wholly amalgamated by white paint, although composed of a large number of component pieces—pieces that are band-sawn to curves, turned to radiused shapes, and virtually carved into "eggs." It is the literal replication of the egg shape as a distinct piece, dangling from expressive brackets spawned by the unrelenting stepping, articulated column shaft, which are the quiet universalist touch that allows all the hyperactivity of these columns to find a *raison d'être*. Perhaps spawned by the same instinct that created pilotis, these universally recognizable icons are overtly utilized as defacto jewelry amid the swelling forms of these multipiece columns. The curvilinear caps of these columns (also turned) are at once vaguely reminiscent of the eggs, and yet somehow more comfortable with many of the cove and crown trim elements found so commonly in shingle style architecture. The final point of connection to the dropped beam that supports the porch eave is a simple stub—a classic "break" between that which is ornamental and that which is structural—the beam above. In this way the spanning piece acts (not unlike the egg) as the simple counterpoint to the multiplicity of parts presented in the column shaft. In one intense 4-ft construction—layered, corbelled, crenelated, bundled, agglomerated—these columns poignantly proffer the iconic eggs. The eggs gain ceremonial interest as they are intended to be removed at the end of the summer season and slipped back into place when the summertime arrivals occupy the house.

It is in the realm of the Small that the typical intern architect can find an extraordinary expression. In this case, fortunately enough, the intern involved had a wealth of hands-on personal experience in building many of the things he had already designed in his brief career. Because of this experience, there is a cleverness and ebullience effected which is undeniable. Note also that the drawings originally effected for this piece showed a far more "architecty" construction, one where the eggs were to be affixed and the transition from column shaft to egg-hanging bracket was to be far more classically ornamented and far less overtly assembled. As Kimo Griggs learned in the act of making, there is an elegance of evolution which allows an open mind to fertilize preconceptions with craftsmanship.

Figure 3 Context. Set in an entry portal to a vacation house, these columns seem dissociated from the shingle style architecture and yet somehow spikily coherent with the octagonalized porch-entry form itself. The overall effect is almost templelike, but definitively beckoning, evocative, and celebratory. (Courtesy of the architect.)

"The columns are structural, but they are also intended, through the stepping and egg motifs, to announce certain themes of the house; namely stepping up to the fabulous view out to the water that is only available from the upper floors, and the feeling of rebirth that the place kindles in the owners. The eggs are detachable to be brought out and hung at the beginning of each year's stay."

3

POOL HOUSE

Bohlin Cywinski Jackson, Architects

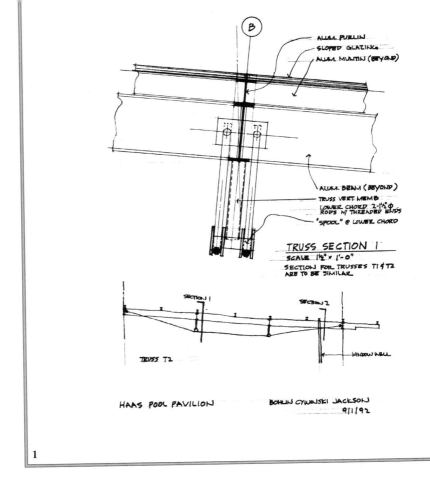

1

An essential challenge for architects, whether during initial inspirations or in the final determination of a project's detailing, is figuring out "the rules of the game." Obviously, when the predominant criteria for success is aesthetic expression (versus cost containment, environmental integration, or even functional accommodation, for example) the onus is on the architect to produce something which has few, if any, compromises. Bohlin, Cywinski, and Jackson are architects whose work is not compromised by a lack of vision or the size of the budget. In this particular case, money and vision were both available, so there was no paucity of innovative, invigorated, and celebratory expression of both materiality and architectural detailing. With the simplest of programs—adding on a pool house-spa to a large residence—the architects provided an extraordinary glass and metal compliment to the original home's stoic stucco presence, simultaneously creating a pavilion that expresses an extreme amount of architectural articulation and some of the commonsense detailing savvy which is the hallmark of good detailing.

In creating something which is an objectified presence set onto the landscape versus a project which is integrated or woven into its context, Peter Bohlin and company have allowed for a simple combination of three materials—glass, metal (predominantly aluminum), and stone. Stone and glass are set in blissful contrast to each other, the latter addressing views, the former restraining earth and providing flooring, and an intertwining lattice of metal framing uses both standard I-beams and ingenious customized trusses utiliz-

Figure 1 *Truss and roof detail. Stock elements are arrayed in a simple coordination to create a lightly invigorated and yet thoroughly practical approach to a relatively long span.*

Figure 2 *Overall view. An aluminum structure is animated in its angled orientation but regulated by its two dimensional pattern. Note the custom cruciform column (center) and the simple truss formed by stock components (upper right). Note also the simple animating gesture of crenelating the window and door wall to the left, as the stock HVAC ducting is allowed to meander and infest the upper areas of the space.*
(Courtesy of Karl A. Backus.)

ing stock turnbuckles and tube stock to facilitate long spans. Cruciform columns are utilized and, when all is set in concert to the zig-zag raked angle ethic of a permutative gridded layout, the final product is extremely kinetic and yet thoroughly controlled. When the requisite HVAC duct system is applied in serpentine self-expression, one has the sense that this is a project which is thoroughly examined and enlivened.

As with many pavilions, this is essentially an assemblage of many details, but as the drawings indicate, none of them are excruciating to execute or unforgiving to the builder and, in fact, the detailing utilizes stock pieces and connections that are "tweaked" in ways that make them memorable versus predictable. And, as with all good architecture, it is the overall layout and organization that allows the standard to become the unexpected. Note that aluminum is used in almost all the structural work, obviating the problematic aspects of galvanic action between differing metals and using a material which is extraordinarily easy to cut and form.

In celebrating the simple act of immersion into the water and the natural environment itself, the architects succeeded in creating a third reality—the participation in an architectural event.

3

"Technically rigorous, yet elusive in spirit, the pool pavilion is both delicate machine and languorous landscape, liquid and stone, reality and illusion."

4

Figure 3 Column and window wall. Columns that are set in blissful ignorance to the patterning of the floor below and yet are aligned to provide for easy orientation support a lightly manipulated aluminum structure. Note the simple details for the joinery between all the stock channels of the window wall and I beams above as well as the inherently "bypassing" quality of the column capitals—a simple box that is cut to receive the angle of the roof itself. Note also that the bottom edge of the collecting beams is cut to create a lightly cantilevered T section which, in turn, supports the glass supporting members of the roof at the uppermost level (upper right). (Courtesy of Karl A. Backus.)

Figure 4 Outside view. Looking back into the pool house, the full benefits of a point load metal framing system can be seen in a thoroughly open diaphanous quality that allows the heavily articulated stone wall to slip by the glass membrane simultaneous with the water's ability to do the same in-and-out action as well. (Courtesy of Karl A. Backus.)

Figure 5 Roof/HVAC. The sinous ducting weaves under, around, and through the rational structural system employed. (Courtesy of Karl A. Backus.)

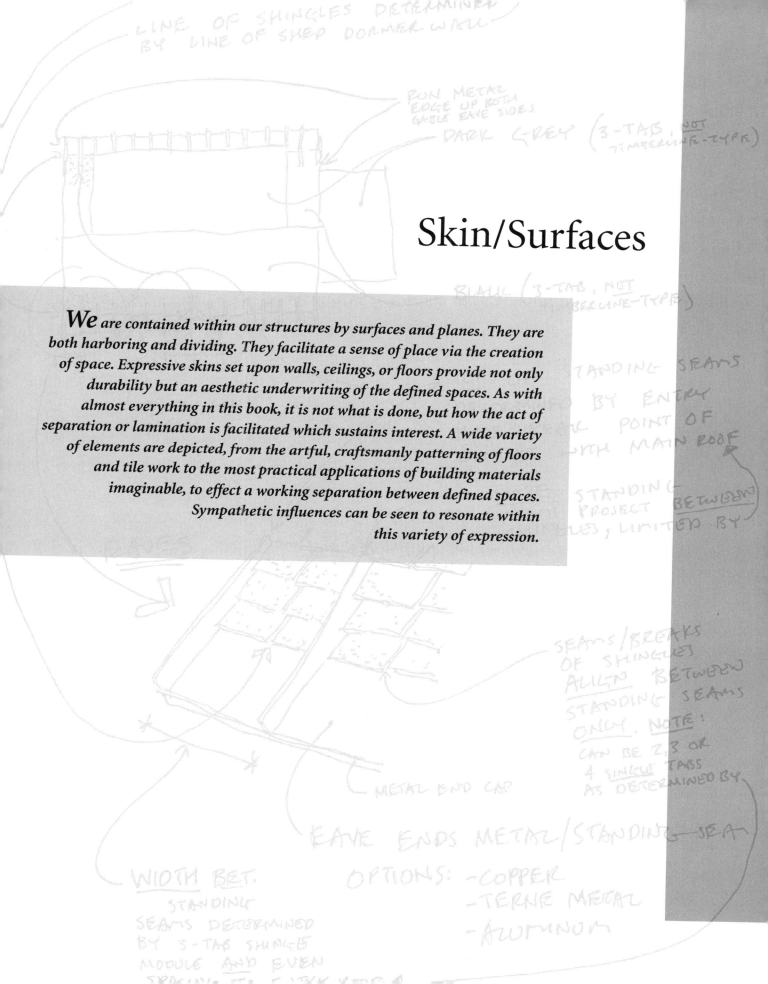

Skin/Surfaces

We are contained within our structures by surfaces and planes. They are both harboring and dividing. They facilitate a sense of place via the creation of space. Expressive skins set upon walls, ceilings, or floors provide not only durability but an aesthetic underwriting of the defined spaces. As with almost everything in this book, it is not what is done, but how the act of separation or lamination is facilitated which sustains interest. A wide variety of elements are depicted, from the artful, craftsmanly patterning of floors and tile work to the most practical applications of building materials imaginable, to effect a working separation between defined spaces. Sympathetic influences can be seen to resonate within this variety of expression.

EAVE DETAIL (VENTILATED)

Herman Hassenger, Architect

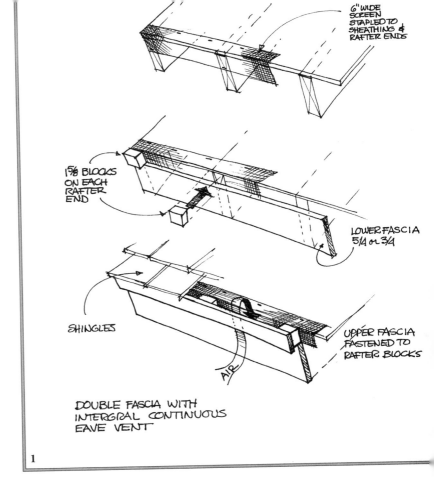

6" WIDE SCREEN STAPLED TO SHEATHING & RAFTER ENDS

1⅝ BLOCKS ON EACH RAFTER END

LOWER FASCIA 5/4 or 3/4

SHINGLES

UPPER FASCIA FASTENED TO RAFTER BLOCKS

AIR

DOUBLE FASCIA WITH INTERGRAL CONTINUOUS EAVE VENT

1

One of the most disappointing details in inexpensive contemporary architecture is the gutter/eave/venting seen at the edge of the gable roofs applied to small and medium-sized buildings. Often simply a mute combination of prefabricated parts, the result frequently looks like a poorly detailed automotive repair where joints never align, bends and crinks are always evident, and surfaces seem to be in collision rather than coordination. Unfortunately, it is assumed that once anything custom is attempted, affordability is left in the dust, and often the potential for a more elegant or effective detail is moot. In and of itself, each prefabricated part employed serves its purpose—the perforated aluminum venting keeps bugs out and lets air flow, the preformed aluminum or plastic gutter redirects water and sometimes provides a pseudo-trimmed edge to the eave, and the prefabricated aluminum drip edging applied to the shingled roof does allow shingles to have rainwater drip off without wicking back against the eave facia. Given the relatively flimsy quality of each of these components, getting them coordinated is nigh on to impossible. When trying to obtain all the benefits of providing roof cavity ventilation, preventing water from cascading down on people's heads or insinuating itself between the layers that compose the roof structure (and thus causing rot), there is often very little that an architect can do without busting the budget to make an elegant solution.

Never let it be said, however, that ingenious architects do not know how to make good details cheap. Herman Hassenger of Moorestown, New Jersey, has

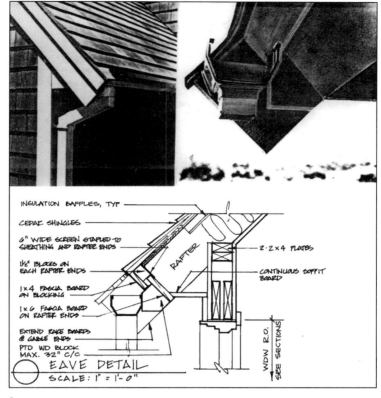

EAVE DETAIL
SCALE: 1" = 1'-0"

2

"This is a way of integrating the gutter detail into the facia. First you have to determine that there will be gutters and where they start and stop. Extend the gable end barge board to cover the ends of the gutters. The horizontal facia can be square cut or plumb cut depending on the design. It helps if the downspout is coordinated with the cornerboard. (Why let these happen by chance?)"

created a system whereby extremely standard materials can act without evidencing themselves in a way which is awkward. Hassenger uses a method that might be called "blind layering." Rather than have prefabricated items slip into or attach onto surfaces, different stock raw materials are laid one upon the other (with all the concomitant benefit of a lack of a need for perfect fit). Beyond ease of construction, this detail facilitates a multitude of shadow lines and coincidences while providing all the desirable benefits already mentioned. By simply wrapping the leading edge of the sheathing and the ends of the rafter tails with fiberglass screening prior to the installation of an eave facia or the roofing itself, ventilation can easily be accommodated. Blocks are applied above the facia line but below the eave line, a layer of wood shingles are applied over this extended blocked out eave facia above, and air is allowed in, while visual penetration is held off. The leading edge of the shingle is pushed out beyond the face of the eave facia by over an inch and a half, thus preventing any wicking of rainwater from carrying back up into the roof cavity. By utilizing wood blocks that are set below the extended facia mentioned earlier, gutters can be set directly to the eave facia without the need for strapping, which is both unsightly and is often ineffective at maintaining the gutter shape against the elements. In this case, Hassenger uses a standard PVC gutter and hides one of the most visually unfortunate aspects of prefabricated gutters, the end condition, simply by extending the rake facia across its end cap and by continuing a lip of shingles over that extended edge. Although this detail is shown with plywood as the subsurface, traditional solid wood 1 x 3 strapping could be used just as easily for this condition if cedar shingles are applied.

COPPER EAVE

Duo Dickinson, Architect

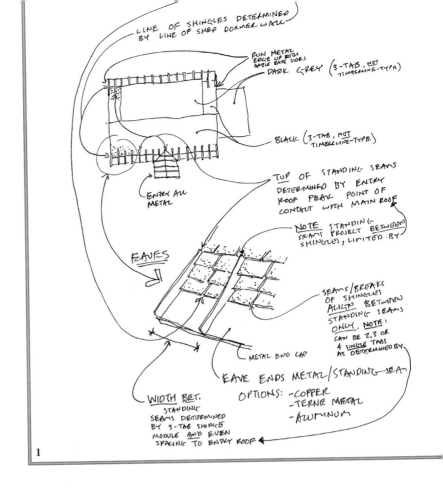

LINE OF SHINGLES DETERMINED BY LINE OF SHED DORMER WALL

RUN METAL EDGE UP BOTH GABLE EAVE SIDES

DARK GREY (3-TAB, NOT TIMBERLINE-TYPE)

BLACK (3-TAB, NOT TIMBERLINE-TYPE)

ENTRY ALL METAL

TOP OF STANDING SEAMS DETERMINED BY ENTRY ROOF PEAK POINT OF CONTACT WITH MAIN ROOF

NOTE STANDING SEAMS PROJECT BETWEEN SHINGLES, LIMITED BY

EAVES

SEAMS/BREAKS OF SHINGLES ALIGN BETWEEN STANDING SEAMS ONLY. NOTE: CAN BE 2,3 OR 4 SINGLE TABS AS DETERMINED BY

METAL END CAP

EAVE ENDS METAL/STANDING SEAM OPTIONS: -COPPER -TERNE METAL -ALUMINUM

WIDTH BET. STANDING SEAMS DETERMINED BY 3-TAB SHINGLE MODULE AND EVEN SPACING TO ENTRY ROOF

1

In the realm of building products, there are two universes—raw

material and processed product. When these are distinct, the former represents unlimited potential (and potentially unlimited cost), the latter offers more tightly circumscribed opportunities with a definitive price range. When the two meet, the joint can be excruciatingly "clunky." When reroofing a 1932 Connecticut cape—a building which offered a paucity of innovative ambience or fresh appeal—there was a concommittant paucity of funds available to infuse the building with anything "zesty."

However, the general contractor involved had just enough shingles left over from a previous job to roof this house. Given the fact that the large quantity of shingles purchased three years ago. The price tag was lowered by the benefits of pre-inflation large quantity unit pricing, there was a little wiggle room in the budget for expressive detailing. The problem was that these were large-scale "Slate Line" shingles—not surprisingly designed to have the ambience of slate. On such a small building as this 24-ft x 32-ft cape, such a roof might seem to be overwhelming unless some lustrous detail could lock it into the existing form. So a second material was chosen for the eave conditions of this little structure.

Metal clad eaves are used wherever heavy snowfalls occur to facilitate the automatic removal of snow and ice from the area of the home where it will cause the most damage—the leading edge of the roofline. The sheet metal effectively "lubricates" this condition and minimizes the amount of icicle buildup which might occur along the roof edge as well as mitigating the potential for "ice damming," which can circumvent any flashing condition and often does great damage to roof conditions. The

Figure 1 *Quick sketches to obtain a budget bid prior to the attainment of the left over "Slate Line" shingles that facilitated the ability for this particular detail to be afforded in copper. Note that the final detailing would allow these standing seams to impose themselves on only one run of shingles, versus the three indicated. Otherwise, all of the dimensioning criteria remain the same. This is a classic builder friendly sketch using longhand versus pseudo technologically sophisticated encryption. Although not necessarily the best for competitive bidding, when a builder is in hand its warm and fuzzy overtones facilitate a favorable disposition (and convey a great deal of knowledge despite its lack of anality).* (Courtesy of Mick Hales.)

Figure 2 *A photo of the detail flanking the entry. Note the simple insinuation of the standing seam within the context of the large format three-tab shingles and its aggrandized center point, a renovated existing entry (the custom turned columns have been dubbed "the asparagus order" by a friend of the architect). Note also that these gutterless eaves mandate the use of a gravel bed placed over filter fabric, complete with aluminum edging minimizing splashback onto the clapboard walls and preempting the possibility for dirt buildup at the sill plate level (a classic rot generator).* (Courtesy of Mick Hales.)

2

"normal" detailing for such a sheet metal edge is a fold over, flat seam joint between the pieces of sheet metal—often of terne metal or galvanized steel. The other fundamental detail is a simple overlay of the roofing material over the upside edge of the sheet metal, covering its fasteners and allowing the two materials to effectively bypass each other. Given the extraordinarily expressive gaps between the three tabs of the "Slate Line" shingles, the opportunity for a meshing of the two materials was immediately evident. In this particular case the three-tab shingle module dove tailed perfectly with the 2-ft-wide copper "pan" available, and the one-tab-deep intrusion of the standing seam of copper facilitated a light but undeniable interlock between the articulated edge and the blank roof. Effectively, this particular detail utilizes the best aspects of the two inherent properties of raw and processed materials. The three-tab asphalt shingle, already less expensive than its wood or stone counterparts, was made even less expensive by its remnant status, whereas the raw copper was kept to a minimum and could be fabricated to fit the shingles' tab gap dimension. The high degree of utility present in the serendipitous meshing of the three-tab shingle module with the available sheet stock minimized waste and highlighted the capacity of raw materials to adapt to specific conditions. Given the ad hoc quality of this construction, it is understandable that no hardline detail was ever drawn up. A prototype was effected which determined shingle orientation (and thus copper seaming pattern) in the field, and the project was quickly executed. Innovation does not necessarily mean high cost, nor does the use of stock materials preclude innovation.

EARTH-ROOFED EAVE

Alfredo DeVido,
Architect

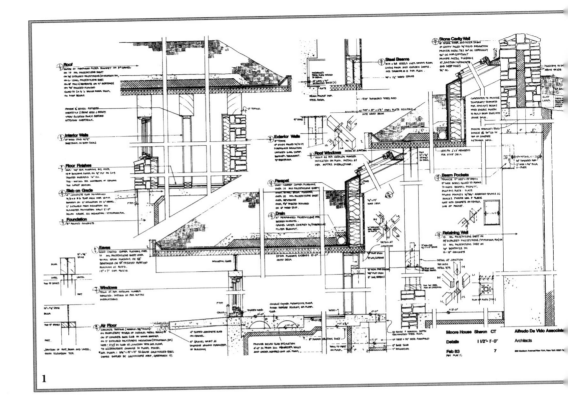

1

Figure 1 This drawing represents the original design intent of Architect De Vido utilizing laminated 2 x 3s (3-in dimension set vertically) to serve as the bottom chord for the multilayered roof structure. Subsequently, 2 x 6 tongue-and-groove planking was used in the underlayment, and an air space was provided for wiring which was then covered by solid-wood 3/4-in x 6-in planks. The finish dimensions and the waterproofing system all remain the same, and the level of intricate flashing, counter flashing, structural expression, and layer upon layer of detail expression are clearly evident in all these drawings. Note the carefully articulated three-dimensional details drawn to facilitate the interweaving column and beam connections in a context where there is no capacity to hide and joint or forgive any misalignment.

Figure 2 The clean, crisp ends of the heavy timber roof rafters proudly protrude from the stoic stone piers that support them. Note the solid wood tongue-and-groove eave underside. From this vantage, the buried aspect of the house is virtually invisible.

(Courtesy of Norman McGrath.)

There is a certain perversity in designing houses that will be intentionally buried. The lowest-tech human accommodation imaginable is a cave—not made, merely inhabited. But the cave is a viscerally comforting accommodation involving a massive monolithic enclosure safe from the elements and yet simultaneously part of them. When humans try to create the benefits of a cave dwelling (the high insulation values, the complete integration with the natural environment, and the poetry of having living material above and around you) *and* at the same time wish to keep water, insects, cave-ins, and decay out of their day-to-day lives, the technical overlay becomes extraordinary (some might even say excruciating). Alfredo De Vido has tackled this task with a vengeance and created a poetically distilled and yet technologically sophisticated solution to the oxymoronic desire to manifest a high-tech cave. Essentially, two methodologies are employed. The first uses layer upon layer of insulating, filtering, and water-shedding products set below the dirt line of the roof. No fewer than four independent layers of plastic products (two layers of polyethylene and two layers of bentonite) are sandwiched around styrofoam, which is used to provide a thermal break (the earth does most of the R value work), and gravel and fiberglass filter fabric allow water to be filtered before it is collected and removed by a new interpretation

of the old "Yankee" gutter system (a gutter that is set behind an eave facia versus springing forth from it). All these high-technology accommodations are, of course, literally buried below the sod roof employed. But what *is* blissfully expressed are the structural consequences of cave creation. Supported by a series of large-scale wood beams (often 8 x 10s) with an occasional steel member thrown in for extraordinary spans, the roof decking employed is at once remarkably simple and extraordinarily expressive. A sandwich is formed to support all the membranes listed. The top layer is ⅝-in pressure-treated plywood, its antifungicidal aspect preempting the possibility of decay generated by dampness. The lower portion of this structural wood deck is formed of stock 2 x 6s laid horizontally with tongue-and-groove joinery. Below them is an air cavity for wiring and a finished ¾ x 6 wood ceiling. The original detail designed by De Vido made the ceiling underside with ganged together finish grade 2 x 3s with the 3-in dimension set vertically, integrating it with the plywood and orienting it to span between the large-scale beams mentioned earlier. De Vido thus attempted to create an image that architects often aspire to, namely the integration of structure, finish material, and expression of the inherent structural conditions present in the overall construction. But as so often happens, the detail evolved to suit changing needs. Without a gap above the finished ceiling, and with no basement, electrical connections and the accommodation of any other mechanical system becomes *very* problematic. This is a horizontal home, almost Wrightian in linearity, providing a conceptual underpinning for the rapid-fire lines of standard wood boards that form its finished ceiling surface. A wide variety of specific joinery conditions are employed, mostly having to do with the layering of materials and the careful non-alignment and gapping of the pieces and parts utilized. Although this is not a low-cost detail (a steel-reinforced concrete slab might be the easiest solution), the inherent problems that are overcome are extraordinary, and the final product has an ambient quality to which it is hard to assign a tangible price tag.

3

Figure 3 Overall view. A meandering glass and heavy timber wall slides underneath a segmented carpet of grass punctuated by masonry piers. (Courtesy of Norman McGrath.)

Figure 4 As seen from this side, the one-way rafter system loses the advantage which affords rafter tail appreciation. Instead, this is a marvelously interweaving system of stoic stone walls and simple wood frame construction. (Courtesy of Norman McGrath.)

4

OUTBUILDING TRIM

Laura Kaehler, Architect

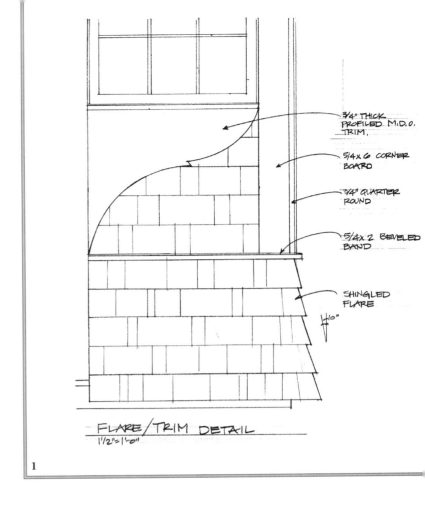

3/4" THICK PROFILED M.D.O. TRIM.

5/4 x 6 CORNER BOARD

3/4" QUARTER ROUND

5/4 x 2 BEVELED BAND

SHINGLED FLARE

10°

FLARE/TRIM DETAIL
1 1/2" = 1'-0"

1

Outbuildings have long been viewed as the one legitimate opportunity for architects to engage in humor and overt irreverence in otherwise more sober contexts. This is doubly true when architects design buildings for themselves. Laura Kaehler is a gifted young architect in Greenwich, Connecticut, and is more often found designing large houses and renovations than minutiae such as this. However, her detailing skill is evident in these pieces, one of which she built for herself, the other built by herself and her father, Herb, for her father's house. For herself, Kaehler explores the interface between the graphic and the built via the use of extraordinarily simple means in the form of some binding bracket trim, aggressively fusing windowscapes on three sides of a studio space. For her father, Kaehler utilizes an attenuated ridge beam and rafter tails to make an otherwise civilized potting shed into something which is lightly energized and animated.

For her own studio, Kaehler intentionally experimented with a variety of trimming and siding techniques, but the most memorable is the use of 3/4-in "MDO" plywood. Normally used for sign making, this is a high-quality plywood, whose veneers are relatively knot free but whose final surfaces are a resin-coated paper intended to accept paint. Rather than having to deal with a combination of solid wood boards that would inevitably gap, and would be difficult to cut with any specific outline, Kaehler used this material in an extraordinarily expressive manner simply by cutting its leading edge with a band saw into a redundant profile which is then mirrored and flipped to

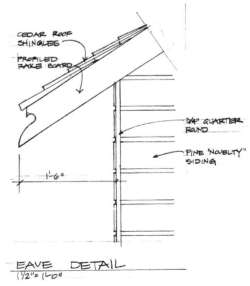

CEDAR ROOF SHINGLES

PROFILED RAKE BOARD

3/4" QUARTER ROUND

PINE "NOVELTY" SIDING

1'-6"

EAVE DETAIL
1 1/2" = 1'-0"

2

Figure 1 *Typical bracket trim. Note the precise coincidence between the top and bottom ends of this reciprocal pair of curves and the chiseled return set between the two forms, concave and convex. A simple flat applied piece of plywood gains great presence when set in concert with windows, trim, skirt, and door opening (left).*

Figure 2 *This is the only "drawable" part of the eave trim discussed, given the sculptural quality of the serpentine ridge attenuations, and this rafter tail is a simple, evocative articulation of a linear piece, evidencing the same sort of folk art detailing which generated the serpentine elements above.*

Figure 3 *Gable view. Four identical brackets and one custom crafted cap piece transform six windows into a singular entity, semireminiscent of Dutch architecture, and simply evocative of the talent of this gifted architect.* (Courtesy of the architect.)

3

bind together a cruciform window array. This binding technique occurs on three sides and has its complimentary cap set above the top of the cruciform window shape realized in the similar method of creative plywood edge cutting. The seaming of the joint between the plywood and the wood shingles is critical and needs to be well formed and thoroughly flashed, but given the extraordinary overhangs that Kaehler utilizes, and given the fact that this is, in truth, an outbuilding and not a residence, there is little room for latitude here. What makes it doubly critical is the use of shingle siding where the vertical grain of the shingle can have real problems when back cut at an angle (glue is often a good idea in such cases).

In the potting shed built with and for her father, Kaehler effected a simpler form but found the opportunity for delicious expression in the attenuation of the structural elements that are present in almost all gable roofs, namely rafter tails and ridge boards. In this case, both have been extended in ornamental fashion and, for the ridge board extensions at least, are simply artful tack ons versus integral articulations. This technique of animating the ridge into a sea serpent sculpture is a direct lift from Scandinavian folk detailing, which, culturally, is intended to ward away evil spirits. Unlike the fusing trim of Kaehler's own studio, the serpentine attenuations of the potting shed are richly painted to flesh out the animistic articulation.

Three intimacies are involved in the creation of these trim details. The first is the architect's hands-on approach, allowing her to become thoroughly integrated into the items that she designed. The second intimacy is in the client-architect relationship, which is either deeply familiar or a single identity. The final intimacy, and the one perhaps most important for this book, is Laura Kaehler's rich knowledge of articulate detailing borne of a long history of creating elegant and aesthetically enriched residences for demanding clients in coastal Connecticut.

4

Figure 4 Corner condition. *When simple graphic pieces are set within replicative coincidence, the places where they meet become quite interesting. There is a positive-negative dynamic implicit in all this work.* (Courtesy of the architect.)

Figure 5 (a) and (b) Serpent head and tail. *Easily bandsawed and delightfully colored.* (Courtesy of the architect.)

Figure 6 Overall photo. *Extended rafter tails and ridge beams take a simple form and sprinkle it with a little bit of magic detailing.* (Courtesy of the architect.)

"These are special places to rest and get away from the hectic noisy world."

5 (a)

5 (b)

6

SHUTTERS

Ofer Barpal, Architect

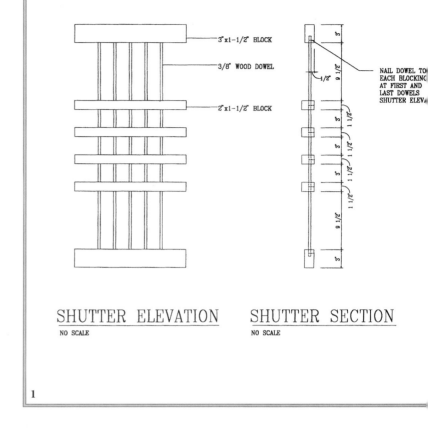

3"x1-1/2" BLOCK

3/8" WOOD DOWEL

2"x1-1/2" BLOCK

NAIL DOWEL TO
EACH BLOCKING
AT FIRST AND
LAST DOWELS
SHUTTER ELEV.

SHUTTER ELEVATION
NO SCALE

SHUTTER SECTION
NO SCALE

1

Architects are seldom wealthy people. They are often, however, extraordinarily creative. When creativity encounters a lack of budget, the aesthetic results are often heightened rather than mitigated. Such is the case with architect Ofer Barpal and his decision to turn the simplest of sliding windows into an exterior event. Shutters have often been used as a "halo" to rude openings set within the context of simple residences. Derived as a protective device, they have now become vestigial remnants used as ornament, whose sizes often would not come close to covering the openings they flank. Nowadays, shutters are often plastic panels screwed to the wall flanking windows that would never be able to utilize their potential protective overlay. Architect Barpal decided it would be a good idea to add a sense of luster to his home, and he utilized the simplest of prefabricated wood elements: $1^1/_2$-in thick stock cut to a variety of widths and $^3/_8$-in wood dowels. Utilizing a minimum of fasteners (and a maximum of friction fitting), he conspired to create shutters that serve as artful (and perhaps humorous) counterpoints to the fairly stark predictability of their context. These oddments are amalgamated into the home's ambience via consistent use of the same paint for siding, trim, and shutter. These constructions are at once expected and lyric. They are also *quite* cheap to fabricate and install.

Figure 1 These drawings are the retroactive reconciliations of a product that was designed in the field of stock components. All the dimensions were keyed to the full-sized tinkering, and all the joints are the image of the easy alignment.

Figure 2 The most basic sliding window and trim assembly gains a sense of enigmatic presence due to the symbolized shutters that are set to align to its outer edges. (Courtesy of the architect.)

Figure 3 Overall context. A simple suburban home has some enigmatic shadow play added to its countenance. (Courtesy of the architect.)

2

"Having to replace the old, broken ones, the intention was to create a light, geometric pattern with large openings so as not to trap moisture and insects. They are attached with hooks to the siding and have performed well."

3

COLLEGIATE GOTHIC FACADE

Nagel, Hartray & Associates, Ltd., Architects

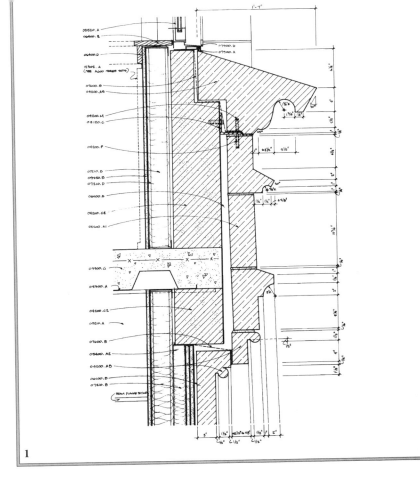

1

Why would detailing that is completely derived from the antique be put into a book labeled "Expressive Details"? Simply because the method behind replicating the preexisting antiquity reflects some of the most ingenious and thoughtful aspects of late-twentieth-century architectural technology. Sixty years ago, when the last Collegiate Gothic buildings were replicated on the campus of the University of Chicago, the gothic facades were merely veneers set to concrete or brick infill. The new work depicted is a veneer also, but it is set to the now-classic heavy gauge steel frame and poured concrete over corrugated steel subfloor system which dominates much multistory institutional construction of this half of the century. This is now a three-layer envelope with insulation and sheetrock facing the inside spaces, an intermediate wall of concrete block that is set to the perimeter edge of the poured floor, and the cut limestone cladding virtually draped in the plane beyond the leading edge of the poured concrete floor and concrete block infill. The concrete block wall essentially allows for the attachment of the limestone skin with steel angle and pin connections, and some of the arched openings rendered on the first level of the construction are virtually self-supporting with the dead load of the limestone skin translated around the window openings by the stone itself. It should be noted that there is little or no direct innovation in the actual profiles or edges used. They are all extruded from the existing adjacent constructions and are set to perfectly align with the buildings that book-end either side of this new construction. The building is thus "locked in," and gains its

2

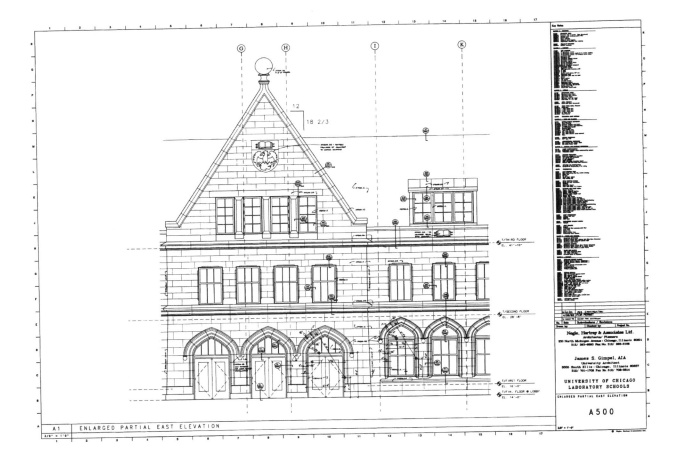

Figure 3 *Overall view. Note the specification key to the right of the drawing. Note also that this is a computer-rendered version of the facade, whereas the seminal detail (Fig. 1) was hand drafted.*

Figure 4 *Context. Flanking buildings presented a precedent that was absolutely followed in this design.*
(Courtesy of the architect.)

zest from the aggrandizement of certain forms and from the redundant articulation of the window forms that have their precedence in the immediately adjacent buildings.

The graphic description of this detail, and, in fact, of the whole project, is a model of late-twentieth-century architectural notation where the numbering system laid out in the Master Format system designed by the CSI (Construction Specifications Institute) in 1963 is used to encrypt virtually all the notations that would normally be written amid the multitude of materials depicted. There is a rigorous graphic encoding as well, where each material is given its own cross-sectional poche. The clarity of the detail depicted in these drawings is striking and allows an immediate and clear interpretation, both at first blush, given its graphic clarity, and upon deeper inspection, given the depth and density of the notations that are encrypted by the Master Format numbering system, which is a model of the capacity for specifications to be both comprehensive and maximally efficient.

Although this building system is relatively standard and time-tested, it is not inexpensive, given the large quantity of custom-fabricated components necessitated by the replication of the limestone skin. However, through the ingenuity of architects such as Nagel, Hartray such potentially ill-defined craftsmanship is rigorously formatted and communicated to the point where misinterpretation could result only from extraordinary incompetence on the part of the fabricator. Thus, this detailing expresses this particular office's dedication to creating a highly controlled expression of reverence for the adjacent buildings.

4

"This Collegiate Gothic facade in oolitic limestone completed the east side of the University of Chicago Laboratory Schools' quadrangle. Conforming to the University's intention to maintain the traditional campus style of the historic quadrangles, it was the first new Gothic facade on the campus in 60 years, and carefully reproduced the decorative elements of that style. The ogee details of the arch defining the window, with its corbeled ball and stone course above the spandrel, matched those in adjacent buildings."

POOL FENCE AND GARDEN GATE

George Ranalli, Architect

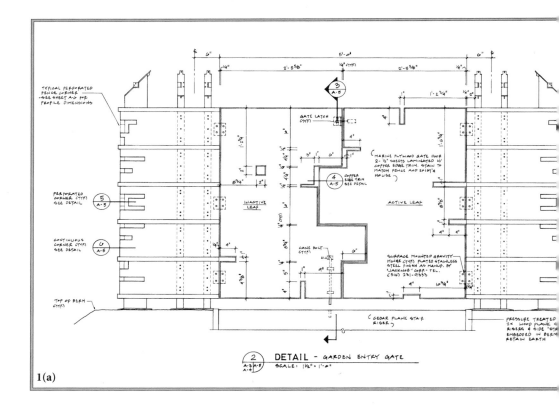

Separating pools from potential drowning victims has been a recent condition of compliance with single-family residential building codes confronted by architects. Often subject to a building official's interpretation of what constitutes a legitimate barrier, these fences or landscape elements can often interrupt the original intent of the architect or mitigate the appreciation of the natural features of sites which accept natatoria. But in some tightly knit communities, these fences can serve in the best tradition of garden walls or other landscape elements that help define and civilize residential adjacencies, such as those present on coastal Long Island. However, if these barriers become rude separations, they neither live up to the macro potentials for spacial and formal definition nor accept the challenge of expressive architectural detailing that sustains visual interest.

George Ranalli, an extraordinarily creative New York City architect, has taken up the challenge of the pool fence with great gusto in this project in second-home-rich coastal Long Island. Rather than simply accept the fate of most of these constructions that the fence should kowtow to the existing architecture (in this case, a classic 1970s vertical-sided, saw-toothed massed contemporary), Ranalli saw the potential in creating a contrasting horizontally linear composition of stock components—namely, stained Douglas fir

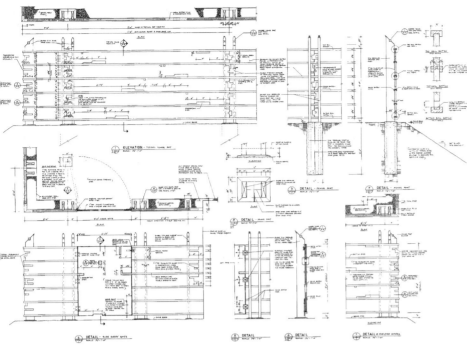

1(b)

2

boards whose joints are obscured with applied battens and whose vertical support comes from similarly standard 2 x 6 pressure-treated yellow pine fence posts. What makes this project unforgettable is its hyperintensive dedication to articulated edges, joints, and corners. Whereas the battens remain perfect and unbroken, horizontally racing around the fence itself, each corner of the fence is both mitered (articulating the wraparound aspect) and irregularly "voided" in an eroding, slotting pattern utilizing the module of the batten to create a variety of gaps just at the point where the eye normally rests. Similarly, the tops of the 2 x 6 pressure-treated wood posts have their shape topped with a rakish angle and custom copper cap piece, with all the microdetailing sympathetic to that which is found in the fence itself. Screw patterning at joints between the horizontal boards and vertical supports are also heavily conspired and defined, relating to the capped doubling up of the 2 x 6 verticals to enhance further the sense of A-B/A-B organization also seen in the contrasting dimensions of the board and the batten.

But the culmination of this fence's hyperarticulated detailing is in the gates that breach its opaque perimeter. These are fabricated from marine plywood and have routed out voidal intrusions similar to the aforementioned corners set and rendered to express the battens' linear impact as a contrasting void to the battens' proud application, and these voids are manipulated to occasionally toss in a bit of irony, preempting a potentially predictable construction. In this way, the most abstract aspects of obsessive grid mania and industrially allusive aesthetics are applied to something which could be painfully generic. The overall effect is of an art piece set in a familiar context. As you might expect, every other landscape element of this project has been thoroughly conspired as well, including poignantly setting the gate's doorstops on the center line of the double column mentioned earlier, lightly reinforcing the articulation of the implicit square defined by the two verticals in the concrete footing, and using an intermediate crushed stone band that follows through on the depth of the column as set back from the outside facing wall plane. Despite the implicit cost in microdesigned projects such as this, where every angle and orientation is critical, some aspects of this design make it more affordable than it might have been, including the use of standard materials that are at the lower end of the cost scale (in this case, pressure-treated yellow pine and Douglas fir). Although the doors themselves are exquisitely patterned and carefully laid out, the material utilized (a double layer of [fr3/4]-in marine plywood) has a very good "bang for the buck," considering its resistance to the fairly aggressive weathering of a coastal environment. In addition, all components are lapped onto one another—most prominently, the board and batten surfacing, but also all hinging and fastening to the vertical supports is overlayed, versus integrated, doweled, mortissed, or "let-in" connections—avoiding the need for precise dimensioning and labor-intensive joinery. The screwing pattern, although intricate, is repetitive and thus easy to lay out. Perhaps the hardest detail to execute in this construction is the mitered corner, which needs to be perfect to prevent separation and checking over time. Also, the copper channel that is let into all the cut edges of the plywood doors needs to be executed skillfully.

The project evidences bold strokes of direct architectural control on a large scale and reflects the fascination that Ranalli has for creating objects which are superficially simple yet, when seen at a closer vantage, extraordinarily vibrant and vital. Note that this articulation is expressed not only at the corners of the project but also at the joints between the horizontal boards set to the double verticals, as well as intermittently, with some areas enigmatically and consistently un-"voided" and other areas subjected to the unrelenting impact of Ranalli's voidal intrusions.

3

Figure 3 Corner view. Simple battens form unbroken lines about the perimeter of this opaque shape, while intricate erosions at corners and other points attract attention and invite curiosity.
(Courtesy of the architect.)

Figure 4 Gates. As the board and batten walls are ringed in shadow, these double gates gain presence by their opacity and their vertical violation (in contrast to the horizontal-linear articulations of the flanking walls).

4

"An attempt is made to form a strong connection with the land at the existing house. It is intended for the new architectural forms to be sympathetic to the house, and yet remain autonomous structures."

TWIN DECK RAILING

Kevin Mason,
Architect

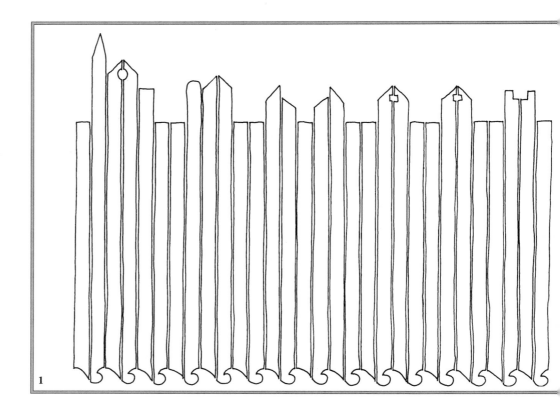

1

Pressure-treated yellow pine is flooding our visual consciousness. When this ubiquitous material is detailed via the recommendations of a large number of standardized texts and publications targeting homeowners and novitiate carpenters, there is an easy standardization of our national backyard ambiences. The encroaching (some might say infesting) sea of grey-green knotty pine is taking over the backyards of suburban America. The virtues of pressure-treated wood are easy to understand—the wood can remain untreated for its lifetime, come in contact with dirt, be relatively strong, and it's still inexpensive. Its downsides are relatively obvious to the thoughtful observer as well. It *is* a sickly green for its first few years of exposure (unless you take the time and effort to apply an appropriate stain, thus defeating the zero maintenance virtue). The wood that best accepts the injected preservative, yellow pine, is often cut from young trees, frequently resulting in center cuts or wild flat-sawn grain patterning, providing intense warping and splitting and a lot of knots unless an expensive grade is used. Whenever these grain characteristics are combined with a very high moisture content, due to the injection of the preservative after kiln drying, the tendency of pressure-treated constructions to blow themselves apart as they dry out is a common problem.

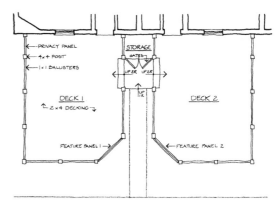

2

3

How do you embrace the virtues without falling prey to the vices? In a project which involves side-by-side decks facing the ocean off the New Jersey shore, architect Kevin Mason has applied the most essential tool any architect can to any design problem—his informed perspective. First, on the macro level, Mason realized that "cost is king," and all his detailing had to be inherently cheap, involving overlay and lapped joinery and face screwing (versus mitering, mortising, or other forms involving precision fit between parts). In addition, the perimeter of these decks is relatively square with but two bevelled aspects, simplifying the need for customized connections.

If that were the only perspective that Mason employed, the decks would look like any of the other backyard constructions that continue their unrelenting march to take over our collective backyards. However, in the best tradition of thoughtful architectural detailing, Mason applied a carefully crafted solution to the deck detailing involving low-tech means and methods to transform a potentially bland or predictable circumstance into an invigorated and thought-provoking solution. First, he recognized that these were two decks, even though they were to be detailed sympathetically given that their common background buildings had a fairly uniform (and blank) context. In addition, power lines, roof vents, flues, and window patterning all celebrated a macro center to this one area of the row building serviced. Mason realized that there would be a dynamic between a common center line and the two owners served by that center line. Bevelling the preliminary threshold to the common access allowed for an easy transition from the parking lot directly adjacent to the deck. In addition, making the railing spacing at that point more opaque allowed for a reinforcement of the division between the decks at their point of connection. Once again, had Mason stopped at that point, there would be nothing special about this construction. He knew, however, that any materials ganged together to create a single plane could become a fabric ripe for creative expression, no matter how redundant or prosaic the constituent parts are. Given that the boards available which are relatively knot free are quite small (perhaps 3-1/2-in width overall) there could be a fairly intricate pattern devised in the one area of the deck which has the ability for easy manipulation *if* you can reject the almost sacrosanct railing and caps seen in most decks. Eschewing the by-the-book rail detailing, Mason simply extended the top edge of the vertical boards. In this particular case, Mason allowed one side of extended board edge to have an overtly seashore motif (a redundant dancing wave pattern) while on the other side of his bevelled signature piece is an abstracted skyline, cityscape, architecturally symbolic profile. In the latter, Mason utilized photographs of local buildings to generate the motifs employed. For this (and for the dancing wave design) he drew full-sized templates and finetuned them on cardboard prior to cutting them out in the field. Furthering this ethical approach, he (plus two friends) built both decks themselves over the period of a few weekends.

Beyond the bevelled feature panels, Mason created a combo gateway involving a modest square demi-pavilion which included lighting fixtures and a common gate, executed two level changes (stepping up into the area described by the pavilion and then up again onto the decks themselves), and allowed for an area of storage to be set up against the houses serviced by the decks and this entry.

All the other elements built by this intrepid deck builder and designer are extremely prosaic, involving the sort of railings, height manipulations, and screens that are now seen all across the American landscape. Architectural detailing need not be expensive to be evocative, and, in this case, the most modest of means created a memorable event when careful planning and full-scale design work overcame a tiny budget and less-than-elegant materials.

Figure 4 *Wave edge pattern. Note that there are only two lines employed to create a pattern which effectively captures the wave motion that the deck beyond this railing views. Also, note the extraordinary variety of graining patterns (and egregious knots) found in the inexpensive wood employed.* (Courtesy of the architect.)

Figure 5 *Context. The blankest of building fronts gains a sense of special treatment via the specialty panels, raised threshold and gateway and focal storage area, light fixture, and trellis.* (Courtesy of the architect.)

4

5

"At the corners (of the twin decks), oiled pine board panels interrupt the railing to speak of contrasting images from the natural and built environments here. On one panel, repetitive waves obviously refer to the Atlantic Ocean on view to the east of the deck. On the other, seemingly haphazard pickets are composed as a less obvious reference. To the west, beyond the actual view of the sunbathers, the owners' parish church, its rectory, and a string of condominia make up the streetscape that is abstracted here. While adults ponder the mismatched panels, children easily identify the likenesses and delight especially in the diminutive skyline. Several severe storms have ravaged the beaches and splintered the decks, yet the wooden waves and bite sized buildings remain unharmed to remind the owners of favorite features of their summertime hometowns."

PORCH EDGE DETAIL

Robert Bast, Architect

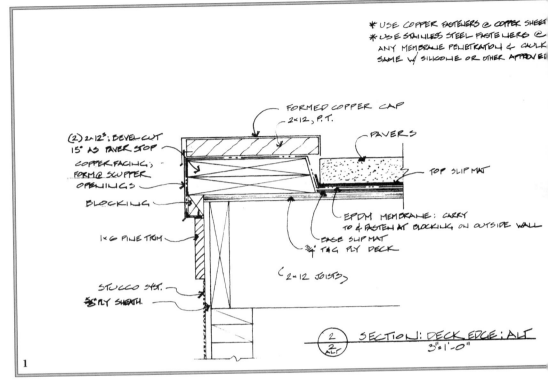

* USE COPPER FASTENERS @ COPPER SHEET
* USE STAINLESS STEEL FASTENERS @ ANY MEMBRANE PENETRATION & CAULK SAME W/ SILICONE OR OTHER APPROVED

FORMED COPPER CAP
2×12, P.T.

PAVERS

(2) 2×12's BEVEL CUT 15° AS PAVER STOP

COPPER FACING; FORM @ SCUPPER OPENINGS

BLOCKING

TOP SLIP MAT

1×6 PINE TRIM

EPDM MEMBRANE: CARRY TO & FASTEN AT BLOCKING ON OUTSIDE WALL
BASE SLIP MAT
¾" T&G PLY DECK

(2×12 JOISTS)

STUCCO SYST.
⅝" PLY SHEATH.

2 / 2 ALT   SECTION: DECK EDGE: ALT
3" = 1'-0"

1

When an architect once declared "God is in the details," one assumed that the architect was a lens through which divine inspiration might create a microcosmic symbol of all that is potentially beautiful or poignant in architectural design. Thank goodness many details can (and do) evidence that sort of distilled symbolism of creative genius. More often than not, architectural detailing has to do with some of the most basic mechanical or functional problems imaginable, almost always under the ever present bludgeon of budgetary accountability. So it is with an edge detail of a porch designed by Robert Bast, a Vermont architect, that was added onto a very clean Georgian home in Vermont. Two baseline design criteria that had no godly intervention or expression were the genesis of this detail. First and foremost, this is an elevated porch extending from the common areas of the house which, due to the site's contours, end up projecting a full level above the surrounding grade. A garage bay and walk-out basement door are set directly below this porch. And yet the owner was desperate to have a true Federal style porch and thus selected brick as a dominant theme in the manifestation of the porch floor. With infinite funds, the brick could be laid over an elevated continuous concrete pad, inherently watertight and monolithically appropriate for traditional support of a brick veneer. Unfortunately, the budget would not allow such a solu-

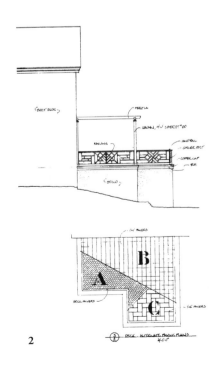

2

Figure 1 The detail. The critical aspect of this detail is its invisibility. Cast pavers are set above an EPDM waterproof roof membrane and alongside a pressure-treated wood curb that is capped with copper. Note the interleaving of the EPDM on either side with slip mats for the base and top, allowing the EPDM membrane to be unscored by the pavers above and allowing the membrane to move above the 3/4" tongue-and-groove plywood deck.

Figure 2 Context and material options for the pavers were given to the client who chose option A and that not only do the pavers give the illusion of solidity but the stucco coating over the plywood wall that forms the sides of this wood-framed terrace does as well.

Figure 3 The critical detail. The 2 x 12 pressure-treated board that rests below the copper allows for the complete acceptance of the prefabricated column plinth plate. Note how the herringbone chevron pattern is allowed to interact with this applied curb, and note also that the stair rail floats above the fray and is attached to the column for support. (Courtesy of the architect.)

3

tion, and a traditional terrace support of backfilled earth or rubble would cut off the garage and basement access. Faced, then, with a hard-edged client-based requirement for a material that would, with "normal" detailing, impossibly violate the house and bust the budget, Robert Bast looked to an alternative building technology for answers.

The last 20 years have seen a remarkable progression in the ability of low-pitched roofing materials both to adapt effectively to site conditions and to provide a relatively sound seal against the elements. One of the leading components in creating low-pitched roofs that don't leak are EPDM membrane roofs, a flexible material which adapts to existing conditions very well when it is allowed to "float" above the surfaces with which it interacts. However, this material is quite fragile when encountering anything that might perforate, score, or even crease its surface, as any weak spot will inevitably open up and allow water to cascade into the space directly below the membrane. Consequently, EPDM is a "no-no" for walk-out roofscapes unless special detailing can be applied. Bast realized this and consulted many roofers about the possibility of utilizing this roof under cast pavers—pavers that would simulate the brick look that the client so desperately wanted to have as part of her house. Ultimately, it was determined that this would be a viable detail *if* both the membrane and the pavers could be allowed to "slip" to bypass their adjacent surfaces, never allowing the membrane to have direct contact with either the pavers above or the wood sheathing below. Once the two interlining sheets applied on both sides of the EPDM membrane became part of the roof design, it then became a simple exercise to follow the manufacturer's recommendations for tying down the edges of the membrane and providing counterflashing. Material choices were also quite easy, as materials needed to be traditional wherever they were visually accessible (copper for all capping material and counterflashing) and zero maintenance where not seen (stainless steel for all fasteners and pressure-treated wood for all that rests below the roofing). Washers were utilized to prevent the capping members along the edge from creasing the material. Because the deck was pitched in a single direction, two details were utilized—one with a modest curb to simply head off the pavers, and the second with a greater curb to control the water more aggressively. This curb not only directs water but also supports a line of perimeter columns that, in turn, supports a shading trellis above and allows a "Chinese" patterned railing to be directly mounted to it. Not only is this detail a structurally and technologically sound approach, it also facilitated another owner request—that she be able to lay the pavers herself in a herringbone pattern. It is remarkable that so many essential and nonaesthetic influences can come together to create a detail that is successful in its invisibility. By simply allowing the pavers to "strut their stuff" and be the dominant visual influence, the overall ambience of the house is enhanced, and the detail in question becomes background, even though it is critical to the success of the entire endeavor.

4

Figure 4 Context. Note the use of copper not only to form the base of the columns but also to make their capitals watertight. If you did not know otherwise, you would assume this was a view of an earth-filled terrace and not one supported by dimensional lumber. (Courtesy of the architect.)

Figure 5 Exterior view. Note how the interleaving flashing and counterflashing and the stucco skirt below never allow for the full appreciation that this is not a masonry construction but one made of dimensional lumber. (Courtesy of the architect.)

"There is a lot of room for expansion and contraction, and care has been taken to ensure durability. In general, the detail has been proven to be imminently practical so far. It has weathered beautifully and performed to expectations. The important point, though, is that the detail was a considered response to a client's choice of finish material and, in that case, the architect's role is to try to make the unseen part of the project as durable as those bricks."

METAL CORNICE

Kent Bloomer,
Architect

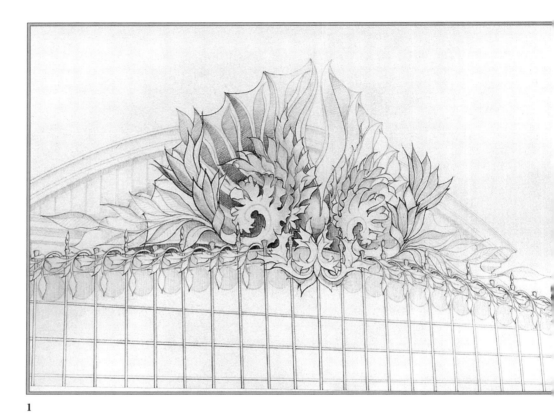

1

This particular project breaks several of the implicit rules of this book. First, the vast majority of details in this book are residential in character, or at least in scale, and this detail is virtually gigantic in comparison, being dozens of feet tall and multiple dozens of feet wide. Second, almost all the details in this book serve to respond to direct functional quandaries, either facilitating movement, providing illumination, allowing weather to be kept out, or simply underscoring some architectonic identity, whether it be structural, technological, or even social. But in this extraordinary piece of artistry designed by Connecticut architect Kent Bloomer, for the Harold Washington Library in Chicago, an unapologetic ornament takes on a sense of presence and identity which fuses sculpture and architecture in a way rarely seen and thus deserves special appreciation. Although it represents a level of architectural detailing which approaches sculpture, ultimately this detail succeeds because it is meshed with the architecture that it is draped upon, and it derives its most potent impact and presence from its context. However, it is in the articulation of the detailing itself that some of the almost lyric (and perhaps even ironic) aspects of this construction are giddily expressed.

2

3

A gigantic library set in the midst of a major urban center is automatically a symbol. Libraries such as this are simultaneously repositories for our collective past, a positive statement about our present, and implicitly convey the fact that we have a common future, either as residents of the city or even simply as members of civilization. By definition, libraries are the product of the collective brain's left lobe—they hold the documentation of our achievements and thoughts. The design for the Harold Washington Library, by Tom Beeby, won an invited competition simply because it so fully manifests the latent potential for architecture to serve as the nexus between our past, our present, and our hopes for the future. Its form and detailing are rooted in many of the traditions of Beaux Arts civic architecture, and the grandeur and sweep of its facades communicate a sense of reassuring precedence while the edginess in much of its detailing conveys an optimistic sense of vitality.

In creating such a monument, often the last element considered is that of ornament. Many Modernist architects simply abstract the linear or graphic elements of a building to the point where they become silly appliques. Post-Modern architects take this one step further (or backward) and provide tacked-on, wallpapered gratuities of intentionally humorous (and often awkward) tongue-in-cheek architectural one-liners. Much of the detailing of this library is overtly historicist. There is an application of precedent that is grounded in architectural history and can be seen as quite comforting to those used to having modern architectural monuments confront their city. It is in the eave and roof that Tom Beeby's design gives us the sense that there is a bright and effervescent future for the city of Chicago. Semisuper graphic lettering is effusively applied to a curtain wall set within traditionally outlined pediments in a semiabstracted and definitely kinetic manner, all regulated by the lines of the mullions employed. Finally, all these energetic moves are set in contrast to Kent Bloomer's extraordinary sculpture and detailing. If this were simply traditional iconography utilizing literal bas reliefs of historic figures or noble symbols (the American Eagle, the National Crest, the "Great Seal" of Chicago, and so on), this would be predictable and unremarkable work. But in the fresh, exuberant, almost effervescent utilization of standard aluminum sheet stock, and custom cast pieces, there is a celebratory rawness to the overlapping forms employed. In the utilization of the owl as an aviary symbol of knowledge, Kent Bloomer's work is both exciting and fascinating in its form and detailing. In boldly responding to the scale of this large building, these huge elements can sustain interest amid the volumes they crown. In positioning and overall form, they have precedence in classical Greek temple architecture. In reality, though, these forms are thoroughly American in their brash sophistication. There is an extraordinary practicality in the fabrication of these elements as well. The potential for the "cut and twist" manipulation of sheet metal to unseen armatures attached with simple welds, maximizes the "bang for the buck" of the elements employed.

Designed from a large-scale model, these elements gained richness as Bloomer personally supervised their fabrication at a local metal works shop. Although designed to crown a monumental building, the success of this project can be seen in terms of its abstract aesthetic appeal and the fact that its succeeds on a variety of levels, including the ingenious craftsmanship of its extraordinarily standardized components, its artful integration with the mullions and pediments employed, and its ultimate ability to attract attention via its scale, visual vibration and sustain that attention with its rich integration of shapes, forms, and density of detail. The art and craft of architectural detailing *have* progressed since "the good old days," and this particular project evidences the best potentials of large-scale architectural ornament as it both dovetails with and transforms its context.

Figure 4 Fabrication. Utilizing simple welding techniques involving clips, some bent small scale stock channel pieces, and, above all, sinuously bent sheet stock, the project is aglomeratively formed in layers, creating elements such as this. (Courtesy of the architect.)

Figure 5 The crowning achievement. Set in effusive celebration above an abstracted glass curtain wall pediment with multiple iconographic messages below, this detail shimmers in the sun and becomes the ultimate expression of the architectural aspirations of this building. (Courtesy of the architect.)

Figure 6 Large scale modeling. The thoughts derived from sketches were preliminarily "reality-checked" via this large-scale model. (Courtesy of the architect.)

4

5

6

"To articulate the Classical idea, as well as to provide an economic plan, the entire building is conceived in the outline of an immense Greek temple. Upon the pediments and at the corners of the roof are metal sculptures representing the ancient Greek antefix and acroterion silhouetted by the immense feathered outline of palmettes, which are probably descended from conventionalized representations of leaves of the ancient Egyptian lotus. In ancient Greece, a burgeoning of foliage above a temple form expressed a renewal of life after a death or a sacrifice. Foliated palmettes often embellished the roofs of monuments in which venerable beings (perhaps the authors and books belonging to this library) are enshrined. Signaling the entrance and guarding the four corners of the roof are the figures of five owls, emblematic of wisdom. The eave unites the roof ornaments into a cartouche that rhythmically engages and absorbs the finials of the fluted vertical mullions. The intent of ornamenting the physical structure of modern building is to pursue the greatest wealth of spatial language innate to architecture. To design architectural ornament, it is necessary to gather, conventionalize, and distribute super-added or adventitious spatial symbols, many of which have been formulated over thousands of years. That is exactly what a writer does in the choice of words and grammar in the composition of a text. Modern building can indeed be utilized to support the millennial life of ornament as long as the linguistic logic, rather than merely the structural 'facts' of western architectural Classicism, is understood."

PLUG AND
PLANK FLOOR

Kevin Mason, Architect

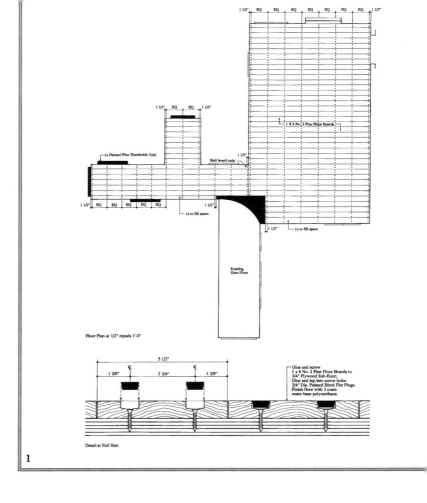

How do you install a wood floor? When the boards are small, nails can be hidden within the context of each piece's tongue and groove edge detailing. When the floor boards get big, the natural acceptance and rejection of moisture by the wood causes the wood to "cup," "check," and "wane." In layperson's terms, the bigger the board, the more it *warps,* and the more a floor board warps, the more it will try to bust its restraints. When dealing with soft wood floors, like the pine floor depicted in this project, the movement can be extraordinary and the forces extreme. Thus the least expensive way to provide sound fastening for most wide board floors is through "face nailing." Often, heads of the nails in face nailing are left raw in older buildings, but the connection between board and fastener is often covered with wood plugs (boat builders call these "bungs").

Without the overarching mind set of an architect's desire to both control the design and liberate the spirit of the work designed, a simple fastening solution such as this is a rude response. In this case, Kevin Mason, a New Jersey architect, has taken the smallest of design criteria—the fastening between a floor board and a subfloor—and turned it into something which has an overarching contextual integration (the spacing of the fasteners) and a delightful enhancing contrast to the materials used (the plugs are prepainted blue in concert with the color scheme of the rest of the project—along with the thresholds into the spaces that are covered with the wood flooring, which

2

Figure 1 Given the on site micromanagement of this particular detail, there were no working drawings per se. These are reconstructions from what was installed. Note the use of painted thresholds throughout, painted the same color as the aggressive plugging pattern that is seen. Note also, the double plugging adjacent to the entry hallway where available length of pine flooring had to achieve a butt joint. Normally avoided at all costs, this aligned butt joint seam becomes a feature in this project. Note the simplest form of flooring was used, noninterlocking, low cost, and replete with knots, pitch pockets, and other figuring. Oriented in a pattern that was made independent of the floor joist below via the use of 3/4-in plywood subfloor (and the fact that each board was individually glued down), the patterning evidenced is allowed to mesh perfectly to the variety of conditions in a marvelous act of wall to wall coincidence that has to bespeak the careful and ingenious overview of the designer.

Figure 2 Context. For all its impact in the drawing, the subtle yet regular dot pattern effected to allow no variation between dot spacing, despite the intervention of the seaming of the flooring itself, quietly underpins the entire ambience of the room. (Courtesy of the architect.)

Figure 3 Sap wood and hart wood figuring, quarter sawn and flat-sawn wood grain, random knots and pitch pockets all serve to flow about the extraordinarily regulated and precisely rendered plug patterns of painted birch plugs. (Courtesy of the architect.)

> "This is an updated version of a random width peg and plank floor that, unlike some of the fake versions available, expresses its actual construction."

3

are also painted blue). Given the softness of the wood and the variety of the graining present in No. 2 pine, the unrelenting clarity of the patterning of these painted wood dots is exhilarating. The result is a wonderful dance between the consistency of the patterning and the aggressively organic nature of an inexpensive wood floor.

FLOOR/TRIM

Duo Dickinson, Architect

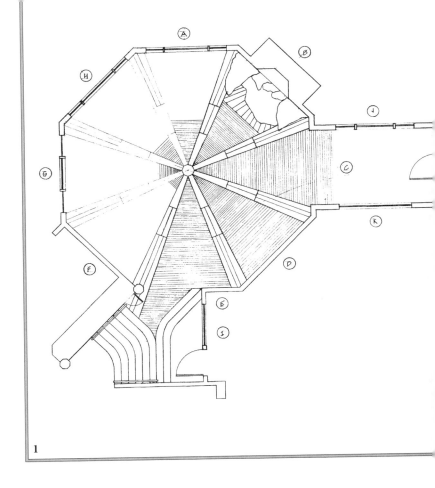

1

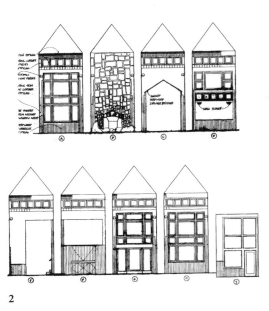

2

Many architects have sought to interconnect spaces, shapes, planes, and lines via the use of integrating materials and geometries. "Architectural detailing" is the general title for areas where small-scale elements are arrayed with large-scale intentions, often using the commonality of application for a wide variety of specific conditions addressed. Whether Wright's hexagons or circles, Corbusier's Modular, or Kahn's circle-in-square, architects tend to think geometrically and graphically in organizing elements that are often three dimensional. The project depicted here had several areas of large-scale concern, both spatially and visually. As a part of the new entry sequence for a house in New York, a new "ballroom" was to be viewed initially from below and ultimately from above. The desire was to create a "unified" space—one that had large-scale cohesion and a presence which was overtly spiritual and centering. It soon became apparent that given the outscaled qualities of the room itself (a 28-ft-across octagonal drum that is 22-ft high at the spring point of the ceiling), a large-scale gesture needed to be applied which could allow the full presence of this room to be made clear to those the space initially encountering it and those who viewed the space from above as they processed through the new entry sequence.

Flooring and trim are often made of the same material—namely, wood. Flooring cannot ethically afford the economy of an opaque finish (paint), and costly hardwoods, so often used in floors, are not typically used in residential construction as window and door trim. Given the zestiness of this octagonal

3

Figure 1 *Plan. Like spokes in a wheel, the octagonal room generates rays of black walnut. The center octagon depicted here is rendered in purple heart with the 2-1/4-in flooring forming the pie shapes defined by the rays being ash. Note the wide board radial black walnut set to the large stone fireplace hearth.*

Figure 2 *Elevations. As each of the eight facades crank about the room, the black walnut rays ascend and relate to the various window, door, and opening dimensions.*

Figure 3 *Elevated prospect. Intended wall and floor plane and increase the sense of the ceiling's disappearing act, these walnut rays catch the eye and interrelate a room that has a wide variety of openings set within its octagonal context.* (Courtesy of the architect.)

Figure 4 *North facing window array.* (Courtesy of the architect.)

4

ballroom, it was clear that the scale and sweep of the room could accept a fairly bold move—namely the fusing of trim and flooring material and the integration of windows, wall, floor, and the overarching octagonal geometry while expressing materiality, joinery, and a high degree of craftsmanship in its final form. Polygonal forms, not unlike circles, suggest a common center point. In the direct relationship between horizontal and vertical planes present in a direct vertical projection of a polygonal form, there is an obvious relationship between the corners of the room and the center point of the room's polygonal outline. The trim and flooring motif depicted in this detail simply takes the inherently radial aspect of the flooring and "connects the dots." That expression is defined at one end by the spaces between the window walls (trim) and at the other end at the center point of the floor itself via the use of contrasting materials and radial geometric projection. Solid black walnut rays perform the linear connection and spring from a purple heart wood octagon set at the "core" of the octagonal space itself. Solid ash flooring is set between the rays. Perimeter trim around the windows is painted out to match the walls, and as the ever decreasing size of the windows employed to vertically ascend ultimately gives way to the carefully considered absence of detail in the octagonal ceiling, it was determined that the interconnecting rays of solid walnut should also progressively "dematerialize" themselves and allow their boards to step and integrate with the aforementioned horizontal lines of the windowscape. Thus, a simple beckoning gesture, black walnut on a white wall, greets the visitor when this room is seen from below. Its full vertical presence is felt once the intermediate floor level of the ballroom itself is attained. And once the final aspiration to the existing second floor is achieved, the graphic interconnection between walls and floors is there for all to see with the big payoff being the central purple heart crux. It should be noted that the black walnut flooring is cut radially, with ever increasing board widths, while the ash in-fill is simply 2-1/4-in stock material. Walnut is expensive, and cutting it into rays with close to perfect joinery makes it doubly so. The act of cutting relatively inexpensive ash flooring to an ever-increasing pie shape is not inexpensive either. Finally, the careful coordination of the transitioned black walnut trim as it registers to the regulating lines of the windowscape and other specific wall conditions allows for a wide variety of fairly intricate joinery to occur with expressive seaming used to highlight the variety of conditions encountered. A simple lesson can be learned from this project. Woods of all different color values, graining, and textures are available *without* artificial staining. In addition, there can be significant integration between flooring, trim, and paneling so long as the distinctions between the elements are kept clear. In this case, thickness is varied between the elements employed by increments of 1/8-in, allowing redwood wainscoting to remain shy of the black walnut striping and painted window trim. In this particular case, raw, naturally finished material is given enormous vitality by the imposition of overarching geometries and carefully crafted, field-fabricated detailing. Although the results are not cheap, they are dramatic and fit the context of a unique space in the way that no standardized detail solution could ever begin to approximate.

5

Figure 5 *Prospect into connector.* (Courtesy of the architect.)

Figure 6 *Center point. A purple heart octagon simultaneously receives and launches the black walnut rays which subdivide the clear ash set perpendicular to the angle bisector of each pair of rays.* (Courtesy of the architect.)

ZOO PAVING

Bohlin Cywinski Jackson, Architects

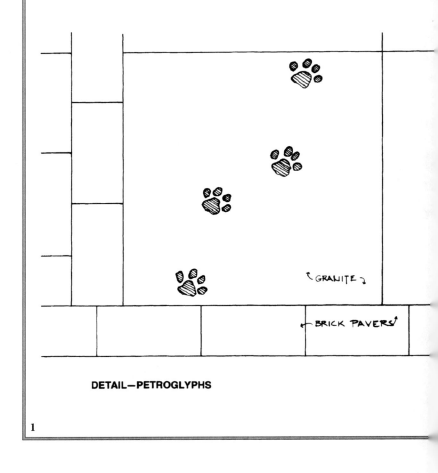

DETAIL—PETROGLYPHS

1

One of the joys of architectural detailing is that it can be as simple as the light bulb appearing over a designer's head. As part of the Carnivore Exhibit for the Philadelphia Zoological Garden (there are two other examples of Bohlin's work on this project elsewhere in this book), the architects involved had one simple idea. In an architectonically organized paving pattern involving 2-in x 2-in granite pavers and standard brick highlighting and edging, why not add a touch of whimsy? In this case, whimsy was simply the sandblasting of the granite surface to "reveal" a pseudo fossilized paw print.

These petroglyphs are pure whimsy. No explanation is offered nor needed. Their mere presence speaks volumes about the emotional bond between those who venerate the animal world via its controlled exhibition and the animals that are both celebrated and yet confined.

Figure 1 Drawing. The simplest sort of detail indicating the location of paw prints that would ultimately be laid out in full sized by the architects.

Figure 2 An ingenious application to a very stock paving pattern. (Courtesy of the architects.)

TILE WORK

Duo Dickinson, Architect

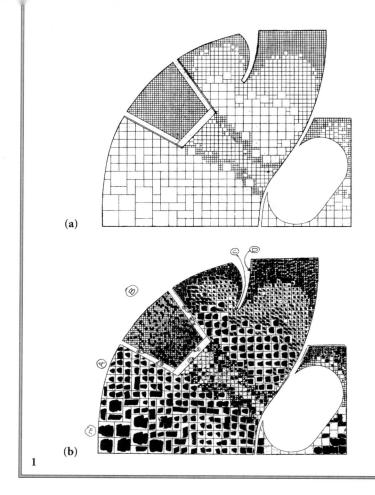

(a)

(b)

1

Custom tile work has schizophrenic origins. Absolutely redundant components can be arrayed in absolutely idiosyncratic ways, allowing the twin world of stock tile and nonrepetitive patterning to infuse each other with the best aspects of each item's inherent properties. Tiles, to many architects, represent a module—square tiles even more so, and square tiles whose sizes vary with modularly conspired increments more so still. Most architects view the invocation of an overarching modularity upon a free-flowing design as a way to integrate seemingly irrational gestures with an existing built form's rectilinear geometries. Thus in a relatively small (16-ft x 16-ft) master bath, eight tile sizes and eight tile colors, totaling 8000 tiles, have been conspired to create swirling patterns evocative of water flow, raw geometry, and elements which are vaguely allusive to landscape. Every tile had to be located and every color had to be chosen. To make matters more interesting, curvilinear and angular elements were juxtaposed and interwoven within the context of the bath's design, and the patterning had to transition from horizontal to vertical spaces without interruption. At the same time, no tiles could be made to bend around or into corners, and no tiles could be cast to conform to specific idiosyncratic conditions. Therefore, all tiles needed to be carefully laid out so that the pattern-to-wall corner avoids unfortunate remnant bits or inarticulate joinery between surfaces. Fortunately, the secret to all random tile layouts is that variation in grout line width over enough tiles can compensate for a great deal of problematic integration. So it is with this particular bathroom where

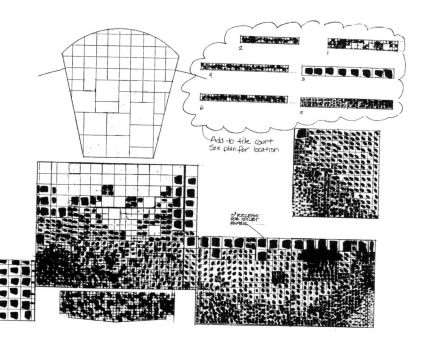

2

Figure 1(a) and (b) Once the tile patterning had been determined, color selections could be made as indicated in the rendered plan (1b).

Figure 2 Every elevation was drawn in intricate detail representing every tile, and every tile had a color applied to it. Note the hidden elevations indicated in the clouded area in the upper right corner.

Figure 3 (a) and (b) Curvilinear tub surround and its equally curvilinear backsplash serve to frame and animate a tile pattern while an effervescent flow of lighter and smaller tiles bubbles across the room. (Courtesy of Mick Hales.)

3 (a)

3(b)

Figure 4 The bubbling "overflow" of the top (see Fig. 3a) seems to be collected by this architecturally delineated shower. Note the floating vanity to the left that allows tiles and tile pattern to occur uninterrupted and the fact that the backside of the shower itself is a niche, recessed from the curvilinear wall from which it springs.

(Courtesy of Mick Hales.)

the variety of colors employed as well as the variety of sizes integrated allowed for enough "play" so that the complete tile layout could be effected with a very modest amount of rectification in the field. Another trick for the ultimate success of this tile work is the use of black walnut and jade green Corian lips and counters to preempt the need for the tile to transition around "proud" corners. "Innie" corners were easy, as one tile could simply slip under another, but at "outie" conditions such as the edge of a tub surround, glazed tiles have a hard time turning a corner and, when there are curves involved, it is virtually impossible, without custom crafted tiles, to allow two rectilinear patterns to interface without an extraordinary amount of painful cutting and joinery—something which is not tolerated well, especially in this "lumpy" form of handcrafted tile. A sense of ordered and conspired choreography is evidenced in this large-scale mosaic. But like the rhythmic metering in orchestral music, this visual melody, while not missing a beat, still expresses joyous spontaneity.

Openings

One *of the contributors to this book, and the man to whom the book is dedicated, Louis Mackall, once said, "Doors are the body, and windows are the spirit." The act of physical passage between spaces natural and constructed is directly related to our bodies by thoughtful portals, and once inside, the ability for our eyes and minds to connect to distant prospects is always framed by openings. As with everything else depicted in this book, the projects presented show that it is not enough to spec the appropriate prefabricated catalogue part that allows our bodies and eyes to pass through walls, it is incumbent upon those who control the design of these essential building elements to make our bodies feel well met and to encourage our spirits to connect beyond distance. In this chapter, we deal with the perforations of the skin and surfaces depicted in the previous chapter, and these openings either stand in concert with or in denial of the structural elements referenced in the opening section of this book.*

CREATIVE CONCRETE

Louis Māckall, Architect

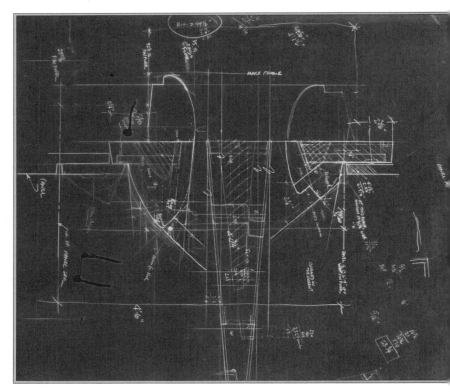

1

Although this project could easily have been put in the "skin" category of this book, it is the windows of this project which represent the most radical departure from a normative concept, thus the entire system is being presented in this piece, with windows as the focal point.

Over 20 years ago, Louis Māckall was just another young architect in search of a place to live. He purchased a piece of land and began building a house, piecemeal, that would ultimately harbor him and his young family. In the intervening time, he has won numerous national awards, and he (and his shop, Breakfast Woodworks) has been recognized as one of the most skilled creators of custom-crafted millwork in the United States. Breakfast Woodworks effects not only his own designs but those of leading architects from all over the East Coast. It is thus ironic that one of the most interesting details Louis Māckall has ever concocted is the treatment of the exterior of his home in Guilford, Connecticut, is made almost wholly of concrete.

Picking up on this obsession with concrete, Māckall decided to custom-fit all his openings into his precast veneer to be applied to his home. To obtain weather worthiness, Māckall decided to utilize a flexible product, frameless plexiglass, to be pulled over an arced concrete form. This approach takes full advantage of the potentials of cast concrete (versus glued and milled wood-

Figure 1 Profile. This was originally sketched as full size to assist the designer and maker (Māckall himself) in the process of forming a full sized template. Much changed during the actual fabrication, but the process of exploration is aptly communicated by this drawing and its informal, almost confessional, notation.
(Courtesy of the architect.)

Figure 2 *Windows. Concrete frames billow out from a precast concrete tiled facade, held fast to the top with screws, pulled fast at the bottom by a bar. Note the cast bottom drip edge that forces any water coming around the plexiglass to avoid insinuating itself back behind the concrete tile. Note also the marvelously thinning side walls that project forth from the flat facade and the registration, top and bottom, of these inserted elements into a heavily gridded context. Given the staggered vertical seaming employed, the upper left and lower right corners register, but their opposite counterparts do not.* (Courtesy of the architect.)

Figure 3 *The billowing windows display their gasketing, drip edge and glistening presence while their second story counterparts, flush port holes set to register within each of the modular concrete tiles, are a bit more enigmatic. Note that each window is one and one-half tile modules wide and, as such, intermittently aligns with the grid superimposed over the facade.* (Courtesy of the architect.)

2

3

work). The methodology employed is very simple: Create a wood positive for this continuous frame, create a fiberglass form from that wood master, and pour in the concrete framework, utilizing steel fibers as reinforcement. The plexiglass glazing is set tight to the top and flexes open when not pulled tight to the concrete frame via a wood lever connected to a string pull. Neoprene gasketing is used around the frame's perimeter to make a good weather seal. The final product is the inverse of a classic bay window, tapering top and bottom versus side to side. Although this window was designed prior to the energy crisis and thus, in and of itself, does not have the appropriate thermal resistance, Māckall retrofitted glass storm panels on the inside of the window to bring it into compliance with energy standards. Although these windows appear to be effortless in their final form, elegant curvilinear appointments on a flat skin of concrete tile, they were produced using two rigorous methods of reality checking which apply to any details that must be weather worthy, involve moving parts, and/or must be affordable.

The first of these design methods is the use of full-sized drawings for the most important cross sectional aspects of the work to be built—in this case, the profile of the window itself. In both aesthetic and mechanical terms, this detail was taken about as far as it could go on paper before Māckall went into the second mode of reality testing. This second mode of design determination, often employed when creating sculpted or intricate details, is the fabrication of a full-size mock-up. In this case, the fabrication method itself necessitated the need to create a casting form, and Māckall, using his woodworking skills, was able to create a full-size dummy/prototype that enabled him to fine-tune all his assumptions and details. The mastery evidenced is subtle and yet exacting when it comes to the perfect mesh with the siding and the ingenious method of closure.

The irony of designing details (whether or not God is present within them) is that noble or rarified ideas need to be grounded in the here and now of fabrication to the most exacting degree present in architecture. It is the fascination with such grounded aspiration that has guided Louis Māckall's career and allows details such as this to exist. Were it not for his, and others', desire to actually build good ideas (as opposed to sketch or talk about them), a lot of our collective creative spirit would be left unbuilt and thus discredited. It is not easy to "get your hands dirty" doing the "R & D" necessary to effect details such as this, but it is the only way conceptual art can be made buildable.

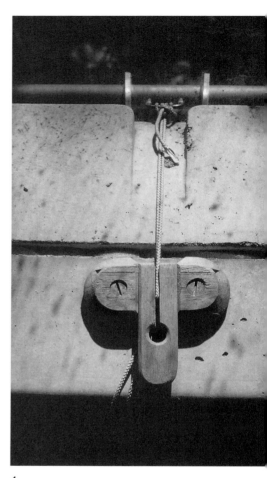

4

5

Figure 4 *Stay. A teak lever handle pulls a nylon cord which, in turn, is tethered to an aluminum bar which, in turn, is fastened through the plexiglass and pulls its flexible form tight to the gasketing which is set to the plexiglass's perimeter edge. When flipped in the out position, this lever allows the plexiglass to regain its "memory" and approach its original flat state, thus pulling away from the curvilinear frame that, in cold weather, keeps a fairly tight barrier against the outside elements—this is critical, given the window's proud presence.*
(Courtesy of the architect.)

Figure 5 *Context. A wood frame building is thoroughly clad in precast concrete elements. There are no overall symmetries present, but a variety of openings and projections allow a blank facade to celebrate its status as literal "wall" while the gap between the two forms announces entry. Note how the tiling had yet to be completed at the far left side and how the traditional galvanized flue for the heating plant is similarly clad in concrete to announce its form at the point of juncture between the two forms' curvilinear stair and edge of rock outcropping.* (Courtesy of the architect.)

Figure 6 *A fairly traditional oak door is set within a custom cast frame. Its major distinguishing aspects are that all perimeter edges of the frame are rounded to reflect the nature of its cast concrete frame. Subsequent to its construction, this frame was painted a pale purple and heavily articulated cotton curtains were stretched across the glazed opening to provide privacy while allowing translucency. Note that this door is centered in the overall grid of the wall. Note also that the paving below is cast (similar to the wall cladding), thus allowing the tile work to be inviolate to grade.*
(Courtesy of the architect.)

6

"When I was doing this house, I liked the idea that Bernard Maybeck had, which was to take burlap bags and throw them into a washing machine that had a cement, sand, lime (or whatever) mix, then take them out and hang them on wires on studs, and that was the siding. I figured if I did that, I wouldn't get a mortgage, so this idea then became pre-cast in a form—concrete panels, ⅝" thick, 21 wide by 27 high with a ship lap or sort of dipping back upper edge over which the next course set. Each of these panels is screwed to 1 x 3 lathe on top of the 2 x 4's with two galvanized screws to the upper flange. The vertical joint is sealed by some 60 ml. BSG rubber, which was glued to the back side of the abutting panels as the panels were installed."

END WALL WINDOW

Louis Mackall, Architect

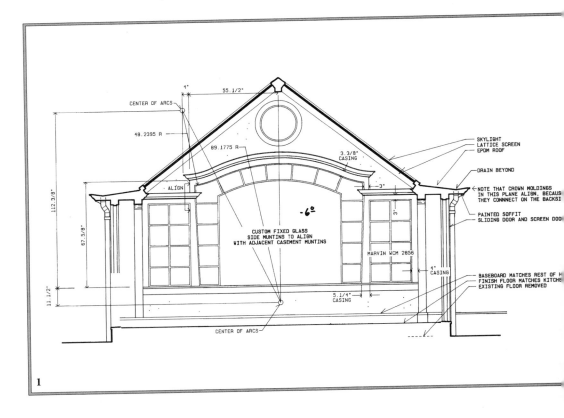

In a small family room addition, Louis Mackall took a standard window company (in this case, Marvin) and animated its generic detailing to manifest a sense of careful articulation which is rare for companies which produce mass quantities of windows, even one with aspirations for customized applications. The irony here is that although Louis Mackall virtually owns his own woodworking shop, he recognized that to make this window affordable, he needed to run it through a production house which had a built-in economy of scale. In the process of adapting his craftsman's mindset to Marvin's standard fabrication techniques, Mackall discovered that "innie" corners are not feasible for therma-pane glass. Two mullions were required in the place of the "innie" corners, and a tapered vertical between two windows ended up with parallel sides. Despite these compromises, there is a striking quality to this design. First, custom-milled crown trim was used to highlight the curve of the center fixed window, and, simultaneously, the same profile is used to meld both side walls and gable wall and, in fact, when the ends are mitered back over the glass, its line is visually extended through the corner panes of the center fixed window to align with the crown that forms the exterior soffit. This effect is blunted by the client's choice of a dark brown trim paint on the outside (versus the white on the inside), but the overall effect is still present. In aligning all muntins between the standard flanking casements and the cen-

Figure 1 *A standard glazing system, Marvin, is manipulated by Mäckall's deft hands to provide a counterflexing ascending center fixed unit. Note that the angled sides of this central unit were straightened, and the final articulation of the bottom edge of the subdivided paning forming the eyebrow top to this fixed unit became more mullion than muntin due to the fact that "innie" corners could not be made in this glazing system. Note the crown returns that interface between center fixed unit and operable flanking casements.*

Figure 2 *Custom fixed windows and trim (center) flanked by stock components. The curvilinear aspects of this project are highlighted by the top lighting provided by the large scale fixed skylighting involved, emphasizing the shadow lines of the crown employed and the mullions utilized.*

(Courtesy of the architect.)

2

3

tral fixed unit, there is an extraordinary degree of integration. By resisting the desire for a simple arc in favor of counter-flexing the ends to a right angle connection at the corners, a predictable window becomes subtly animated and plastic in its manipulation. There is also a light resonance in this curve to the backs of chairs set before this window.

Given the abilities of today's custom window manufacturers, only an architect's limited vision prevents a creative result at a reasonable price. In this particular case, with the addition of years of experience in dealing with sophisticated joinery and careful application of trim, the product becomes thoroughly memorable, despite its stock origins.

"I was trying to stretch the opening and make it feel as big and graceful as I could and still keep the whole thing plausible."

Figure 3 *Context. This top lit celebratory dining and living area is the focal point for the entire back side of the house and its bright ambience filters back through to the existing interior.* (Courtesy of the architect.)

Figure 4 *Exterior. Not only does this window's presence transform the interior space, it provides a potent focal point for the exterior as well. Note the integration between the eave trim and the flanking head trim of the casement windows that form the outside edges of this ensemble.*
(Courtesy of the architect.)

4

TREE WINDOW

Duo Dickinson, Architect

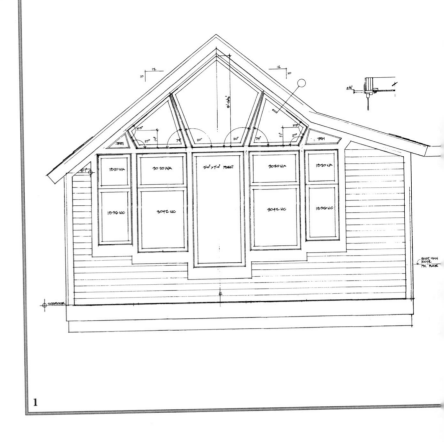

Adding on to older homes can be difficult for architects. The urge to safely copy the existing architectural details begs the question of innovation. However, an "in your face" rejectionist aesthetic simply mocks the parent building, creating a yin-yang composition with all the subtlety of a comedian's one-liner. Despite their charms, architectural antiques offer some significant drawbacks. The couple who owned this antique had lived in it for 20 years and had been squeezed by the 7-ft-2-in–high ceilings, and their views were funnelled through small windows composed of tiny panes. They sought spacial relief when they asked me to design a family room for them, with the culmination of that room being a large window facing their back yard. In "architecturally correct" fashion, I played with designs for this end window that took the muntin patterning present in the existing windows and greatly mutated them to respond to the aggrandizing of the end windows' size to the point where the majority of the end wall of this family room addition would be glazed. When I presented this approach to the clients, they had a disappointed look on their faces. Thinking I had overstepped the bounds of legitimate interpretation, I said I would go back and simply "tone down" the lightly animated glazing I had proposed. "You don't understand," said one owner. "We *hate* the windows in our home! Blow it out!" The window that resulted was undivided thermal pane glass with several operable units. What makes it a suitable exercise for this book is that it uses a standard window company product (in this case Pella) and, by simply angling the sides of some of the

Figure 1 Large scale drawing that was in turn laid out by full size format. Note that the window types went from Marvin to Pella specification, and in so doing, because some problematic aspects with field dimensioning, a transom was added to the middle vertical fixed glazing.

Figure 2 Tree and window. It is at this vantage that the interrelationship between the focal tree and the newly created opening can be best appreciated. Stepping sills and splaying transom pay homage to this ancient tree's poignant form.
(Courtesy of the architect.)

2

window frames utilized and thus tapering two mullions, a splaying upper transom is effected. Along with the staggered sill height employed, this expanding clerestory is intended to have an immediate cross-reference to the natural focal point of the window, a 100-year-old apple tree axially oriented to the addition.

Although there is no excruciating reinterpretation present in this window's small-scale detailing, its large-scale ordinates are completely responsive to the form of the addition, as well as reflecting the natural context and the owner's mindset. Fulfilling these idiosyncratic design criteria with a simple reinterpretation of window shape represents the sort of creative thinking on a budget which can allow for a high degree of personalization. Moves such as this can be made by architects who have limited experience or confidence in their ability to "reinvent the wheel" when it comes to making expressive weather-tight fenestration.

Figure 3 *Interior. A wall of glass has its mullions animated while its lines are backlit by a demidormer of top and relocated existing windows to the left.* (Courtesy of Bob Perron.)

Figure 4 *Context. The new wing (right) utilizes a sympathetic roof pitch and form to the parent building (left) but eschews the tiny openings that were present, as well as the even tinier pane divisions of the original eighteenth-century home.* (Courtesy of Bob Perron.)

3

4

CIRCULAR PLAYROOM WINDOW

Bart Prince, Architect

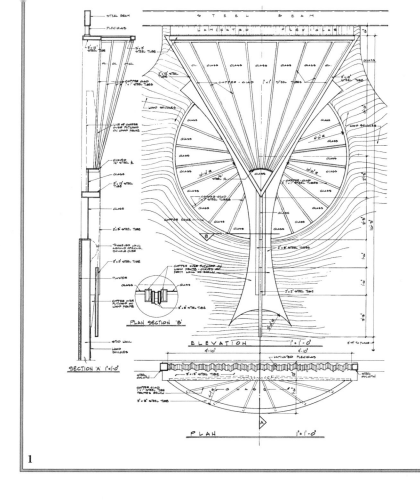

1

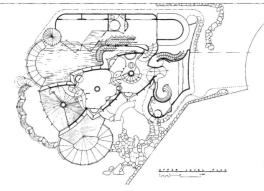

2

Architects like to use the word *fenestration* to describe the holes in a building—namely doors and windows. When an architect like Bart Prince "fenestrates," he does not let the pseudo-scientific flavor of the nomenclature depress his outlook. In fact, nothing could depress Bart Prince's outlook about anything architectural, and nothing proves this designer's obsession with materiality, shape, organic expressionism, and, most important, valid craftsmanship and buildability, than this perforation set within the interior of a home built in Corona del Mar, California. Set at the juncture with a stair and an interior wall, this perforation becomes a focal event in an extraordinarily evolutionary context. Every aspect of this 16-ft high construction has been examined and articulated. Rather than spanning the void with pieces of glass in the form of an uninterrupted sheet, Prince first uses multiple thicknesses and divisions of plexiglass to defuse the light in a way which fully animated the ambience. The stacked plexiglass "halo" rests above individually segmented pieces of sheet glass, all canted in reference to the overarching geometries employed. Rather than choose one simple geometric influence, Prince allowed radial, circular, angular, and organic forms, lines, shapes, and motifs to infuse his window with an extraordinarily effervescent sensibility. The window remains coherent by the use of an all-powerful center line, a tough task given the hyperarticulation of the potentialities employed and the wide variety of metals, glass types, wood species, and joinery utilized. This

Figure 1 *An articulate rendering of a highly effusive detail, one that combines intricate joinery on a grand scale (note that the overall detail stands well over 16 ft high).*

Figure 2 *Context and plan. This interior window sits amid an extraordinary home—one whose prismatic radial motifs are naturally integrated to the lines of the window itself. Set between the two stairs seen in the upper central portion of the plan, this window serves as a focal point to those who ascend and descend the stairs which rest on either side of it while allowing light to filter in and around the window into all its adjacent spaces.*

Figure 3 *Undulating wall surfaces, flowing stairs and overtly kinetic spacial flow all move about this centering form that is at once a void and potent presence.*

(Coutesy of the architect.)

3

"Rather than having the window be a cutout in the wall, I wanted it to have a three dimensional quality both as the glazing meets the wall and within the window itself."

project represents the highest level of craftsmanship (and thus cost), but the bang for the buck is still undeniable, and the creation of a focal point for an overwhelmingly expressive house justified the intensity of effort and effect manifested by architect Prince.

DOORS

Arne Bystrom, Architect

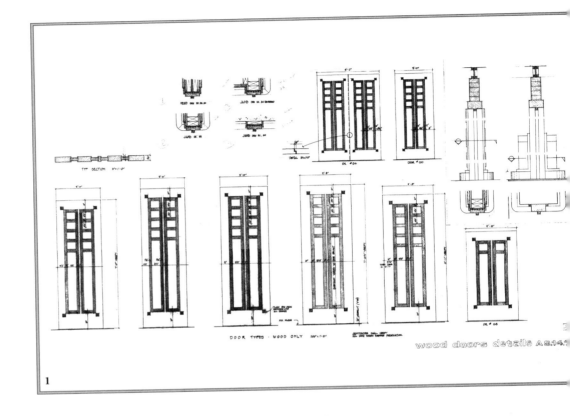

Doors have been the subject of many stylistic attempts at articulation and expression. It is pretty clear that doors are a very simple reality—namely a portal for human accommodation. When made of solid wood, most doors have to deal with some elemental aspects of dimensional stability because in response to changes in humidity wood moves a great deal when measured across the grain (typically the short dimension of each board) and hardly at all in the direction that parallels the wood grain (typically a board's long direction). We have traditionally used almost iconographic raised panel doors in order to deal with the potential of solid wood constructions simply to blow themselves apart when boards are set in the same plane but at orientations that are at right angles to each other. The accommodation of the movement of the raised panels set within the relatively stiff wood frame composed of horizontal rails and vertical stiles is almost forgotten amidst the desire for a stylistically familiar door. Alternatively, modern architecture uses plywood, where stability is gained from lamination, to simply obviate the need for any aesthetic articulation of wood's differential shrinkage patterns. However, it is in the crafts tradition that wood can gain enormous presence through the expressive application of multiple species, grain orientation, and even the expression of end grain (where the wood is cross cut versus the more normal

Figure 1 *The rigorous rectilinear patterning of the multitude of door sizes is accommodated by the consistent use of the typical section seen in the upper left corner of this drawing. Via the simple act of providing for a slipped joint between the proud fir frame and the recessed linear redwood, a simple dado detail allows for the solid wood to move, and the difference in coloration of the materials used gains a great deal of visual presence. Note the squared corner projections, which are all end grained redwood set flush to the frame.*

Figure 2 *A typical door. Note the complete integration between the linear elements which define walls, floors, windows, and structure.*
(Courtesy of the architect.)

2

flat grain, quarter-sawn wood where wood is cut parallel to the lines of the growth rings of the tree). In this series of doors designed by Arnie Bystrom for a house in Idaho, the typical perimeter of a door (rails and stiles) serves as the secondary frame for the expressive use of specie and grain orientation. Rather than accept the simple solution of floating panels set in a frame, Bystrom utilizes individual pieces of wood to form two planes: 1-1/4-in thick stiles and rails form the perimeter frame and interior subdivisions. Let into these thicker elements are 1-in thick lines of wood, with but a 2-in exposure. These "floating" linear pieces are redwood, set in contrast to the clear fir which composes the rigid frame. Articulating the corners of the stile and rail, end grain fir provides sparkle as well. The orientation of the detailing respects the orthogonal shape that most doors naturally follow to mesh with stick-built framing of the walls the doors are set within. Bystrom allows all the doors' parts to expand and contract without any blow-out as the thinner redwood sections are let into the thicker fir pieces by a 1/2-in reveal. Given its overt graphic sensibility, this style of detailing can adjust to the multiple sizes and shapes of doors required for a large custom house. In this way, Bystrom almost makes the wood itself the stylistic denominator of the doors he creates. Going beyond the simple craftsmanly tradition of elegantly articulated joinery, these doors are semiabstracted in their layout, while thoroughly indicating their materiality via the expressive use of grain and specie.

These are doors "using patterned recesses, vertical grain fir, end grain fir and redwood in combination to create rich visual pattern."

3

Figure 3 Detail. *Recessed redwood contrasts with flush quarter sawn fir in a near graphic articulation further highlighted by the deed and dark end grain redwood which is slipped into the flush fir as a perfected square. The joinery is virtually perfect, as is the wood which is used for these doors.* (Courtesy of the architect.)

Figure 4 Context. *The extraordinary integration of virtually every aspect of what might be used to build this house, as evident from the relentless use of banding, square end grain motifs, and orthogonal patterning that goes from large to small, infuse the entire house with the sense of complete coordination and absolute control by an architect at the peak of his powers. Note that all wood is clear finished and that the specie and grain orientation provide the only contrasting aspect* (Courtesy of the architect.

4

PLOWSHARES DOOR

Louis Mackall,
Architect

1

Sometimes, politics and architectural detailing can have a blissful marriage. In negative terms, Albert Speer related Fascist fantasies to architecture with buildings that were as cold and brutal as the people who occupied them. In other, more positive environments, societal symbols can be rendered in architectural ornament in ways which are uniquely political. So it is with the door for a room at a conference center in Massachusetts. Louis Mackall's children had gone to this conference center as part of a summer program for years, and when the center asked him to help them create a special place, Mackall's first response was to donate a door. The door he designed and fabricated was not the product of overwrought architectural detailing but rather the simple, heartfelt expression of Mackall's own personal political passion—namely, the elimination of nuclear weapons and thus the metaphoric beating of swords into plowshares. The room was to be called the "Plowshares Room," and Mackall took his design skills and meshed them with his gifts as a hands-on fabricator to create a plain door with a simple "hook." This is a custom-fabricated hollow core door with a stock lever handle latching mechanism applied to it. It has a single glazed opening, within which is a sculpture designed and carved by Mackall that, at first blush, is pleasant but unremarkable. What makes it and the door absolutely memorable is that Mackall had

Figure 1 The focal point. A combination of window, sculpture, political statement, and ultimately an expression of the hardware employed as the sculpted anvil lifts when the door is opened and comes down upon the sword that is draped across the anvil. Note the delicately articulated fasteners and gasketing around the perimeter of an extraordinarily blank door. (Courtesy of the architect.)

Figure 2 Door. A thoroughly blank context provides a focal point for the window cum sculpture, and additional bite is provided overhead by a stock transom. (Courtesy of the architect.)

2

the presence of mind to link the door's movement with his hand-crafted frieze-sculpture set within the window itself. By animating the carved hammer with each swing of the door, it physically hits the sword as it sits upon the symbolic anvil, which, in turn, becomes a plow. The frieze is expressively carved by Māckall to articulate each pass of the chisel and then "whited out" to create a relatively abstracted symbol. Given the completely neutral door face (painted plywood), and the articulated joint between the glass opening and the door itself (via gasketing and some expressed screw fasteners), Māckall has imbued this politically potent focal point with the power to sustain visual interest. In the use of articulate but crude carving techniques, whitewashing, stock hardware, and the flat hollow core style door, and by considered application of hinge placement (doubling up of hinges at the head of the door), Māckall has made this expression of his heartfelt ethical and social values economically possible. Architectural detailing can do so much with so little, including expanding into the realm of ideas which have nothing to do with aesthetics or architectural technology.

Figure 3 *Door inside prospect. Note the inscribing on the back side of the door to allow for the final appreciation of the focus of the work, namely, the anvil transforming its shape into that of a plowshare whose lines are incised below the bottom edge of the glazing. Note also that, in this picture, the anvil is in its upright position as the door has been opened* (Courtesy of the architect.).

3

RIDGE SKYLIGHT

Alex Varga, Designer

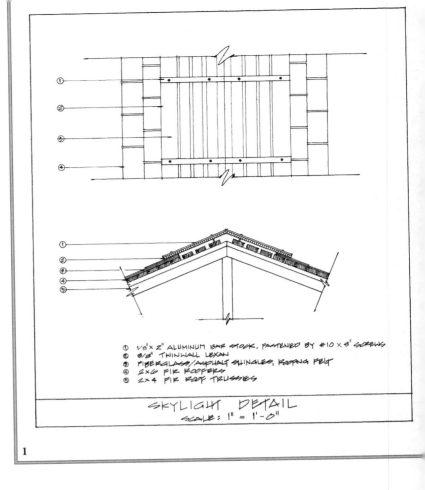

① ⅛" x 2" ALUMINUM BAR STOCK, FASTENED BY #10 x 3" SCREWS
② 3/8" TWINWALL LEXAN
③ FIBERGLASS/ASPHALT SHINGLES, ROOFING FELT
④ 2x6 FIR ROOFERS
⑤ 2x4 FIR ROOF TRUSSES

SKYLIGHT DETAIL
SCALE: 1" = 1'-0"

1

When you are in architecture school, you are desperate to express your-self in something that is built (versus something that is thought of and sketched and mused about amid other people who can only muse along with you). Sometimes, just the act of building can give students sustenance in lieu of expressing whatever design talents they might have. When Alex Varga was going to architecture school, he built a screen porch. He conceived of the roof support for this structure to be treelike in its triangulated, three-dimensional, diagonal expression. But it was only when he came close to finishing the rough framing of the project that he realized that there was the chance to really get some "kick" into his work. Given that the underside of the roof sheathing would be highly visible in this open, uninsulated construction, Varga used solid 2 x 6 tongue-and-groove boards for sheathing. Attempting to get light into his struc-ture (without baking the occupants), he found it difficult to figure out where a skylight could elegantly be set into place, given the expressive continuity of his roof structure. During construction, as each piece of 2 x 6 sheathing went into place, Varga realized that he had the means to the end of light intrusion literally in his hands. By simply gapping the sheathing pieces with increasing spaces as they neared the ridge, and by laying a piece of plexiglass over the sheathing and gaps to form a simple ridge cap, Varga allowed light to come in which was fil-tered by his structural expressionism and yet provided top lighting of it as well.

There were, however, several potential problems in Varga's design. First, there was no way to know whether the plexiglass (in this case Lexan, a very

Figure 1 This drawing is a retroactive documentation of something designed in the field. The ridge skylight depicted effectively utilizes stock materials in a way to animate their individual presence and complements the structure below while top lighting the triangulated construction below and articulating the roof sheathing method. Note that 3/8-in twin wall Lexan had the capacity to simply be bent in the field and held down via aluminum bar stock.

Figure 2 A fairly animated presence, this simple increased spacing, provided by the gapping of the sheathing, seems a natural progression from the construction techniques employed and highlights those areas where the architect focused a great deal of his attention, namely, the expressive use of triangulated framing work and tongue in groove solid wood sheathing, facilitating wider than normal framing bays. (Courtesy of the architect.)

durable product) would actually bend to meet the roof's angle, but by utilizing $\frac{1}{8}$-in x 2-in aluminum bar stock and screws set directly to the roof framing pattern, the 6-in-12 pitch seemed shallow enough to allow the plexiglass to bend without heat. Second, the success of this skylighting technique depended on the absence of a ridge beam or ridge plate. Even with the truss work that Varga insinuated, which has inherent stiffness due to its three-dimensional properties, some stabilizing influence would need to be applied to prevent the potential for racking or having the rafters simply rotate away from bearing upon each other or upon the truss work involved. Varga tripled up on every other framing bay and applied $\frac{1}{4}$-in-thick steel plates at these multiple layer bays to create an intermittent stiffened frame that preempted the need for a continuous ridge member, thus freeing up the central gap that formed his skylight for complete solar access. The net result is effortless, one that is made of off-the-shelf products, with no fussy detailing. Because it overlays the crown of the roof, there is a minimum opportunity for any ice damming or buildup at the intersection between the asphalt roof shingles and the plexiglass ridge cap, and because Varga was able to bend a single piece over the crown of the roof, there is a marvelous sense of openness—a celebration of the ascendance of his roof sheathing pieces.

Fresh young minds might not have the depth of experience to execute intricate and interweaving details that solve multiple problems with the depth and breadth of knowledge that is often awe inspiring, but fresh young minds are also unencumbered by preconceptions, allowing a simple insight to have a dramatic impact without the overlay of affectation or preconception.

> *"I had earlier conceived of the roof trusses as mechanical versions of the tree branches which the porch looks onto. I thought that the solution to the skylight question should come out of the same line of thought. I chose to gradually space the last four rows of 2 x 6 roofers to produce slits along the entire ridge of the roof through which sunlight would seep into the interior. I chose to cover the exterior surface of the ridge with sections of 4 x 8-ft twin wall Lexan sheet, held in place by $\frac{1}{8}$-in x 2-in strips of aluminum bar stock on 6-in centers set in silicone and screwed through the Lexan into the 2 x 6 roofers."*

3

FELINE DINING ALCOVE

Robert Orr and Associates, Architects

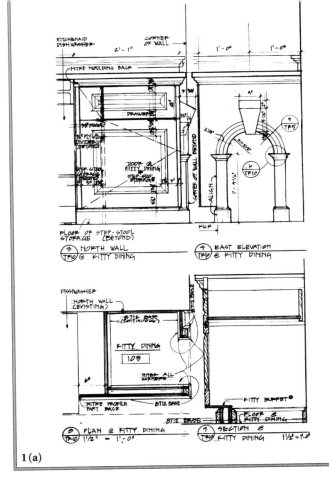

1 (a)

In a tiny seventeenth-century Federal style townhouse in Greenwich Village, New York, Robert Orr was asked to "finish" the interior space in such a way as to maximize utility and amenity while minimizing the sense of "pinch" one might have in such a tightly sized residence. Orr responded in two ways, both detail intensive. First, he condensed all the "serving" parts of the home (including kitchen, bath, and storage units) into tight, custom-built elements. Second, and almost more important, Orr made this efficiency imperative delightful by the use of some animated Georgian detailing. Historically, detailing may be a visual cue to predictability via precedent. However, nothing could be further from the truth for this particular domicile, and the freshness of mindset and the application of familiar motifs can best be seen in one corner of the galley kitchen. Space was so tight that the precious 2-ft x 2-ft area in which the owner's cat could eat his fill needed to have a functional double dip via the extension of the kitchen counter top over this corner space. But rather than simply cantilever a slab of counter over a bowl or two of Purina's finest, Orr decided to transform this simple accommodation into art through the use of cleverly scaled details providing a keystone capped archway leading to the "kitty buffet" for the storage of feline food products. This playful detailing of a potentially predictable end cabinet is just one of many elements in this house which bring the scale down to that which is smaller than the norm. In addition, the seemingly solid kitchen-facing side of the cabinet is, in fact, a door allowing full access for cleaning and food preparation for the beloved pet.

Figure 1(a) and (b) Set within the context of a classic set of architect-derived cabinetry drawings (one level shy of shop drawings but several notches up from the classic architect's drawing), a special condition is rendered involving some aggrandized elements as well as ones that might be described as demitasse in scale—all derived from a feline perspective. Note that inside the cabinet the toe kick recess becomes a surface for dining, and the door that normally allows for storage within a lower cabinet becomes an access hatch to provide more food and maintain hygiene, all provided without interrupting the use of the upper third of the cabinet for a drawer as well as the full use of the space above this alcove for counter use.

Figure 2 End cabinet and cat portal. Note that the finished product had its vertical legs reduced a bit, providing a starker, more opaque context for its insinuation. Note also the crisp transition from toe kick to pilaster base seen at the lower left.
(Courtesy of the architects.)

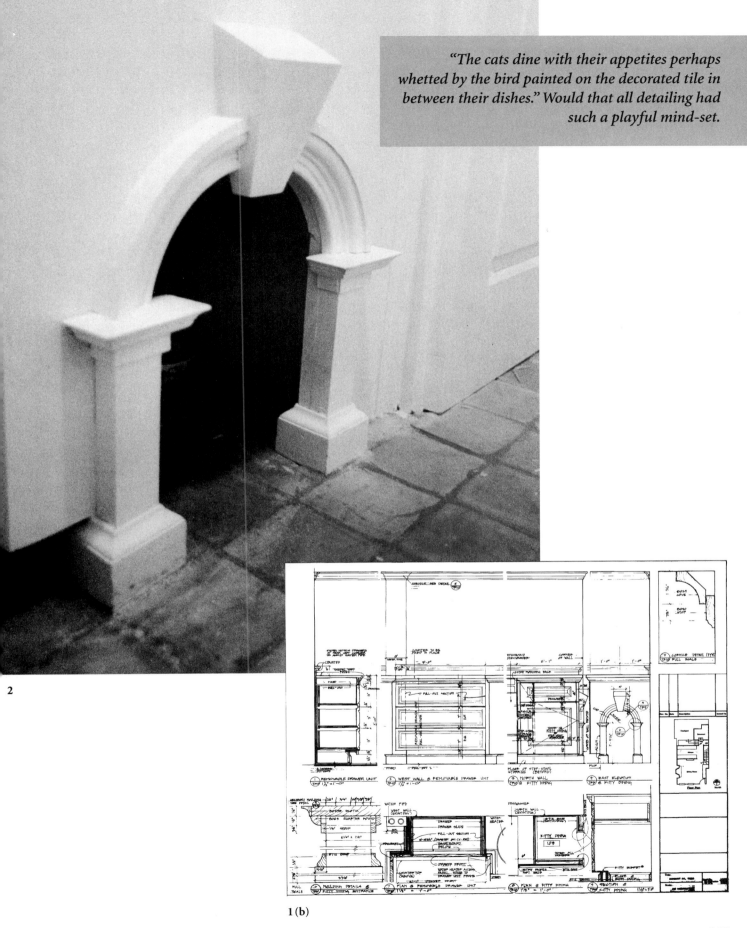

2

1(b)

Movement

If structure makes a building, surfaces define spaces, and openings allow passage, it is stairways that best reflect and facilitate the act of human movement. Stairways have provided some of the richest evidence of architectural innovation and are often seen as mediators between the large-scale act of construction and the small-scale acts of craftsmanship and detailing. The richness of these examples is directly attributable to the complexity of structural, ergonomic, technological, and material aspects which cross-pollinate and infuse these often intricate constructions with a sense of thoughtful detailing and expressive manifestation which is often all too rare in our buildings. Because of the multiple design criteria that must be addressed for a successful vertical transition, stairs represent some of the more fascinating examples of architectural detailing presented in this book. In addition, railings direct the flow of traffic, and, although less compelling in form and use, they offer real opportunity for creative expression.

RAILINGS

James Kimo Griggs, Architect

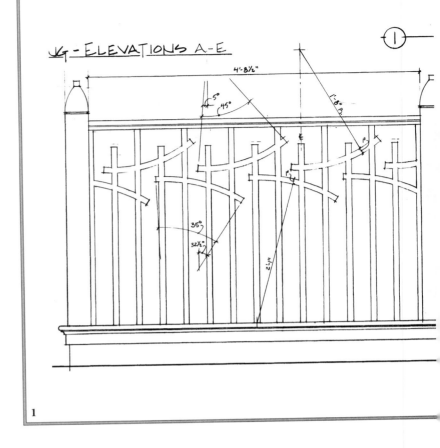

The function of a railing (a physical barrier to prevent self-destruction via an abrupt level change) is so elementally obvious that it often blunts the spear of potential innovators. In other words, something that could be (and often is) effected via a 3-ft-high stud and gypsum board wall, can be easily overlooked as potential for aesthetic expression. But architect Kimo Griggs's spear remains sharp as seen in this railing for a new studio. This railing has as its mute counterpoint the classic half-wall at one end point. Perhaps it is this sort of dynamic contrast which reveals the creative potential of any architectural detail. In fact, beyond the stark contrast between the low wall and this railing, there is contrast present between the individual components comprising the rail itself. In fact, there is even contrast between the lower two-thirds of the balusters effected and the upper one-third, where all the creative expression announces itself. It is these sorts of internal contrasts, utilized to maximum effect via the application of color and material change, that help any architectural detail to gain presence and distinction. In fact, this railing gains a great deal of mileage with a minimum of distinctive and contrasting elements. Born of standardized components (1-in x 1-in square balusters, 4-in x 4-in newels, and a simple 1-1/2-in x 3-in railing), these elements are creatively rendered by the judicious use of color and shape. Few curves are employed, and there are no "random" or non-geometrically defined shapes.

Breaking down the construction into its three basic components—newel, rail, and balusters—one can see the value of the designer's clarity of perspective. As said, the rail is a simple and straightforward linear element. The newel

Figure 1 *Repetitive baluster spacing gains a level of intermediate distinction as every other baluster touches the handrail above, with those balusters held short attached to their full-length counterparts by arced lines arrayed to form a botanical sensibility. Note that these arcs are half lapped with their vertical counterparts. Note also the precision with which they are laid and described.*

Figure 2 *Railing. The coincidence of the generic (the low wall to the left) and the custom crafted (the rail, center right). Note how newels are rendered as centering influences on the botanically lilting arrays of arcing as well as the low and horizontal intermediate stiffener. Griggs rendered his newel top as a nascent bud. Contrast is employed between the aforementioned wall, the natural wood floor, the dark green newel and rail, and the white baluster system.* (Courtesy of the architect.)

2

> "I endeavored to allude to a vine or garland in order to satisfy the client's desire to bring nature inside the building in some form. This desire is also reflected in the newel post caps which are made in the form of large, green buds."

is similar in its simplicity but has a lightly geometricized cap piece—its four sides tapered in an arc with a reveal set between the beginning of this taper and the square shaft of the newel itself. The balusters are essentially a two-part construction where every other baluster spans from floor to railing underside, with those between the full-span balusters being held the same distance below the rail as the balusters are spaced apart (4-in). Linking these full-height balusters to those held short are simple arced pieces that, by their careful alignment, become botanical in their ambience. In reality, these simple inflected lines are unabashedly graphic and are oriented symmetrically about the newels in an array which aggrandizes their input and is allusive to the implicit bilateral symmetry so often found in nature itself. Besides providing the linkage between full-span and held-short balusters, the simple expression via projection of the end points of these arced appliques communicates a controlled animation and craftsmanship which resonates well in the simple, painted final product. Attachment to newels is straightforwardly expressed via half balusters which are screwed into place. The working drawings precisely locate the angle, arc, and vertical orientation of each one of these pieces while reflecting a graphic communication of something which was designed at full scale.

Coming early in Kimo Griggs's career, as part of an overall design for an artist's studio, this railing proves that modest means can effect expressive results and communicate subtle notions of botanical ornament, graphic abstraction, and, most important, the craftsmanship needed to guarantee a buildable construction.

STAIR

House + House, Architects

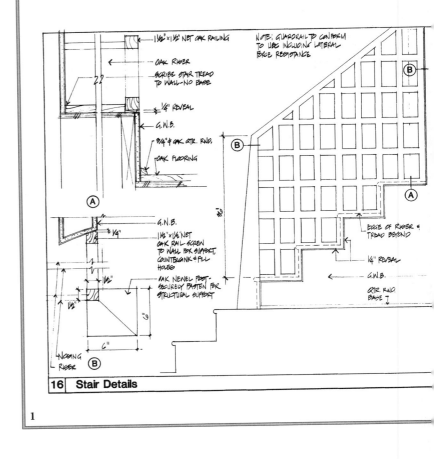

NOTE: GUARDRAIL TO CONFORM TO UBC INCLUDING LATERAL FORCE RESISTANCE

1½" x 1½" NET OAK RAILING

OAK RISER

SCRIBE STAIR TREAD TO WALL-NO BASE

¼" REVEAL

G.W.B.

¾" ⌀ OAK QTR. RND.

OAK FLOORING

G.W.B.

1½" x 1½" NET OAK RAIL SCREEN TO WALL FOR SUPPORT, COUNTERSINK & FILL HOLES

OAK NEWEL POST-SECURELY FASTEN FOR STRUCTURAL SUPPORT

EDGE OF RISER & TREAD BEYOND

¼" REVEAL

G.W.B.

QTR. RND. BASE

NOSING RISER

6"

16 Stair Details

1

It is hard to remain fresh and yet grounded when designing architectural details. The easiest path is simply to follow an isolated muse, one that is both rejectionist in its aesthetic predilections and futurist in its technological expressions. Often this attitude can create more failure than success as elements become so "Space Age" that people feel they cannot touch or "know" them. As such, in architecturally expressive building, the elements often most intimately addressed by people are the coldest and most distant from their own level of comfort. In designing a stair for a new house in an area of California which had been ravaged by fire, House+House, Architects, opted to attempt a light allusion to the Craftsman Mission Revival homes of the early 1900s without compromising their firm's own overtly Modernist tendencies. What was created was part screen, part stair—craftsmanly and on budget. In the selection of material and the basic geometries employed, the architects are quite allusive to an earlier era. Solid oak is used in a gridded format reminiscent of the recently incinerated community's architectural heritage. An extraordinary degree of economy is achieved by using inexpensive stock stair risers and treads and by heading off the outside stringer side of the stair with the aforementioned screen. The difficult joint between stair sidewall and the screen face is mitigated by the use of a stark quarter-inch reveal (the back-set gap allows for misalignment and uses a shadow line to delicately highlight the divergence of materials between painted gypsum wall board and wood). Structural stiffness and light architectural expressionism were served in the

Figure 1 *The simplest of stairs has a grid cum railing applied for the middle part of its straight line run, giving up the bottom two treads to a railless level transition and the top six treads to a condition which is flanked on both sides by walls. The module of the grid is determined by aligning with the riser direction and by bisecting the tread dimension. A stiffening newel is effected by flaring out two sides of the newel to a full 6-in dimension. The detailing is crisp, clean, and simple.*

Figure 2 *The grid is set within a sheetrock and timber interior and somehow resonates with the crisp lines of both.*
(Courtesy of Mark Darley/Esto.)

2

"newel," which projects out to a 6 x 6 dimension from the stock 1-$^1/_2$-in x 1-$^1/_2$-in square module of the lattice work itself. Beyond simple stiffness and formal expression, this is an extraordinarily economic detail as well. Its simple integration into a carefully rendered grid, unapologetically defined by the rise and run of the stairs, is both poetic and powerful. The coincidence of the angled rail (rendered as a flush diagonal running through the grid) creates slightly dynamic patterning of truncated rectangular openings. All fasteners and joinery in this particular structure are obscured with wood plugs to match that which is exposed. Given that the wood has been stained, and given that the railing only has a modest run of nine treads and is held blissfully distinct from its stock stair and standard sheetrock elements, it serves as a quiet reminder of things gone by, reinterpreted by architects whose attitudes are as fresh as can be found anywhere—including California. To welcome hands and satisfy the building code, a standard pipe rail is set on stock bracket supports to the wall side of the stair. The only "tough" detail is when the treads are incised into the sheetrock wall, necessitating a fairly careful joint between natural wood and painted gypsum board.

"The gridded oak railing was designed as a strong geometric element as well as providing a lacy, transparent feel. The railing is painted transparent turquoise to match the exterior siding."

Figure 3 *The simplest of yellow pine stock stairs is flanked by sheet rock on one side and stained oak on the other and gains a sense of solid continuity amid the relative kinetics of its surroundings. Note that the steel handrail (left) provides a code-compliant ergonomic accommodation, whereas the gridded rail to the right is merely viewed as a barrier, given its lack of continuity and distinct rail condition.*
(Courtesy of Mark Darley/Esto.)

3

STEEL RAILING

House + House, Architects

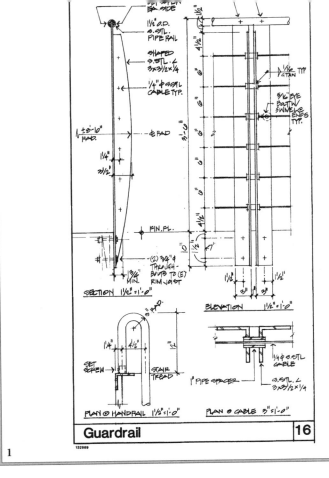

In the late-twentieth century, architects rediscovered steel as a tool for architectural detailing. Its most aggressive form (shown in several examples in this book) provides for a wonderfully light quality, coinciding with the peculiar problems of stair building—tough joinery, three-dimensional stiffness, and specific site constraints. This stair provides an example of both the inherent utility of stock pieces and the undeniable craftsmanship involved in the joining of various types of steel to form a highly customized final product. In this case, the handrail serves a commercial use, and thus its edges and form had to be dealt with on an ongoing basis by a large number of people. The undeniable sturdiness of steel is put to test in this context where crowds move on and around the stair. To provide maximum stiffness, steel welding is used to attach all the components employed, except where the railing is bolted to the existing floor structure. What makes this particular project special is that not only is every piece of steel carefully crafted in its joinery, but human hands are accommodated by the softening of all edges employed, and the potentially ragged, scary qualities of steel construction are mitigated by the wonderfully rendered burnishing applied to all the elements employed. A bit of nautical poetry is applied via the turnbuckle fastening system to post-tension-braided steel cable forming the code-compliant barrier usually provided by balusters. It is the combination of high-strength components and high-tech imagery that makes this an unapologetic and yet poetic piece of craftsmanship with a sensibility that is both uncompromised in durability and in the artfulness employed to create it.

> "Essential materials in sculpted forms lend to the design of this stair railing. The surface of the steel pieces are burnished and ground to provide interesting reflected textures which appear to change as one passes by."

3

Figure 1 *A single detail drawing that provides a clue to the generic application of a standard newel and baluster situation. Since this is a stair that is incised downward between walls, the only barrier that is required is at the top of the stairs, and there is no need for diagonal baluster work. Note the variety of standard components and simple attachments.*

Figure 2 *Overall view. A simple construction that evidences the strength of steel and facilitates easy passage, catching light and providing support while preventing an unwanted level change from occurring.* (Courtesy of Stephen Shepard, Jr.)

Figure 3 *Top-of-stair detail and newel. Note the return of the sinuous handrail is met with the standard turnbuckle detail that provides connection between the "newel" and the braided cables that serve as the barrier normally formed by balusters. By simply extending one leg of stock L-channel up to the railing above, a four-part harmony is achieved between stair, handrail, newel, cable, and horizontal rail. Note the heavily articulated grinding patterns and the thoroughly softened edges.* (Courtesy of Stephen Shepard, Jr.)

STAIR RAILING

Anne Fougeron, Architect

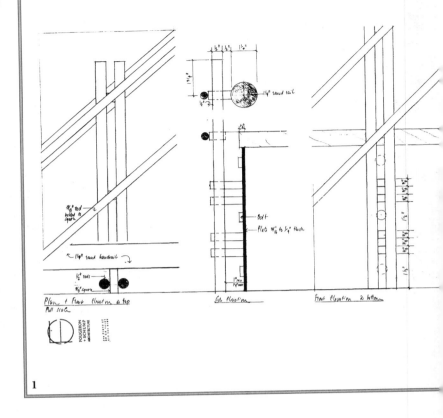

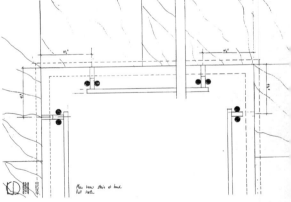

There are two classic ways to save money in doing details . The "safest" way, a method which is blind to experience or expertise, is the much-flaunted use of "stock materials." As any designer who has attempted to make a mountain out of many stock molehills knows, the savings incurred by using "stock" materials versus those that are not "stock" is not great. Typically, perhaps 20 to 30 percent of the total cost of any specific detail can be saved when stock components are used; most often, labor represents the lion's share of the overall cost incurred. However, when the need for savings is imperative, stock materials do help. The second tried and true method of cost savings is absolutely basic to one's understanding of how to make a detail cost effective and does involve the application of knowledge born of experience. For lack of a better term, the technique employed might be called a "loose fit" mind-set. "Loose fit" simply means that no elements have to join perfectly with another. Levels do not have to align perfectly, corners do not have to meet. There is no integration. Everything is set to bypass everything else with only coincidental attachment (versus integral).

Both these techniques are fully evidenced in a hand rail designed by Anne Fougeron, an architect in San Francisco, California. The total hand rail assembly consists of three discreet parts, each attached only to its particular run of stairs. Each piece that comprises each run of the stainless steel construction also bypasses each other piece. Even the type of attachment which is used (welding) does not require predrilling or a perfect fit but can be laid out in a

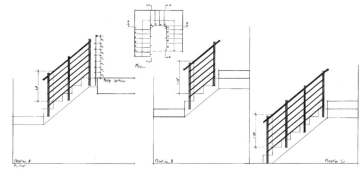

3

4

Figure 1 Composed of lapped bar stock simply welded together and bolted to a stringer, these details are rendered in a rough and ready style which is quite similar to the rather direct detailing employed.

Figure 2 Plan detail. Three independent sections of railing are each attached to their own stringer faces, evidencing the inherent strength of steel, they remain independent of each other until their railings are attached at the top of the newels.

Figure 3 Elevations. These three independent rail assemblies have their angles set by the rake of the stair, they railings located to touch each other, but otherwise have their points of attachment blissfully ignorant of the stair rise and run geometries, allowing for an ease of installation that complements the economy of the material employed.

Figure 4 Linear, yet cranking, these three independent stair rails have identical detailing but customized lengths to register to the runs of the stairs they address. (Courtesy of the architect.)

shop on a full-size template on a work bench. All fasteners of the vertical supports to the stair stringers are expressed steel bolts. All cross sections used (round and square) are stock channels, and the finish employed is a simple light burnishing. What makes this stair artful is that each element is allowed to express itself and nothing is allowed to break the rules of coincidence. The simple lines of the built product are due to this conspiracy and belie the thoughtfulness that has obviously been brought to bear. The linearity of this construction works extraordinarily well with the "lapped over" qualities of the stair tread and riser, qualities which provide a light shadow line against the stringer.

"The stair is made of cold rolled steel and is assembled from stock pieces of rod and square tubing material which are welded together. The design of double rods for the vertical support has many advantages: It creates a space between the rods where the rectangular connectors for the horizontal rods can be welded and yet appear hidden, and it imparts the rail with a visual lightness (without compromising structural integrity)."

5

STAIR

Brian R. Brand, Architect

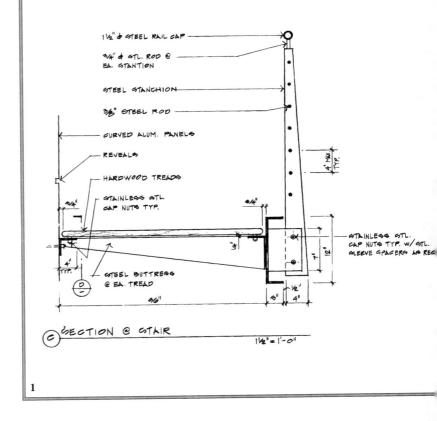

1½" ⌀ STEEL RAIL CAP

¾" ⌀ STL. ROD @ EA. STANTION

STEEL STANCHION

⅜" STEEL ROD

CURVED ALUM. PANELS

REVEALS

HARDWOOD TREADS

STAINLESS STL. CAP NUTS TYP.

STAINLESS STL. CAP NUTS TYP. W/ STL. SLEEVE SPACERS AS REQ

STEEL BUTTRESS @ EA. TREAD

4" MAX TYP.

7"

36"

ⓒ SECTION @ STAIR   1½" = 1'-0"

1

In the last decade or two of the twentieth century, expressive steel detailing has become more than a side show of architectural expression. Once utilized by Modern architects as a symbol of the new technologies present in the exploding Industrial Age of the early twentieth century, steel is now viewed as just another vehicle for architectural expression. This expression seems to have graduated from the realm of symbolic icon of an anti-fine arts aesthetic to take on the subtleties of a more craftsmanly focus. So it is with a stair set within a custom home in Seattle, Washington, designed by Brian Brand of Baylis, Brand, Wagner, Architects.

Steel is an extraordinary material for two reasons. Foremost among steel's unique properties is its extraordinary strength-to-weight ratio. Thin pieces of steel have enormous capacity to sustain loads, both in compression and in tension. Steel also has a unique capacity for extraordinary strength in a variety of connections as well—welded, bolted, pinned, or virtually any other connection one can think of.

In addition, steel comes in a variety of forms—sheets that are rolled, bars that are extruded, fittings that are cast, wires that are woven, and on and on. The strength and versatility of steel has thus caught the imagination of those who create architectural details in an unprecedented way in recent times, and this stair evidences a fine realization of steel detailing for a unique residence. According to the architects, the goal of this particular residence was to serve as a gallery for a professor of art history's collection, and, as you might guess,

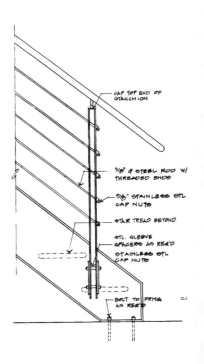

CAP TOP END OF STANCHION

⅜" ⌀ STEEL ROD W/ THREADED ENDS

⅜" STAINLESS STL. CAP NUTS

STAIR TREAD BEYOND

STL. SLEEVE SPACERS AS REQ'D

STAINLESS STL. CAP NUTS

BOLT TO FRMG. AS REQ'D

ⓑ ELEVATION @ STAIR   1½" = 1'-0"

2

Figure 1 *Cross section. A delicate attachment to the wall surface (left) is complemented by the heavy attachment to the solid channel stringer (right). Note that both tread support and newel-baluster both expressively taper and that all joinery is "loose-fit" and predominately effected by a vague manipulation of stock steel components.*

Figure 2 *Elevation of typical newel. Utilizing standard shapes and profiles, the lightness of steel is fully evidenced in the connections and dimensions employed. Note the unapologetic use of "nuts and bolts" fasteners.*

Figure 3 *Detail sheet. There is a latent continuity between the graphic depiction of careful steel detailing as seen in the large scale and small-scale drawings evidenced here.*

Figure 4 *Stair. A kinetic and yet controlled construction, the stair is both beckoning and elegant in repose.*
(Courtesy of the architect.)

4

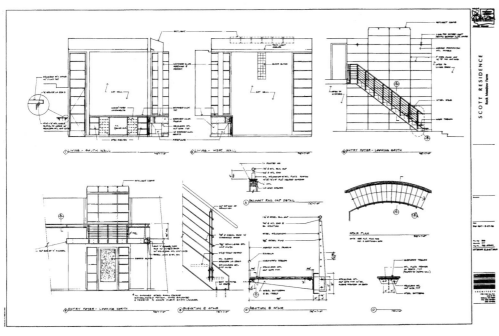

3

most architects would like it if their own work was seen as part of the art on display. The simplicity of the stair's line (using lightly angled treads around a very gentle curve), serves, in a large sense, to animate something which could be predictable. This curve is fleshed out by the use of an aluminum screen/wall that follows the stair's arc. By using a grid which articulates the panelization of the background wall, the curvilinear aspect is metered and highlighted, as is the ascending diagonal of the stair itself. Although steel allows for relatively minimal support, this particular stair (as are all residential stairs) is compelled to comply with certain code minimums, including the edict that no gap in any railing shall be more than 4 in, net (preventing small children's heads from becoming lodged in ways which can prove problematic). In this case, steel rod is used as the barrier, and a relatively tight spacing of steel channel is used between balusters and newels to facilitate the forming of the curve of this railing. Providing the underlying support for the entire stair is a large steel stringer formed as a bent C channel. In truth, every element of this stair is custom-fabricated from stock components, but the utilization of lightly canted cuts and detailing which never forces any component to perfectly align with an edge or plane creates a tangible sense of architectonic sculpture. All joints are expressed (either bolts or welds), and all material connections are "gapped"—using reveals or stand-offs that allow each individually crafted component to be set visually free from adjacent parts within the overall construction. Whereas the heavy inner edge of the stair's curve is the aforementioned solid bent C channel, the edge of the treads going up against the metering aluminum screening presents no visible means of support as each tread is supported by a small steel channel almost invisible from those ascending the stairs. This helps reinforce the dual identity of the inside edge being heavily articulated and expressive while the outside edge, going up against the large-scale blank wall, is more abstracted and quiet and uses the wall as a datum upon which all the steel detailing can occur.

Economy was served by the use of standard steel that is clear lacquered versus stainless steel, which is much harder to fabricate and more costly to purchase. In addition, many of the components that were used in the fabrication of the stair and the wall are off-the-rack stock items. All surfaces are either ground or patterned to present a completely finished sense of final realization (versus something that is more overtly rustic/industrial grade).

Figure 5 Context. *Tucked behind the arching wall, the stair is deferential to the art on display and yet allows its presence to be viewed coyly as seen from the living area of the home.* (Courtesy of the architect.)

"The stairway complements other simple materials in the house which include painted sheetrock, lightly stained oak floors, and exposed ceilings, countertops, and finishes."

5

PIECES AND PARTS STAIR

Alex Varga, Designer

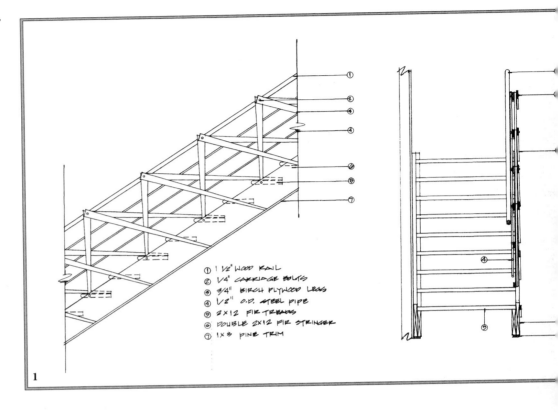

① 1 ½" WOOD RAIL
② ¼" CARRIAGE BOLTS
③ ¾" BIRCH PLYWOOD LEGS
④ ½" O.D. STEEL PIPE
⑤ 2×12 FIR TREADS
⑥ DOUBLE 2×12 FIR STRINGER
⑦ 1×3 PINE TRIM

1

Architectural detailing is often held up to harsh reality checking during the design process, the construction process, or by the particular detail's need to function in its natural environment or accommodate its use. So it is with a stair designed by Alex Varga which is set into an apartment renovation in Connecticut. Varga is a young designer and, as such, could plead that ignorance is bliss when it comes to detailing. His details could be derived from a book's knowledge base or simply from an imitative process that celebrates other designers. But not only does Varga accept personal responsibility for the detailing he executes, he often builds it himself. As such, he has the ability to both reality-test and fine-tune the work he designs. So it is with the stair that he inserted into the apartment to access a new loft. It needed to mesh with an existing stair, be thoroughly affordable, and—because Varga has a passion for personal expression via architectural details—it needed to be energetic, delightful, and expressive of his vision. In the best tradition of architectural design, Varga sat down to design his stair in the classic vacuum of a sequestration, alone with his tracing paper and pen. However, when his best-laid plans began to see the light of day by his own hand, he realized that he had been mistaken in his preconceptions. He thus set about to rearrange the parts that he had painstakingly fabricated out of ¾-in birch plywood in a

Figure 1 More retroactive documentation than a sketch which would determine the design, this drawing accurately reflects the ultimate result of field modifications by architects via the designer-builder to create an effusive accommodation of preformed or stock parts. Each rail support is effectively triangulated by birch plywood pieces that lap either side of the double stringer, with a central piece that is let into its top edge. The double stringer facilitates a simple attachment of the stock 2 x 12 fir treads, and an effective barrier, normally formed by balusters, utilizes simple pipe conduit. All attachments are simply bolted and unabashedly expressed. All materials are clear finished, and the overall impact of the construction is undeniably potent.

Figure 2 Pieces and parts in blissful bypassing interaction.
(Courtesy of the architect.)

2

way which now made sense. The result is at once dynamic, useful, and affordable. A dynamic balustrade is formed by a series of diagonal struts set to either side of a 2 x 12 fir stringer, with a single layer separating them set directly into the first stringer itself. By aligning two of these birch plywood supports to the rise and run of the stair, gigantic metaphoric treads and risers are formed, and by creating the third diagonal stiffening member, a sense of kineticism is enhanced and the stiffness of this solution ensured. Without the three layers, two lapped on both sides of the stringer and aggressively bolted over their length, and a central piece that is let into the top of the stringer, this might be a fairly floppy construction. But given the multiple layers, laminations, and lapped fastening conditions, it has adequate strength, despite its minimal mass and relatively flexible material (plywood). These plywood fins, in turn, support horizontal tubing to provide the code-compliant barrier and an additional stock fir rail that is held off from triangulated supports. The stringer is also elegant in its simplicity. Below the full stringer that heads off the treads and allows the simple attachment of the triangulated pieces mentioned earlier, there is a second recessed piece that forms the classic zig-zag line of tread support. By chamfering the proud corner of this zig zag, and by projecting the 2 x 12 Douglas Fir treads beyond the edge of the stringer and bullnosing that edge, a carpenterly pieces and parts construction is effected—one where each individual piece and fastener is celebrated. Since the existing stair ascends from below, Varga applies a subordinated piece of trim to the underside of these doubled stringer pieces, effectively obscuring their joint. Because of the expressive orientation and shaping of many of the components, there is no opportunity for this to be confused with any kind of "make do" or ad hoc fabrication. Appropriately enough, all this intensive detail work is appreciated from every angle, as the stair is seen from below as one ascends the existing stair, on level as the stair is held as a focal point amid the loft space accesses, and from above as seen from the loft. In this way, there is a sense that this is a possessed piece of art, integrated to its context by the use of the omnipresent and readily available (and thoroughly affordable) Douglas Fir. This piece becomes highly expressive of the personal vision of Alex Varga and it served as a laboratory for his development as an architect. It is often via detail elements viewed as "throwaways" in the design process that young architects find out what they value and what is possible. School cannot teach these things effectively. It is only with the hands-on, reality-based realization of personal vision, the acceptance of misconception, and the adaptation to financial, environmental, and human exigencies that students become architects, and architects ultimately have the ability to serve their clients and their craft with the highest level of skill. If details were simply unimportant, there would be no sense in learning from them. Unfortunately, this is the attitude of a great many architects, one that creates buildings that are often architectural one-liners with little chance for visual sustain, affordability, or long-term benefits to the owner or to the profession. By picking up the mantle of personal responsibility for his own detail work, Alex Varga presents the best tradition of the craft of architecture, and his words can serve as a window into the mind of a young architect fine-tuning his own set of beliefs while expanding his knowledge.

Figure 3 Context. An existing stair slides up under the new stringer while the cranking, ascending stair into the loft effectively grabbed attention within the heavily framed view of a large-scale superstructure and the sheet rock infill it resides within. (Courtesy of the architect.)

"I started the railing design process with sketches that I thought would be a techno–take-off on a ship's railing, but done in wood to be consistent with the other finish details in the apartment, and also so I could fabricate it myself on site. From these rough sketches, I laid out and cut some profiles out of ¾" birch plywood to create supports for the handrail and for the immediate piperails. However, when I placed the pieces on the stair carcass in the manner that I had planned, I found that I did not like the visual effect of the way the joints were going to work. Rather than toss the components that I had cut, I began to play with different arrangements and groupings of the pieces until I started to see some images which were more appealing to me. The composition that I finally selected seemed to be a mechanical expression or suggestion of the movement of bodies along the stair's path. Also, the overlapping lattice pattern was fairly rigid and relatively easy to install, which made the resolution of the design that much more satisfying."

3

WALL-HUGGING STAIR

Arne Bystrom, Architect

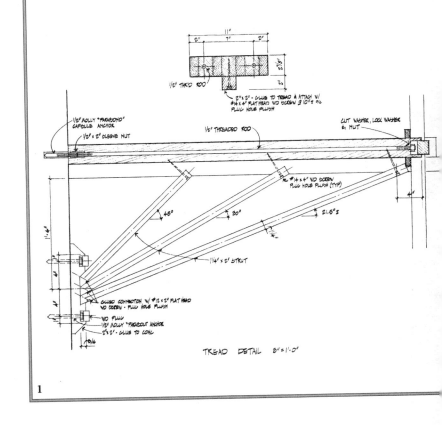

TREAD DETAIL 8"=1'-0"

1

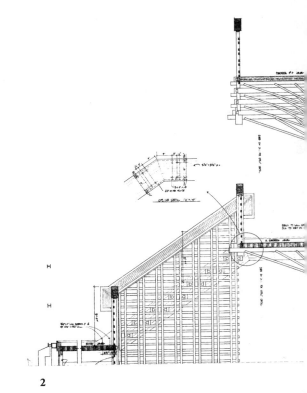

2

Architectural details can be seen as the mediator between good ideas and the built form. In a house where material distinctions are a baseline design determinate for the entire construction, Arne Bystrom has rendered this wall-hugging stair as a symbol of contrast between that which is immutable and monolithic (cast concrete with tile detailing) and that which is kinetic, transitional, and organic, assembled of pieces and parts (a wall-hugging wood stair). Without this baseline material distinction between the opaque wall and the hyperarticulated stair, both elements would lose their "punch." A stolid stair of cast parts laid up against the wall would by definition be a subordinate element, dominated by the context of the space itself. If the hyperkinetic wall-hugging wood lattice stair were set in the context of a space formed of wood lattice and even more wood parts, its extraordinarily articulate wood joinery, fabrication techniques, and raw artfulness and ingenuity would be lost to all but those who could "tune out" the visual noise that would surround it. But instead, Bystrom has set this stair in contradistinction to its context. The obvious solution would be to support the outside edge of this stair with some sort of column system, but in accreting this stair, barnaclelike, to this dense wall, Bystrom not only enhances the spritely lightness of the stair itself but heightens the sense of solidity and massiveness of the wall upon which the stair is applied. By making the stair essentially the coordination of dozens upon dozens of wood brackets, Bystrom takes the module of each individual stair tread and extends it into something which is viewed as a

Figure 1 *The critical bracket and tread detail. 1-¹/₄-in x 1-¹/₄-in sticks of wood are let into an ever so slightly thicker 2-in x 2-in horizontal at their top and, in turn, are let into a common 2-in x 2-in bracket at their base. This bracket is supported at the downward side by ¹/₂-in "parabold" anchors and at the top is held fast via a through-rod connection set directly into the wall at the side and heavily post tensioned to facilitate stiffness. The combination of the post tensioned steel and the wood set to be compressively charged, makes for a minimal, though intricate, support.*

Figure 2 *This drawing allows for the appreciation of the connection between the upper cantilevered run of the stair and its gridded lower component.*

Figure 3 *View. The rationale for floating the stair had as much to do with clearance of the opening below as it did with the artistry involved. The artistry is undeniable as the dancing stair tread assemblies contrast with the organizing banding of tile set in the concrete face of the surrounding walls.* (Courtesy of the architect.)

Figure 4 *Tread end condition. Virtually every structural aspect of this construction is evidenced both in the geometries employed and in the wood species and grain orientations effected. Fir brackets support cedar verticals, which in turn are let into cherry wood and oak treads having expressed maple dowels let in over the end conditions of the post tensioning rods. Almost every expressed section is square, and the contrasting wood species highlight an already articulate form.* (Courtesy of the architect.)

4

serpentine whole but also as a meandering series of linked components. The brackets employed (simple sticks of wood, each joined to its own wood mounting plate bolted into the wall) serve to stiffen treads and platforms of laminated wood which are in turn linked to the cast wall via post-tensioned threaded steel rods. Either system alone might have been adequate had its dimensions been "beefed up"—either a massively thick series of laminated tread and platforms attached with multiple post-tensioned steel reinforcement, or fatter, deeper, more massive brackets independently supporting each other with a thinner, less stiff surface material applied to them. But by minimizing the size of *each* constituent part, Bystrom allows for the maximum impact of the two systems employed. And when the detailing of endlessly bypassing constituent pieces is applied to the stair rail employed (also using a laminated wood rail and a lattice, baluster, newel), an extraordinary choreography of material and craftsmanship is evident. It is hard to imagine a stair of this complexity and richness being designed by anybody who does not have the complete command of knowledge that Bystrom has. His long career of dealing with wood is reflected in the power, presence, and complexity of this construction. How ironic it is to think that when most architectural interns come into the profession, completely inexperienced and inarticulate in the ways of architectural detailing, they are often given the task of stair detailing.

Although this stair was definitely uncompromised by cost considerations, the ingenuity of its design, using modularized, semi-prefabricated components, and the stunning reality of its visual presence set a very high standard for any architect to aspire to in the world of architectural detailing. And although the results are amongst the most articulate imaginable, the motivations are extraordinarily basic.

5

Figure 5 *Bracket-to-wall connection. A simple assembly of radial wood is set to a chamfered ended bracket with expressed plugs set over mounting bolt heads.*
(Courtesy of the architect.)

Figure 6 *Context. A fabulous tracery of material, light shadow, and line amidst all the definitive orthogonal control this dancing stair has an animated presence.*
(Courtesy of the architect.)

"The easiest way to support the stair was to cantilever off the concrete wall. Solve this by using wood braces and a tension bolt in an expansion shield."

6

CIRCULAR STAIR

Arne Bystrom,
Architect

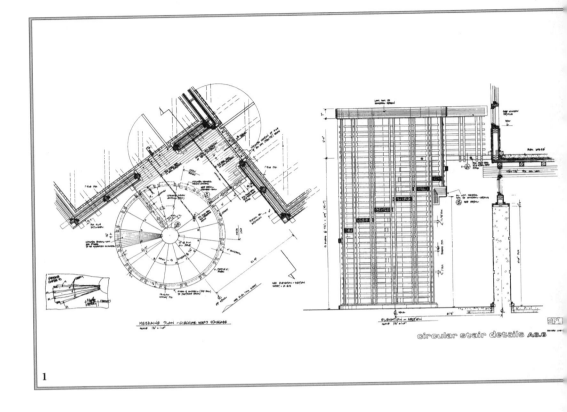

Figure 1 *Plan elevation. A simple construct gains intense density vie the use of heavily organized and thoroughly animated component parts. Note the architect's own squiggly line sketch at the lower left of the plan indicating his desire for unequal lamination widths and the insinuation of cherry and maple into the treads.*

Figure 2 *Stair. An object that is definitively larger than furniture and yet comfortably reposing within the scale of this large space, this stair provides simple access between levels and yet is a three-dimensional articulation of some of the extraordinary banding/gridding/linear interweaving that this exquisite house offers up.* (Courtesy of the architect.)

Wood is an amazing material. It can be detailed to be quite strong despite the fact that it is an organic material where defects can be unseen and yet integral, compromising the strength of any particular piece to the point of structural insufficiency. Whether by disease, graining pattern, or simply an unseen split, wood can have its strength undercut invisibly and completely. Two techniques can help mitigate wood's potential for structural insufficiency: The first is the lamination of multiple layers of wood, continuously glued together to form a single entity of mutually reinforcing parts. Recent years have seen "engineered" wood products dominate many elements of construction that were once the province of steel. By lamination, potential flaws are buried within the context of multiple layers of consistent and predominately nonflawed layers of wood. In addition, the dimensionally unstable characteristics of warping and shrinkage are simply eliminated by lamination. The other element employed to foster strength in wood construction is a geometric orientation. A wood construction that is arrayed in a curve can utilize the shape's inherent strength to defeat the inherent flexibility of wood. The stiffness of curvilinear wood can be seen in a barrel, where both the circular cross section of the barrel itself and its slightly arced shape allow the wood to be held in continuous compression by metal staves, thus stabilizing each individ-

ual piece and preventing it from flexing. Turned wood columns are another example where wood gains enormous rigidity from simply providing an interlocking curvilinear orientation of each piece. Utilizing both of these methods, this circular stair designed by Arne Bystrom for a spectacular custom house in Idaho can be seen to be almost a diagram of how small pieces of wood can be arrayed in a structurally stiff way—providing a distilled, almost symbolic catalog of wood joinery and expressive detailing. As with much successful architectural detailing in wood, all the elements in this particular construction "bypass" each other. They are not mortised, dove-tailed, or scarf-jointed together. In this way, the entire construction can be seen to be laminated, where layer upon layer is either woven or directly applied to every other layer, and where many, many small joints create a single stiff construction. The wood treads employed are actually made using the techniques of prefab glu-lam structural members where dimensional lumber is glued together to form a construction of a much greater strength and stiffness than any one of its constituent parts. By the use of contrasting woods (cherry, redwood, and maple), there is a conspired depth to this construction. Using a tartan grid composed of laminated thin members whose ordinates are based solely on the height and width of each tread's width and thickness, the entire perimeter is modularly defined. Each tread is let into a center post of (what else?) laminated wood and is thus pinned to a common pivot point, one that is as solid and opaque as the perimeter is multiply pieced and diaphanous. All the constituent components are of small manageable pieces, typically 1-in thick, with horizontals

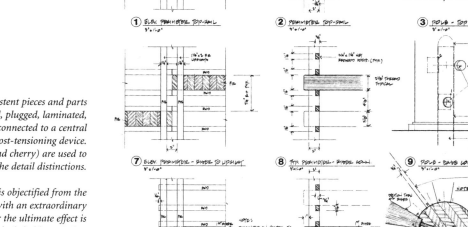

Figure 3 Details. *Extraordinarily consistent pieces and parts (as small as 1-3/4-in x 3/4-in) are lapped, plugged, laminated, and in almost every way possible, interconnected to a central lamination post using steel as a buried post-tensioning device. A variety of woods (fir, redwood, and cherry) are used to highlight all the detail distinctions.*

Figure 4 Inside the stair, that which is objectified from the outside becomes spacial on the inside, with an extraordinary sense of developed enclosure. Whether the ultimate effect is space age or craftsmanly is up to the beholder to judge.
(Courtesy of the architect.)

3

4

of 3/4-in x 1-1/4-in redwood and verticals of 2-in x 3/4-in fir. Almost all fasteners are expressed via protruding plugs, and virtually all edges are lightly relieved and beautifully clear-finished to facilitate the direct expression of their materiality. This stair manifests the inherent helical quality of a classic spiral stair while fully fleshing out its implicit cylindrical nature.

Although this is not an inexpensive construction, the money invested reaps extraordinary results, and the essential lessons of the inherent strength of lamination and of curvilinear orientation are always recognized and never hidden or denied.

"The glu-lam guys made it. The 1-1/2-in piece was going to be too hard to steam bend, so they took three layers laminated to make the curved pieces—laminated and curved, structurally double dipped for strength."

LADDERS

Arne Bystrom, Architect

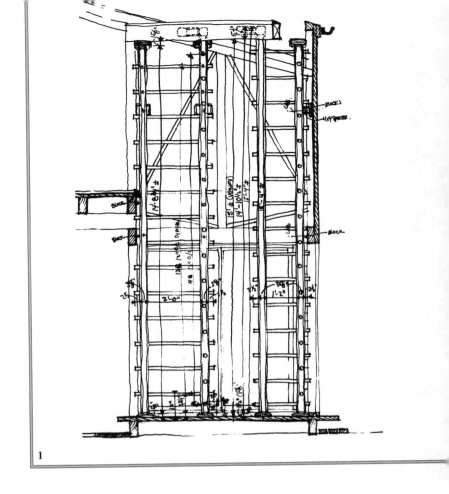

1

When designing their own houses, architects often take a few liberties
in detailing their work—allowing for experimentation at the expense of durability or predictability. When Arne Bystrom was designing his own vacation
home, he felt it was incumbent upon him to design *every* aspect of it—right
down to the method of joinery between each stick of wood. In contemplating
all the moves to be made, Bystrom realized that since he was going to be
doing a fair amount of the fabricating and installing himself, he simply needed to figure out what needed to be done rather than to present it in such a
way that it could be communicated to someone who had no idea what was in
his mind. The elements depicted in this piece are series of ladders forming
two corners. Given its rural location, these ladders needed to be made of easily obtainable stock pieces of wood (sometimes of indeterminate species).
From the outset, Bystrom set out to create a minicatalogue of materials that
would facilitate ease of construction and, he hoped, evidence the casual craftsmanship from which the rest of the house benefits.

Several abiding rules are present throughout the entire construction. All
edges are heavily chamfered, making it easy on grasping hands. No end points
"meet." The details employ bypassing parts, allowing for imperfect joinery
and alignment without anyone noticing. All connections were made as lapped
(versus mortised or hidden with screws or other fasteners), thus facilitating
ease of installation once fabrication was complete. All pieces were sized to
standard dimensions that are readily available. Bystrom then proceeded to

3(a)

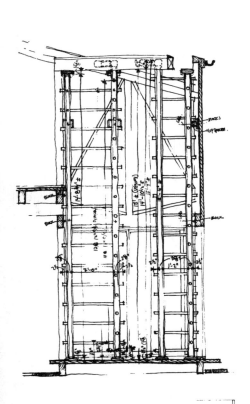

Figure 1 What could be rude lattice work becomes crafty millwork. These ladder forms create corners and are linked by their "treads," in reality, simple closet pole stock. Although the drawings are quite gubby, they are absolutely determinate in their dimensions and clear in their intent.

Figure 2 Overall sheet. Note the catalogue of parts on the far right and the indication of drill holes for the verticals involved, as well as the explicit sizing and quantity of screws.

Figure 3(a) and (b next page) As merely one more part in an animated construction, the expressive use of every modest element (including proud wood plugs), fosters a sense of considered carpenterly logic that facilitates a sense of hand hewn, aesthetically conspired design. (Courtesy of the architect.)

2

3(b)

create a set of softline drawings that described everything right down to the screw type (and quantities!) to help him and members of his family in fabrication and installation.

The ladders seem at once to provide structure and filter light, although neither function is really the origin of their form. Compared to the muscularity of the home's structure, these ladders are made of smaller components with far tighter details, and they use an orthogonal orientation belied by much of the surrounding diagonal, triangulated strut work of the post-and-beam frame.

Part screen, part structure, part ladder—this kind of multiplicity of use allows architectural detailing to span the scales of the whole house and its subordinate cabinetry.

"This shows how a working drawing becomes the detail and cutting list all at the same time. It shows how to make a set of stock 2 x 4s and 1-⁵/₁₆-in dowel become a ladder."

TEAK STAIR

Duo Dickinson, Architect

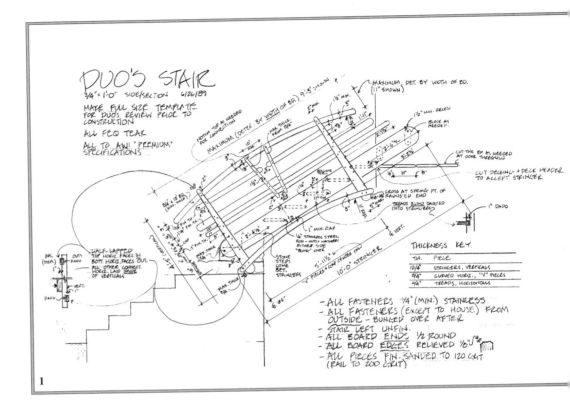

How do you span from outside to inside in an elegant manner when you also have to ascend a full flight of stairs? Architectural details can provide a source of delight, not only in their aesthetic contrivance but also in their physical use. By realizing that this entry stair into my own house needed to be the "jewel in the crown" that both beckoned and sustained interest upon entry to the site and, ultimately, to the house. Large rocks that had been removed to accommodate mechanical lines were built up to form a large-scale, rough-hewn berm, and between these rocks were laid relatively inexpensive broken stone risers and treads. Between this stalagmite-esque launching pad and the cantilevered house form, a wood stair would be the focus of the entire entry sequence. Teak is an incredibly durable wood. Not only does it resist rot naturally, given its high oil content, it also, when harvested and cut properly, has a minimum of knots and defects. Thus it is dimensionally stable and can be found in fairly large thicknesses. Stainless steel is also impervious to rust, and hiding screw heads behind flush plugs provides even less chance of future problems. When any wood is completely covered, via an overhang, much wear and tear is avoided. Lastly, if laminations can be avoided, problematic glue joints can be avoided as well. All these aspects were applied to this teak stair, which leaps from its built-up lower portion to gently cling to an incised

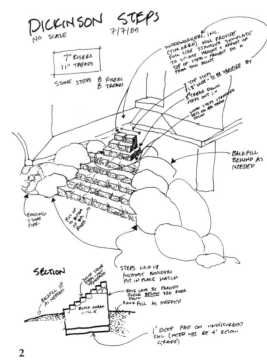

3

Figure 1 Composed of individual pieces of nonlaminated teak, this stair rests one newel upon stone while the other floats. The arc of the rail and the arc of the newel stiffening strut set below the closed stringer seem to vault from stone steps (lower left) to the home's entry. As such, this stair is part bridge and has a fairly animated countenance to complement the fairly stolid and stoic elements it mediates between. Note that the stone steps come up between the two closed stringers and the length of the stringer was held far shorter than indicated in these drawings as the 12/4-in teak available would not allow the additional 2-ft plus extension into the entryway.

Figure 2 The complement to the teak stair is its "launching pad," a set of stone steps set between bermmed rocks. Note the distinction between the drawing meant for a mason (softline and three-dimensional) versus one meant for a woodworking shop (with every dimension laid out hardline).

Figure 3 An animated construction of singular pieces, all edges bevelled and each oriented both for safety and art's sake.

(Courtesy of Mick Hales.)

entryway. Each piece of teak utilized was sized by available stock, including the closed end of the stringer, which was formed out of 12/4-in teak (this thickness allows for complete reception of the individual 8/4-in teak board treads a full 1 in into the body of the stringer itself, post-tensioned by threaded rod to hold the assembly together). Railings are located to allow a multitude of ages to have a place to grip, and the final lines of the stair are both invigorated and familiar, involving a modest pair of arcs top and bottom, and two splayed verticals at their center point. Tapering newels also act as points of support at the bottom of the stair, as attenuated stringers straddle three treads that rise up between them. Although the available wood preempted the ability to project the stringer as far as was originally hoped, the overall effect is quite positive and, at the time, was code compliant. In the late 1980s, the requirement was to prevent any 6-in ball from passing through any area of a given stair, and this stair accommodated that. Now, the requirement has shrunk to 4 in, but two young children have survived thousands of safe passages along this stair, and, so far, the wear and tear has been minimal. Although not inexpensive (the stair cost more than my first new automobile), it *is* the exterior focal point of the entire house. As such, it was aesthetically worth the cost, and, because the materials and details were chosen to effect an ethical design, the investment will sustain itself for a long time to come.

Figure 4 Individual pieces of teak serve to animate the joint between architecture and organized rock. By its imposition, the stair helps prevent those at the top of the stair from going from the latter to the former. (Courtesy of Tracie Rozhon.)

Figure 5 Inside view. A closed stringer was intended for young children to run toy cars down. The next horizontal line was for those who were "cruising" (toddlers), the next horizontal line was for young children, the next rail up was for those who are not quite adolescent, and the crowning arching railing for adults and those who are anxious to be adults. All projections met the 6-in diameter opening standard of the late 1980s when it was built but would no longer be code-compliant due to the new 4-in overall standard. (Courtesy of Mick Hales.)

4

5

NEWEL AND RAIL/ OLD AND NEW

Duo Dickinson,
Architect

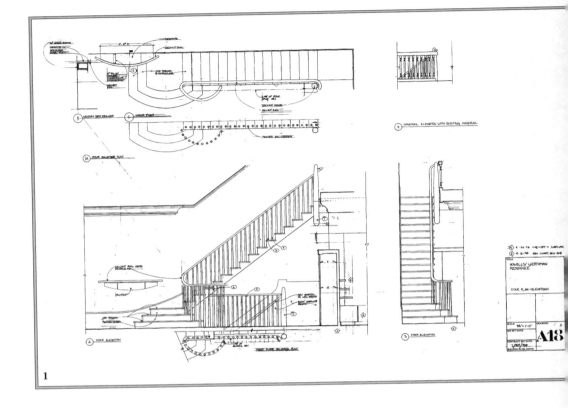

It might be said that there are two essential mind-sets when encountering the built environment. The first mind-set is one we all share—a sense of memory and history and that most objects are either literal icons or metaphoric symbols. This is the familiar in our lives. The alternative mind-set is the attitude that innovation should strive to break any preconceptions at all costs. This outlook equates precedent with boredom and tradition with intellectual and creative laziness. Overt Modernism was born in the early twentieth century simply because late-nineteenth-century architects had found so much solace in the past that new materials, technologies, and social values were unaddressed by their work. For almost a century since then, the sense has been one of "either/or." That the existence of one made a mockery of the other. Almost always, it was Modernism sticking its tongue out at the "fuddy duddy," hidebound traditionalist outlook—one that in some way is found to be stultifying at best and a "cop out" at worst.

Recent times have seen an aesthetic relativism take hold where traditional motifs can be freshly applied in ways which have integrity and evidence innovation, and rote Modernism has given way to more animated (as well as more socially and environmentally sensitive) expressions. In truth, rather than "either/or," the best attitude might be simply labeled "and." In this combina-

Figure 1 *A new stair has its ultimate influence at stair top by a newly imposed code-compliant handrail which, in turn, interacts with a preexisting (and below-code-required minimum height) handrail. The intersection is both carefully coordinated and thoroughly indirect.*

Figure 2 (a), (b), and (c) *New rail rises and turns at new newel while the existing baluster rail has its preexisting curve cut so that it seems to pay homage to the same new newel. Old is heavily figured, new is softly abstracted.*

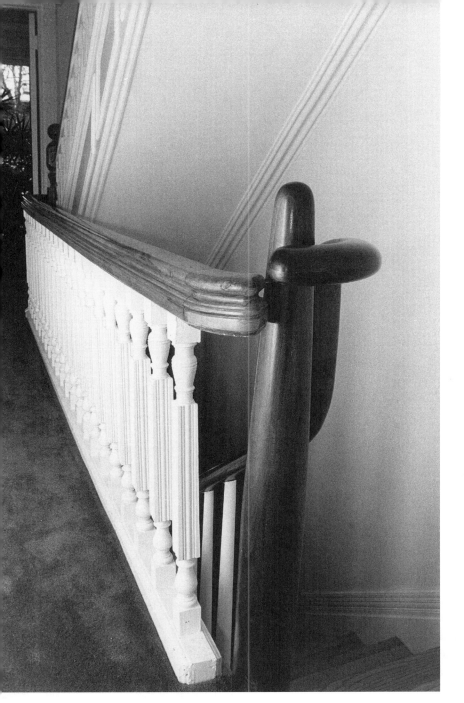

2(a)

2(b)

2(c)

tion of a preexisting 1880s line of balusters and rail with a new stair newel and rail, the nineteenth-century decorative arts are held distinct from the 1990s geometric abstraction. Painted, stained, and carved wood lightly caress a clear-finish and linearly attenuated Modern counterpart. This is a modest dance, almost a handshake rather than a contest between parts. Either system alone would lack the presence of this combination. Rather than seeking joinery and continuity, this little dyad seeks to allow for peaceful coexistence—*not* blissful ignorance nor overt choreography, but the simple recognition of the ancient need to rest one's hand at the top of the stair (newel) and continue the slide down (stair rail) as well as provide a barrier to an opening (horizontal rail). So function, material, and motif are interwoven without compromise.

TREE RAIL

Michael deStefano, Designer

1

Figure 1 *A botanic element allows for safe passage. Note the consistency of linear elements and the elegant swoop of the trunk-newel, stabilized by the overhanging "roots."*
(Courtesy of the architect.)

Figure 2 *Stair top. Note how the bend in the branch-railing facilitates a transition normally effected by a "goose neck" or an ease over. Note also how the final bend in the branch allows for direct attachment to the wall, providing stiffness, and how the interweaving and billowing minor branches provide code-compliant separation.* (Courtesy of the architect.)

It is rare that sculpture, craft, architecture, and movement come together, but in this particular case, that is what a gifted metalsmith executed. This is a commission that provides a code-compliant separation at the edge of a stair while providing ergonomically viable support for those using the stairs. Architecturally, Michael deStefano and his company, Art & Metal, Ltd., of Jupiter, Florida, provided a marvelous counterpoint to the normative detailing of a standard open stringer stair. Essentially, a client showed deStefano a picture of a Baptismal font formed of a tree shape and asked him to fabricate a handrail for a new house based on that approach. The elements employed to form this artistry are also quite simple, with perhaps the most problematic aspect being the creation of the "trunk" of the trees involved. This was accomplished by simply fashioning trapezoidally shaped $1/8$-in pieces of steel. The tapering shape of each was bent and hammered while hot to create an organic surface that is pleasing to the touch and delightful to the eye, and when welded together to form a trunk, the result is a thoroughly organic, nongeometric shape which is thoroughly sculptural in nature.

The "branches" that billow out from this "trunk" are forged $1\text{-}1/4$-in, $3/4$-in, and $1/2$-in "wire" stock. Such work is not so much "detailed" as it is artfully enacted. With nothing but quick sketch drawings and a great deal of articula-

2

tion in the field, the result is visually sustaining due to its contrast with the raw oak treads and the painted wall and riser surfaces that it lays up against. The careful coincidence of branches wrapping around walls for support and "roots" spreading upon the bottom tread and down its riser to form a stable connection are simple botanical metaphors which make latent visual sense. It might be conceptually nice to state that this project was the manifestation of an overarching theory of contrast between the built and the botanical, but in reality, this is simply functional ornament. It is the direct articulation of a bold idea in a thoroughly artistic and yet craftsmanly way. In its simple use of standard materials and its thoroughly consistent application of a gentle organic motif, deStefano creates something which is both barrier and sculpture, an ergonomic assist and a visual delight. Gaining stature by contrast and finding logic in its consistent use of artful line, deStefano maximizes the impact of a minimum amount of design criteria. As a direct application of art over architecture, this particular project could have been affected, awkward, or perhaps even silly, but in its ingenious integration with the form of the stair itself, the final result is both a stand-alone piece of art and an integral element in the ambience of the stairs that it services.

> *"The entire railing consisted of two main pieces which were treated for a thorough sand blasting with extra fine sand and a hot oil-bees-wax-clarant-who-knows-what-else mixture that was hand-rubbed once over. All told, the approximately 22-ft long railing took less than 100 hours to complete, including installation. However, the most rewarding part of this job was seeing the client's reaction upon first seeing the railing installed. He was elated, and everyone who saw it was quite taken with the design. Overall, and in every respect, this is a truly pleasing job. I only wish all jobs would turn out so well."*

Figure 3 *Trunk and roots. Expressive stabilizing (note this is at the bottom the double run of stairs).*
(Courtesy of the architect.)

Figure 4 *Top view. Two discreet runs of sculpted stair provide a dynamic counterpoint to the sheet rock and oak context. Note the splayed branches at the upper right set to stabilize the lower stair rail.*
(Courtesy of the architect.)

3

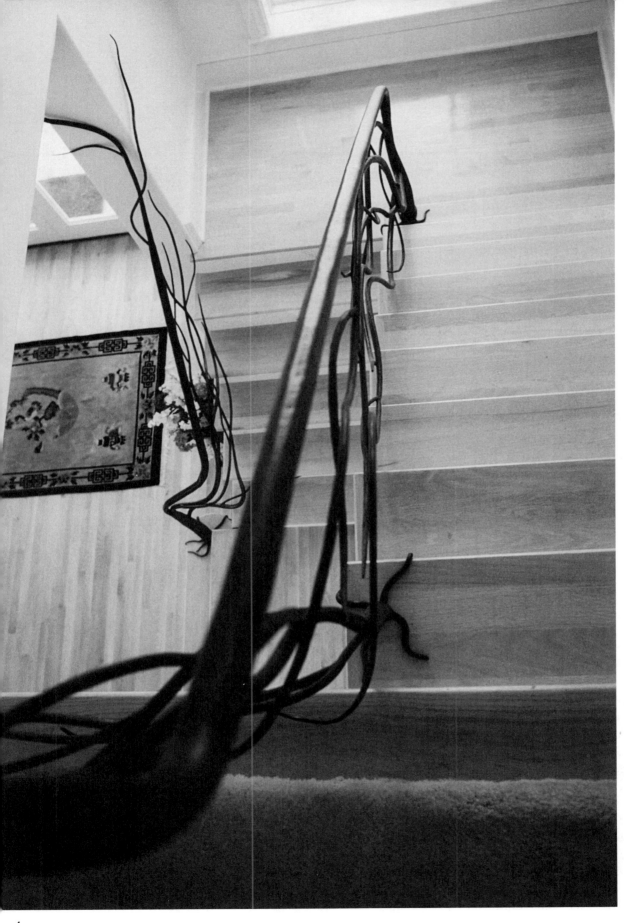

4

STAIR

Bohlin Cywinski Jackson, Architects

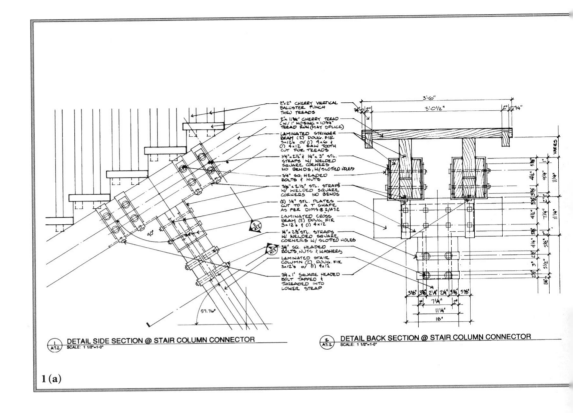

1 (a)

In creating architectural details, there are two basic tools in the designer's hands. First, and arguable most important, is the materials selected for use. The second can be said to be relative sizing of the components employed to create jumps in scale—micro to macro. The interface between these two tools is often the essence of what creates expressive detailing.

No project better illustrates the capacity of an architect to manipulate both size and carefully selected materials than this stair designed by Peter Bohlin of Bohlin Cywinski Jackson for a rural retreat in the Endless Mountains in Lake Winola, Pennsylvania. Not only is the structure diagrammatic and outsized, but the detailing is simultaneously micromanaged to the point where the stoutness of the diagonal strut that reinforces the stringers is made to feel even more outsized and gigantic, especially when it is integrated with the patterning of the stone flooring. Although it may be said that all the elements used in the stair are bigger than they need to be, it is via the use of relative gigantism that relative intricacy can be appreciated in a project such as this. Often it is best simply to let the architect describe what is going on, and in this case, Peter Bohlin's words provide an articulate insight into the genesis and realization of the project. "In this design, the details are about how to take a functional object such as a stair and make it an object or a construct. The stair is a study of celebrating connections and how to express the parts of a whole.

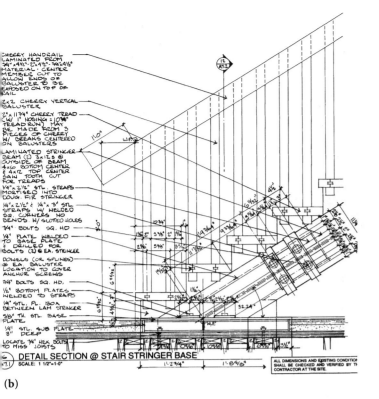

(b)

2

3

Figure 1(a) and (b) *Part of an extensive set of drawings where virtually every dimension and material were expressly called out. These drawings represent the kind of micro-managed control that allows for a near-perfect finished product if (1) the explicit directions are correct and reasonable and (2) the artisan chooses to respect the drawings. Note the extraordinary attention paid to allowing every joint to be both "slipped" visually and yet, in a design and engineering sense, absolutely "locked in."*

Figure 2 *Stair backside view. A stout Douglas fir strut supports an equally stout pair of Douglas fir stringers, upon which treads and rails are set to extend almost mechanistically.* (Courtesy of the architects.)

Figure 3 *Side view. The interface between floor and stair is expressed via their independent structure and yet integrated via consistent detailing of the railings.* (Courtesy of the architects.)

"*Positioning and detailing make this stair a construct in its own right, as it expresses its nature, its parts, their connections and its relationship to the whole.*

Seen from the entry, the open steps permit a view through to the glazed east wall of the great room. Sharing the timber construction of the house, the structure of the stair sits firmly on the stone floor, its weight supported by a prop of milled Douglas Fir. Along with the fireplace the stair inhabits the living space, openly connecting it with the balconies above.

As with the column base plates throughout the house, the stair uses steel strapping to connect its heavy timber structure. Slotted holes and steel straps slide to accomodate the shrinkage of Douglas Fir members.

Tactile surfaces, the treads, balusters and handrails are distinguished by the use of Cherry. The 2 x 2 in balusters extend through the handrail and read flush with its upper surface. Because of greater shrinkage across the grain of the cherry rail, these flush baluster heads extend slightly above the surface, so that the handrail is used a tick-tick-tick becomes both a tactile and a visual experience. The balusters also pass down through the cherry stair threads, reaching below their bottom surface. Thus the stair reveals how it is made and celebrates its use."

Figure 4(a) and (b) Stair bottom. A large custom steel plate supports two massive stringers below while outsized laminated rails and balusters stand in bold invitation to ascend. Note the custom steel work that straps everything together and has every aspect of its design articulated either by off-set or lateral extension to provide a clear identity for each piece. Note finally that bolt heads are twisted for orientation to the geometry of the strapping. (Courtesy of the architects.)

Figure 5 Central brace. Large-scale solid wood members are interconnected via custom steel strapping. Note how the wood checking becomes an aesthetic feature in contrast to the consistent and rigorous use of steel and in the context of the interfacing rectilinear geometries of tread and rail and stringer and strut. (Courtesy of the architects.)

4 (a)

4 (b)

5

ZOO RAIL

Bohlin Cywinski Jackson, Architects

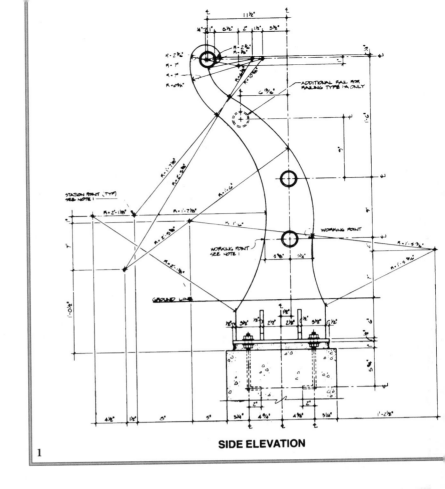

SIDE ELEVATION

1

Architects are often given difficult problems that can be solved only with clever detailing. Such is the case with the railing that Bohlin Cywinski Jackson, Architects have executed for the Philadelphia Zoological Gardens in Philadelphia. Two other details from this project can be seen in this book as well. Funding is seldom plush for such projects, and this project manipulates stock materials in direct and dramatic fashion utilizing available technologies. A series of tubular steel sections and flat stock steel components are cut and bent to follow a curvilinear path meandering about the animals. The railing is a consistent element that traverses streams, encounters rocks, and flows in and about the natural environment within which it serves to direct visitors. The detailing here is not aggressive or intense, but it is obviously organic in its ultimate ambience given the sinuous botanic quality of the vertical brackets that are used. Its ability to adapt itself to a variety of different conditions is keyed to its ingenious manipulation of its steel base plate which is either continuous or isolated, wrapping around corners, or set to the ground. The actual form of the sinuous rail verticals is itself determined by a large quantity of intersecting radii. The horizontal tubing which serves as the method of restraint is manipulated to extend to natural features; members are eliminated where not needed to facilitate view access and added to provide additional restraint at bridge areas. Thus, this project is user- and builder-friendly *and* enhances the sense of animistic, organic expression that is wholly appropriate to a zoo.

2

Figure 1 An extraordinary array of dimensions that micro-define
    something that looks effortless in its final product. Note the
notation of variable options of railing presence or lack of same.

Figure 2 At the bridge (right), bent stock channels support the
base. Where the bridge ends, the expressed steel channel ceases and
the more standard direct connection to the train (left) begins. Note
the sequential elimination of two horizontal tubular restraints at
the terminus of the bridge. (Courtesy of Otto Baitz/Esto and the architects.)

Millwork/Minutiae

When thinking about architectural detailing, some details are essential parts of our physical accommodations. Structural support, weatherproofing enclosures, openings for view and passage, and stairways all have hard-edged, generic identities which are, to a great extent, self-defining. Standing in contradistinction to these "bottom line" elements are the elements which enrich our daily lives, allowing us to gain a sense of intimacy and connection with our built environment. Whether it is in the form of trim, hardware, or simply a decorous appointment or appurtenance, it is these small-scale items which, although not essential to physical accommodation, provide a sense of reward and enrichment and often allow for an ease of use in our day-to-day lives. Although "nonessential," they are none the less the raison d'être for taking the time, effort, and expense to do anything more than rude accommodations of our physical requirements. They may be the frosting on the cake, but they are essential to our aesthetic nutrition.

UPPER CABINETS

Cheng Design,
Architects

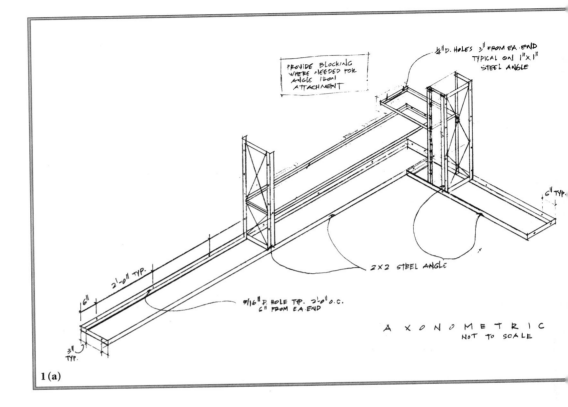

1 (a)

In kitchen design, it could be said that the upper cabinetry has consistently missed opportunities for expressive detailing. Upper cabinets are at eye level and often form the first impression of the space in which they are set. At worst, these cabinets are rendered as stark carcasses, simply tacked on a wall. They often have a stylistic applique crudely "wallpapered" upon them—raised panel, flat panel, plastic laminate, stainless steel, natural wood, or simulated or stained wood veneer—all are relegated to the role of "box" when these cabinets are applied to the walls of a given kitchen space. There are simple reasons for this, namely that unlike their base cabinet counterparts, upper cabinets do not need to be continuous—they do not need to support an unbroken line of countertop. Second, it is quite expensive to integrate any cabinet into any context—usually involving customization or hyperarticulation of detail to mesh the cabinet into its context. In most cases, therefore, whether the kitchen is custom-crafted or out of a catalog, upper cabinets are rude impositions on a space which often serves as the functional fulcrum of the American household. Rather than surrender to a perceived *fait accompli*, Cheng Design, of Los Angeles, California, has opted to reinvent the upper cabinets in this California kitchen in a way that is not only aesthetically expressive, but affordable and visually distinctive. Beyond simply creating cabinet space, the detailing

Figure 1(a) (above), (b), and (c) (see page 167) These are extraordinarily effective working drawings, as they are relentlessly recognizance of three-dimensional realities and provide for a very simple interpretation that would be readily understandable by a small shop. In fact, their very character recognizes the low-tech skill required to produce such an armature.

Figure 2 A logical result of the ever contrasting materials used, the upper cabinets of this kitchen are simultaneously abstracted in form and integrated by detail to the surrounding materials and cabinetry around them. The crispness of line and clarity of organization stand in distinction from many similar kitchens where "style" often leads to cabinets that resemble chests of drawers screwed onto walls more than something which is a part of its context.

(Courtesy of the architects.)

employed provides several ancillary benefits as well. To facilitate affordability (while expressing the inherent qualities of natural wood) it is often necessary to use veneered plywood. This use of plywood can be apologetic and imitative of solid wood construction via the use of ornamental trim to simulate wood frames or, as in this case, the wood graining can be held in crisp abstraction as cabinet fronts are detailed to be absolutely frameless and visually detached from their surrounding context. The veneered wood grain direction is set either to provide continuity between fronts or rotated 90 degrees to provide a distinctive end condition. Whereas the wood cabinets themselves are held in contradistinction to the context of the walls (via heavy contrast with the wall's heavily figured and dark slate tile or blankly painted surface), it is the unifying element of a steel frame that makes these cabinets both unforgettable and extraordinarily innovative relative to other examples of upper cabinetry one might typically find elsewhere. Stock steel channel is utilized as an overt linear element to virtually underscore the abstracted wood grain mentioned earlier and to serve as a bracketing counterpoint at the corner condition set between the two isolated upper cabinets in this particular kitchen layout. Rather than the enigmatically invisible attachment that most cabinets have to the wall, this steel bracketing/linear gasketing system serves as a strong visual signal that the wood cabinets are unapologetically rendered to be distinct objects. Essentially an intermediate system of implicit support, these steel frames also serve to provide the often problematic light valance (the visual shield that obscures standard light fixtures from being directly seen) as well as providing support for glass shelving at the corner between the wall units. In one fairly expressive articulation, the steel channel is extended along with some diagonal sheet metal work to provide an easy-access wine rack to one side of one of the upper cabinets. All the materials and detailing employed for these brackets are the simplest imaginable—welded stock shapes with routine ground-welded joinery. The orientation of the steel is always held in deference to the projecting wood boxes they visually support, and this misalignment continues with the extended shelf supports mentioned earlier. Although the methods employed are inherently stark and abstracted, and thus a bit pungent for some households, this detailing addressed a problem that is encountered in the vast majority of U.S. kitchens—the affordable rationalization and mitigation of the inherently awkward presence of the vast majority of upper kitchen cabinetry. And, besides, these particular cabinets are virtually the perfect application for their Modernist, sculpturalist context.

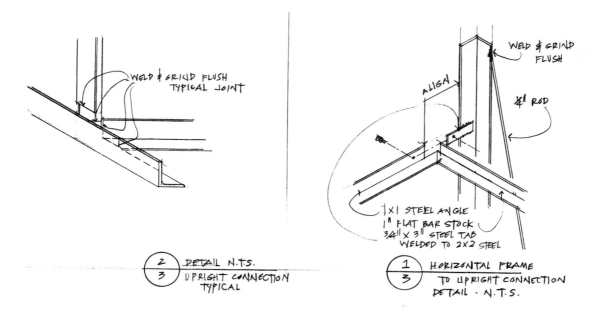

WELD & GRIND FLUSH
TYPICAL JOINT

2/3 DETAIL N.T.S.
UPRIGHT CONNECTION
TYPICAL

WELD & GRIND
FLUSH

ALIGN

¼" ROD

1×1 STEEL ANGLE
1" FLAT BAR STOCK
¾" × 3" STEEL TAB
WELDED TO 2×2 STEEL

1/3 HORIZONTAL FRAME
TO UPRIGHT CONNECTION
DETAIL · N.T.S.

1(b)

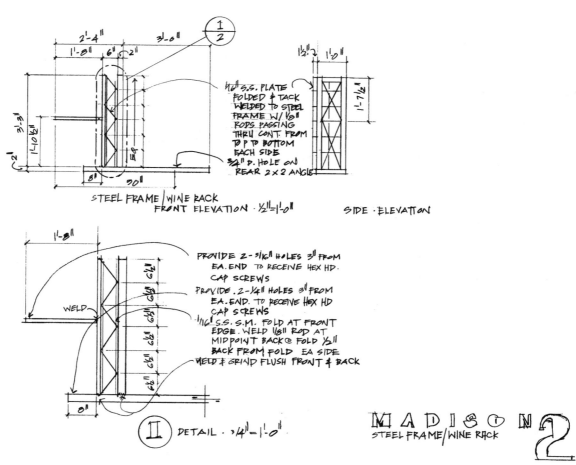

1/2

¼" S.S. PLATE
FOLDED & TACK
WELDED TO STEEL
FRAME W/ ⅛"
RODS PASSING
THRU CONT. FROM
TOP TO BOTTOM
EACH SIDE
¾" D. HOLE ON
REAR 2×2 ANGLE

STEEL FRAME / WINE RACK
FRONT ELEVATION · ½"=1'-0"

SIDE · ELEVATION

PROVIDE 2-5/16" HOLES 3" FROM
EA. END TO RECEIVE HEX HD.
CAP SCREWS
PROVIDE 2-¼" HOLES 3" FROM
EA. END. TO RECEIVE HEX HD
CAP SCREWS
1/16" S.S. S.M. FOLD AT FRONT
EDGE. WELD ⅛" ROD AT
MIDPOINT BACK @ FOLD ½"
BACK FROM FOLD EA SIDE
WELD & GRIND FLUSH FRONT & BACK

WELD

II DETAIL · ¾"=1'-0"

MADISON 2
STEEL FRAME/WINE RACK

1(c)

BATHROOM MIRROR

Anne Fougeron, Architect

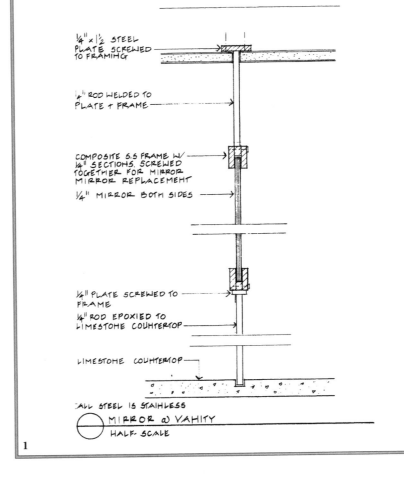

1/4" x 1 1/2" STEEL
PLATE SCREWED
TO FRAMING

1/4" ROD WELDED TO
PLATE + FRAME

COMPOSITE S.S FRAME W/
1/4" SECTIONS SCREWED
TOGETHER FOR MIRROR
MIRROR REPLACEMENT

1/4" MIRROR BOTH SIDES

1/4" PLATE SCREWED TO
FRAME
1/4" ROD EPOXIED TO
LIMESTONE COUNTERTOP

LIMESTONE COUNTERTOP

ALL STEEL IS STAINLESS

MIRROR @ VANITY
HALF-SCALE

1

Mirrors are often used with an exquisitely disingenuous motive, to provide the illusion of space by, at the minimum, doubling up the visual indication of a room's true size while in no way actually expanding the room's usable space. At some point, all architects and designers have been tempted (and have often succumbed to the temptation) to use mirrors to answer questions that are either unanswerable due to a site's context or in lieu of a "better" idea. As such, mirrors can be seen to have a greater affinity with the mindset of creative illusion employed by set designers, rather than the architect's hard-edged design criteria of solving spacial or functional problems. However, like many other materials, mirror has unique properties that creative architects can employ with a wholly innovative mind-set. In this particular case, the creative use of a mirror virtually *hides* its own presence but in no way obscures the true size of the room it sits within. Ironically enough, this application of mirror affords a *true* sense of the size of its context versus perpetrating a cruel joke on the users of the room in which it is set.

In late-twentieth-century America, two-career couples often find themselves confronted with the unfortunate reality of simultaneously doubling up on the available bathroom space for personal hygiene. Thus, it is now more the rule than the exception that master bedroom suites have two sinks. This design requirement can become particularly problematic when renovating an existing home. In this particular case, Anne Fougeron, a California architect, has encountered not only a relatively tight space, but a space that has poten-

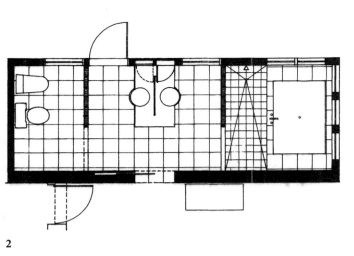

2

Figure 1 *Careful orientation of simple components allows for a minimum of visible detailing. Note that both the rods and frames are set to absolute minimum sizes, thus providing an optimal capacity for the "disappearing act" which is facilitated by this detail.*

Figure 2 *Plan. Note that upon entry, the end of the partners' desk vanity is viewed with the almost invisible end condition of the double mirror directly opposite those entering. Note also that the towel pattern, flanking glass block walls, medicine cabinets, and doors (one fixed and one operable) are rigorously oriented to this same center line. The bilateral symmetry involved facilitates the interconnection of mirrored elements from side to side, thus allowing the mirror to disappear.*

Figures 3(right) and 4(next page) *A sense of complete spacial openness is effected despite the fact that there is an intervening mirror set above the two sinks.* (Courtesy of the architect.)

3

4

tial for a wonderful view. By providing direct access to an outdoor deck, Fougeron did solve the functional problem of bringing the outside in, but when confronted with the need for two large vanity spaces within a tight area, both requiring the requisite mirror upon which the occupants might address their own visage, Fougeron responded with an extraordinary amount of creativity by realizing that a mirror need not be set on a wall, but can be utilized as a free-standing element. By backing up vanity to vanity, "T-ed" off from the wall pierced by deck-accessing doors, and by utilizing a lightly framed two-sided mirror held distinct from the "partner's desk" vanity by standard steel rods, Fougeron created the needed reflectance without the unwanted subdividing bulk of a "real" wall. With light and air floating all about its presence, this double-sided mirror was inherently light in its impact. More ingenious is the fact that when set within a semisymmetrical room, one combining the patterns of tile and glass block and the linear elements of trim cabinetry, there is a virtual "disappearing act" facilitated by the mirror's positioning. By simply reflecting that which is opposite their presence, each mirror replicates what might be seen on either side of the vanity as if the mirror itself did not exist. By reflecting the light present on both sides of the vanity from identical and symmetrically placed full light doors, there is no loss of light due to the presence of this two-sided mirror. In fact, although this mirror does not add to the sense of space within this room, it rejects the notion that a space need be perceivably divided by imposing a plane that separates two areas of a room. All the elements employed in this case are crafted of stock materials, detailed to minimize

"The symmetry of this space works with the floating mirror to create a spacial illusion: looking into the mirror the reflection one sees appears like a continuation of the space, one has the illusion of being able to see right through the mirror. The resulting space is light, spare, and yet visually exciting."

5

any focus on the detailing involved. There are no articulated fasteners or expressed joints. Mirrors are merely fused to a plywood panel and surrounded by a stainless steel frame (carefully screwed together to facilitate replacement in case one of the mirrors should happen to crack or lose its backing). In fact, it is this invisible detailing that helps create the illusion of a nonexistent wall.

Sometimes the most powerful impact a detail can have is that it affords the overall sense of its context to be fully manifest, unabated by the presence of the detail itself.

WET BAR

House + House, Architects

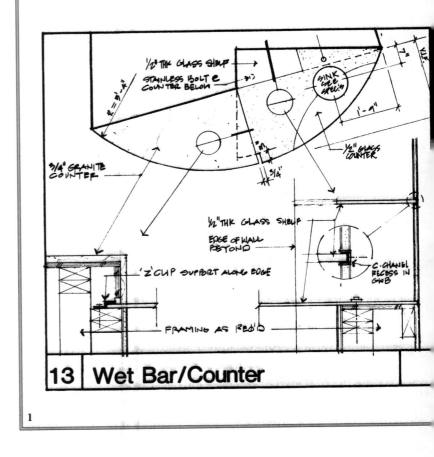

13 | Wet Bar/Counter

1

"**Pieces and parts!** Pieces and parts!" So quotes many an architecture professor when describing "high-tech" Modernist work. If the art of detailing consisted of nothing more than rudely combining industrial, Modernist details, the resulting cacophonous jumble of "pieces and parts" would render the product either useless or, more probably, simply ugly beyond use. In this particular case, a very simple desire (for a wet bar) is incorporated with an extraordinarily deft hand to express the specific component identities of counter, sink, and storage, while addressing all the design elements of line, shape, materiality, and artfulness that are employed whenever successful architectural detailing is manifest. In this particular case, the materials involved are all expressed to the point of sculptural abstraction. A tempered glass counter serves to hold fast a stainless steel sink that has a conical shroud set below it for support of the counter's front. A clever underglass shelf is provided at the back side of this piece that both supports the back side edge of this glass and allows the waste and pressure lines to remain unseen. This glass counter is also set directly into a carved-out niche in a sheetrock wall context and abuts into an extension of the sheetrock system which supports a granite countertop. In addition, a small angular glass shelf is set in the "crotch" or joint of the niche and projection just mentioned. These "pieces" gain presence through their carefully sculpted, rendered forms. They do not rely on the cheap thrills of cacophonous collision to obtain a sense of dynamism. Instead, components are carefully arrayed to be shy or proud of

Figure 1 Single vignetted detail provides large-scale sectional details and a comprehensive plan. The direct teeing of the details to the plan is a clear recognition of the fact that graphic niceties often create problems. The architect's willingness to coalesce all details onto one small graphic device clues all disciplines involved in the fabrication of this piece into its ultimate form. The only item left to the imagination is the elevation, which is not part of this sketch. Otherwise, there is a surprising level of information from such a small piece of graphics.

Figure 2 Sculpted wallpaper-clad gypsum board provides the blank background for several simple moves, both recessive and projecting, which serve to create shapes that reflect light, cast shadows, and allow for clean attachments of disparate materials. This is a clean construction with underpinnings of lively rationalism as a generative influence. (Courtesy of the Alan Weintraub.)

2

each other for ease of construction and a delicate expression of materiality. Some of the most important details in this particular project are the ones that are unseen. Every piece is "gripped" by fasteners that are set behind the sheetrock, and the cavity of the niche allows both shelf and a sink counter to occur with a minimum of visible support. The contrasting textured wallpaper is an inexpensive way to amalgamate all the shapes of the supporting backround gypsum-board-surfaced construction.

The detail sheet for this particular project is wonderfully minimized—simply a plan and some cross sections, all with the barest essential dimensions shown.

ROOM DIVIDER

Tigerman-McCurry, Architects

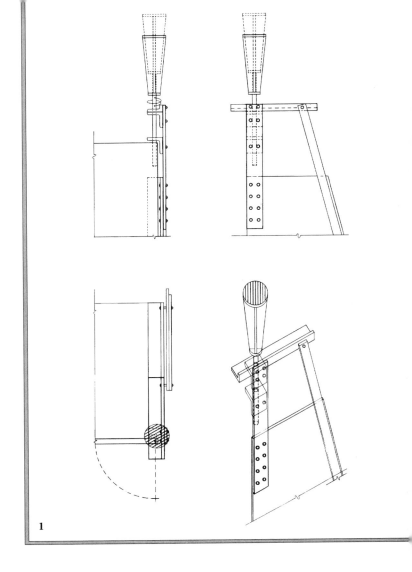

1

Sometimes simple problems make for extraordinary solutions. Often, a single generator for an innovative idea creates an enormous flurry of aesthetic effort that ultimately makes a delightful mountain out of a molehill or two. In this particular case, the architects involved (Tigerman-McCurry in Chicago) were dealing with the subdivision of a large-scale, almost industrial loft via the use of built-in components. They were confronted with one simple problem—the planes of the floors and walls of the loft were at a variety of levels and were, in and of themselves, anything but plumb or level. Creating a plumb built-in unit in such a context is a mechanic's nightmare given that there is nothing from which to register. Such micro problems are often blindly resolved by providing gaps—reveals, spacers, stand offs—between the newly installed item and its eccentric context, allowing any item to fit any space. Rather than address this last level of accommodation as an afterthought, it served as a conceptual launching pad for an enormously creative construction utilizing mostly standardized parts. Steel I-beams provide the "plinth" for this unit, and stock T-sections (aluminum for easy cutting and working) vertically support fairly simple cabinets whose sides and fronts are made of ½-in-thick sheet aluminum. The vertical extensions that provide compressive stability for the entire structure are conical in profile but fabricated from flat stock and

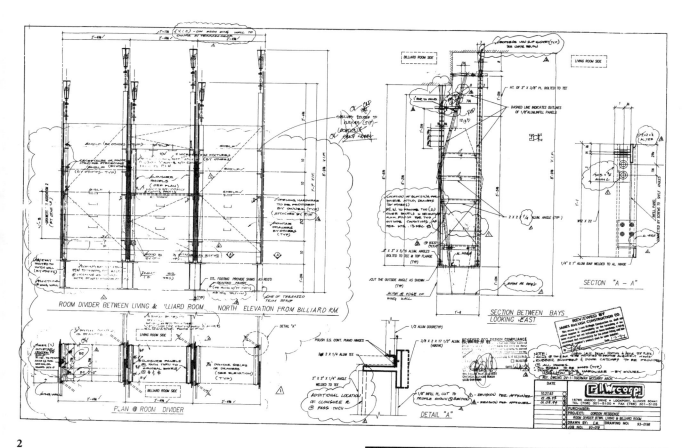

2

Figure 1 *The detail of the retroactive PR drawing, and not a true working shop drawing, the precise drawing techniques are, in this case, absolutely appropriate given the nature of the work to be defined. A variety of specialized parts are formed from stock materials to create something which is mechanistic, animated, and enigmatically technological.*

Figure 2 *Shop drawing. A classic document of interpolation between architects' well intentioned, but often incomplete, attempts at detailing something that is not always fully within their understanding, this shop drawing evidences both rigorous attention to specificity and a careful overview of the architects as they attempt to maintain control and enhance their own design via harnessing the expertise of those who would fabricate their work.*

Figure 3 *The detail. Here, seen at its base condition, a standard threaded rod is connected to a spayed array of heavy gauge sheet aluminum forming a "foot" for the project. Note all the hyperarticulated and blissfully bypassing elements employed with every possible fastener and joint celebrated.*

(Courtesy of the architects.)

3

have the capacity to adjust to the uneven surfaces used to provide stability. A neoprene gasket is set between this movable part and the ceiling surfaces to allow for a tight fit. In addition, a wide range of struts, brackets, stiffening members, and secondary components are all blissfully expressed via the unapologetic use of through-bolted joinery and nonaligned end conditions. Generic stock hardware and fasteners join in thoroughly customized intersections. Creating cabinet doors out of solid aluminum is a novel idea that has resonant aesthetic impact and allows for a latently powerful sense of materiality which no painted wood or plastic laminate solution could approximate. Although budget was not one of the main design criteria in this project, it is clear that the overall aesthetic impact is extraordinary, especially when there are only two functional requirements—that a fair amount of storage is provided and that the unit separate the space within which it sits. It is not often that such simple design requirements can mesh with such custom craftsmanship to form a piece which is at once high-tech and user-friendly. Part of the unit's success is its ability to be blissfully ignorant of some systems (lighting and HVAC grills) and yet be visually married to others by coincidental techno-detailing including a low-voltage suspended wire lighting system, a sliding panel room divider system, even the imposed linear detailing of a terrazzo and aluminum strip floor. The net results convey industrial strength and whimsical delight. Joints are both honest and yet somehow ironic or vaguely humorous. It is via these ironies and paradoxes that memorable details come, and, when found within the safe harbor of a weathertight envelope, the elevation of small design criteria to overarching consequence is thoroughly appropriate and intriguing. One might say that the architect's statement has an equivalent sense of irony and complexity.

Figure 4 Overall view. Intended simply to divide two spaces from each other, the net form is potent, aggressive, and somehow delicate in its attachment. Note the variety of systems expressed in blissful ignorance of each other, including custom terrazzo floor patterning and a combination of high-tech, low-voltage lighting system and the low-tech, catalogue-component derived HVAC grills and heat detectors.
(Courtesy of the architects.)

Aluminum   [< L. *aluminis*]
                  lux, lunien, lucere; lighted light lightning.
To be lighted.   In movement and weight; tracery.

                  Tectonic, tonic
                  [**Gr.** *tonikos* < *tonos:* a stretching, TONE]
                                        of muscular tone, tension. Tonic cond.

[< L. *tonus*, sound.]   A relative height of pitch. Syllable.
Angle   [< **Gr.** *ankylos:* bent, ANKLE]

Arche, Artifice   [< L. *ar-*, to join, fit together, ART, ARM,

                                        ARTICULATE]   trickery.

4

WALL/CHANGING TABLE

*Duo Dickinson,
Architect*

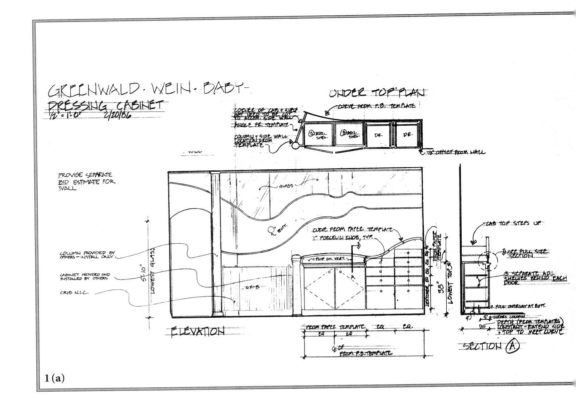

1(a)

There are times when no standard component can be plugged into an existing condition. This is most often true when space is at a premium and when the needs involved are relatively idiosyncratic. In a tight loft apartment in New York City, a newly pregnant couple realized that their one accessory bedroom needed to accommodate two people with extraordinarily diverse needs. One side of the room would be occupied on an ongoing basis by their new baby. The other side of the room would have an intermediate occupancy by sleep-over babysitters or perhaps even a live-in *au pair*. Although the existing room was oversized for either occupancy, it was definitely undersized, in the traditional sense, for both occupancies combined into one space. Therefore, a "normal" wall separating these two spaces would simply make both tenancies implausible. Thus a custom solution was envisioned. Once the doors are opened to nonstandard thinking, innovation tends to infuse itself to a wider context than simply addressing the immediate problem encountered. So it was in this particular case when the inherent problem of storage and the unique needs of a baby's changing table were also put into play. After a variety of solutions were considered, it was obvious that the only way to accommodate all the needs involved was a slightly "bent" wall—one that would allow a widened area on one side of the wall for a changing table, while allowing

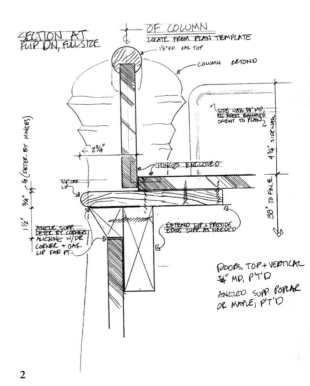

2

3

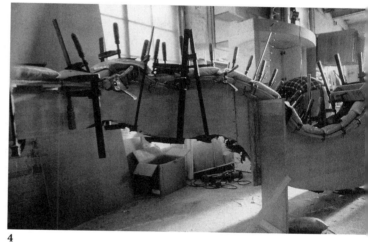

Figure 1(a) and (b) An architect's first stab is gridded (b) and, using this gridding, the curvilinear aspects of this project are blown up to full size.

Figure 2 A full size detail to the changing table edge, where a variety of items have to move, align, and coordinate.

Figure 3 The wall and changing table. The elements are assembled from three sources, the middle wave from a shop in Connecticut, the changing table (right) from a shop in upstate New York, and the binding lower wall and upper plexiglass fabricated on site. Note that lighting and a doorway (far left) were also installed on site, all over a preexisting floor condition. (Courtesy of Mick Hales.)

4

Figure 4 The intermediate section of the curvilinear wall (above a field fabricated stud and sheetrock wall and below a field applied layer of plexiglass glazing) is formed in a shop utilizing two layers of 1/4-inch plywood and a variety of internal stiffeners. The curving upper lip is formed via clamping utilizing lead-shot filled bags to provide even pressure along the edge to be clamped. (Courtesy of the architect.)

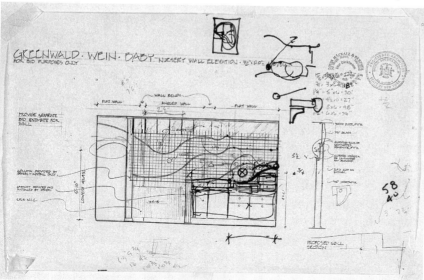

1(b)

existing openings and new storage areas to be accepted at the other end of the construction. Not only was the bend to be in plan, it was also deemed to be a good idea to allow as much light and openness as possible to be achieved on either side of the wall, while achieving some level of sound separation. So it made sense to glaze the top edge of the wall. Even these relatively idiosyncratic needs do not necessarily mean that expressive custom-crafted detailing needs to be imposed. The overlying aspect of this entire project, however, was the desire for the work to be infused with the joyous sense of childhood and the fresh outlook of a transformed family condition in which a couple ceases to be a self-imbued dyad and begins to see the world through the eyes of the offspring. Pieces of furniture can become animated expressions of affection for loved ones. In this case, the innocence and spontaneity of an infantile outlook can be seen in the expressive and curvilinear lines employed to allow a doorway, clerestory glazing, stock crib accommodation, lighting, storage of diapers and other hygiene products, and a changing table as part of this overall construction.

In creating this particular project, the worlds of construction and cabinetry are completely intertwined, and, in fact, there is a literal interface as well, involving three separate fabricators. The changing table itself was the product of a solo practitioner in western Massachusetts, Bill Ritt. The central portion of the curvilinear wall was the product of a shop doing other work in the loft of the apartment (Breakfast Woodworks); this shop had the large-scale capacity to define the curvilinear aspects in three dimensions that the smaller shop could not begin to address given the obvious deadlines of a pregnancy-driven construction project. Last, the general contractor on the job, Rosli Construction, needed to make the intermediate wall components to support the piece formed by Breakfast Woodworks and connect the wall to the ceiling with clear plexiglass. The wall benefits from the stabilizing influence of the changing table on one side and a custom-turned column on the other. The contractor also insinuated a pocket door and provided all the electrification present (a single bulb sconce above the crib and an articulating wall lamp above the changing table). Fortunately, everything was to be field painted, and thus the joinery, while although it had to be perfect ultimately, could be modified on site to accept variations of unforeseen field conditions and the inevitable miscalculations present when so many different elements are combined in ways that are not rectilinear (or even geometrically defined).

The key to the success of this entire project was the use of full-sized templates for all the curves involved. A shared full-sized template was used for both the wall and the changing table, and the contractor-fabricated aspects of the wall were not even attempted until the intermediate strip of millwork was brought onto the site. In addition, all the horizontal curves were laid out full size using the time-honored method of small drawing interpolation with ongoing large-scale overview of the design. Given the curves, this is not an inexpensive undertaking, but the methodologies employed—using the appropriate artisan for the appropriate task and allowing for field finishing of all components involved as well as the lack of any inherently costly materials themselves—allowed for an extraordinarily expressive piece to be insinuated into a fairly stark context of sheetrock and strip oak flooring. Allowing gnarly problems to be infested with an effervescent spirit not only takes care of functional problems but allows innovation to overcome potentially stultifying conditions. So it is with this project and so it can be if care is taken to translate small-scale good ideas into large-scale built form.

5

6

Figure 5 Occupied. With crib in place, the ultimate sense is
one of focusing on a dearly beloved inhabitant, the focal
point of both the linear components as well as
the light fixture. (Courtesy of the architect.)

Figure 6 Context. A new curvilinear entry piece (left) sets
up the curves of the newly applied wall (background right).
Lightly complementary coloring facilitates some simple
graphic underscoring of the lines and shapes applied.
(Courtesy of Mick Hales.)

CORNER
CABINET
AND WINDOW

Bart Prince, Architect

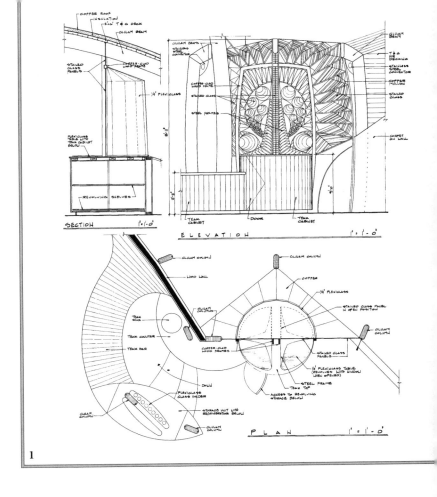

1

There are many ways to look at a building. Often, architects like to segregate or express structure, isolate the exterior envelope, or hold cabinetry distinct from its context—all in neat hierarchial sequencing. Bart Prince does not believe in architectural "food chains." His projects evidence the holistic, organic approach where every element of a building is in concert with, and often "mates" with, every other element. So is the case with this thoroughly invigorated construction in a private residence in Corona del Mar, California. Set in the context of a room with an extraordinary view of the ocean, this particular corner wanted to have its view obscured to allow a non-view-oriented focal point. Prince saw an opportunity to co-conspire the arced micro-lam structural ribs and the copper flashing of the voided corner of this partic-ular part of the construction *and* to facilitate storage within a room where traditional furniture would not be very comfortable. Creating a focal point in a house that is, in itself, a gigantic focal point with a multiplicity of subordi-nate focal aspects to it might seem difficult, but Bart Prince is up to the task and utilizes an extraordinary array of colored glass, geometric permutation, and extreme integration between cabinetry elements involving teak, steel, plexiglass, and copper, all craftily insinuated into a polygonally activated con-text. The colored glass is in truth a screen that opens up to the view when the table top is rotated, and the interior of the curvilinear base is completely accessible via doors (the shelving of which also, not surprisingly, rotates). Although the drawing presented accurately describes every aspect of the

Figure 1 Cabinetry and glazing respond to polygonal, radial, and organic motifs integrating structure, craft, fine art, and the amazing mind-set of Bart Prince. This drawing is hyperarticulate and yet leaves a great deal of latitude for the artistry employed to effect this piece.

Figure 2 Context. An unlimited view (right) necessitated the need for some visual distraction and dynamic with the built-in element (left). Note the sympathy between all the motifs of structure, enclosure, cabinetry, and glazing.

2

design, the extraordinary application of craftsmanly detailing is truly at the highest level and inevitably gives responsibility to the artisans employed to effect a finished product that will stand the test of time. Even an architect with the skill of Bart Prince knows when to allow those even more knowledgeable than he to derive the final level of micromanagement of specific details of joinery and connection.

Figure 3 *Rendering of stained glass work. As
effervescent and articulate as the entire house itself, this
glass work stretches the limits of the craft employed.*
(Courtesy of the architect.)

Figure 4 *Stained glass work.* (Courtesy of the architect.)

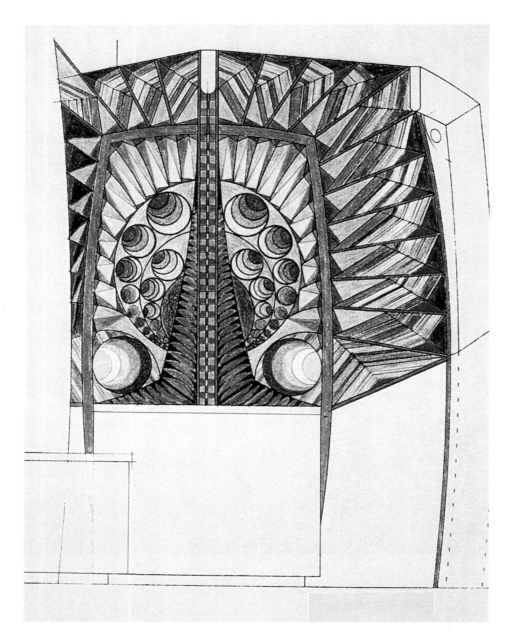

3

*"The problem was to conceal the view of the ocean beyond with a
design that could be open if desired while it appears to be 'fixed'
glazing. The center sections of the window rotate outward into a
multisided glazed cylinder which keeps out the weather and gives a
three-dimensional quality to the corners on the outside."*

4

LIGHT BEAM

Michael Wisniewski, Architect

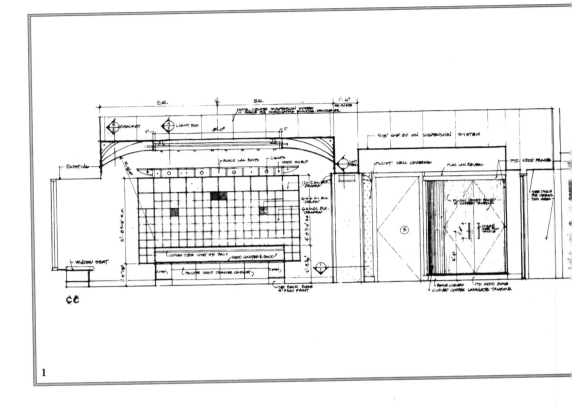

1

Condos are often built to make a ready profit via a quick sale. They are often view-focused and have features seemingly pulled out of an à la carte menu of domestic fantasies. That is to say, rather than thinking about what might delight any particular individual, for-profit, spec-built projects evidence whatever laundry list of desirable products that can be shoved into any given space to seduce a potential buyer into a sale. It is a very uncommon condo buyer who would request an expressively laminated wood ceiling ornament to form light troughs, but it is a talented architect who can see the potential present in a relatively blank space that has been given completely over to a view in the hopes of a quick sale. When Michael Wisniewski of Duncan·Wisniewski Architecture saw this space, he was overwhelmed by the view of a copper-clad church spire set prominently before the large windows that dominate this condo's interior. Given the fact that Wisniewski perceived the building was floating over the landscape with no legitimate direct connection to the ground, he endeavored to sustain visual interest within the condo via a series of architectural millwork details.

The most memorable of these is a rhythmic imposition of eight ornamental ribs that span across the living space of this small unit. Essentially metering approximately thirty linear feet of space, this ceiling ornament not only

Figure 1 *Room elevation. These ribs of techno trim provide infill in a raised portion of the main living room space (upper left center).*

Figure 2 *Details. Created of simple laminations of plywood and of easily formed copper components either of sheet stock, pipe, or wire, these essential sections in three-dimensional view convey the commonsense detailing of the expressive elements employed.*

Figure 3 *Light beams. Decorative brackets flair to receive troughs which, in turn, harbor light, all of green tinted bird's eye maple plywood and appointed with copper accoutrement and is thoroughly integrated with a variety of upshine and downshine light fixtures.* (Courtesy of the architect.)

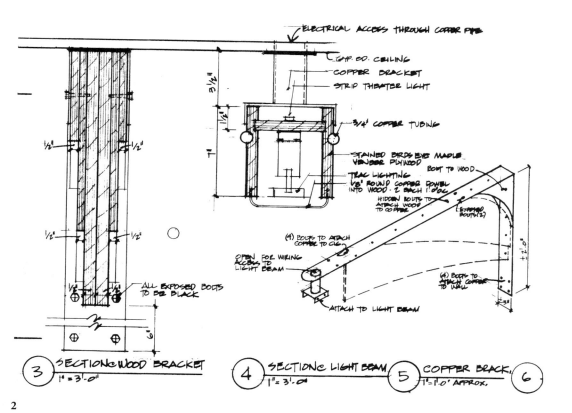

ELECTRICAL ACCESS THROUGH COPPER PIPE

GYP. BD. CEILING
COPPER BRACKET
STRIP THEATER LIGHT

3½"

1½"

1"

¾" COPPER TUBING

STAINED BIRDS EYE MAPLE
VENEER PLYWOOD

BOLT TO WOOD

TRAC LIGHTING
⅛" ROUND COPPER DOWEL
INTO WOOD - 2 EACH 1' O.C.

HIDDEN BOLTS TO
ATTACH WOOD
TO COPPER

EXPOSED
BOLTS (2)

(4) BOLTS TO ATTACH
COPPER TO CLG.

OPEN FOR WIRING
ACCESS TO
LIGHT BEAM

½"   ½"

½"   ½"

½"   ¾"

ALL EXPOSED BOLTS
TO BE BLACK

± 2'-0"

± 3"

ATTACH TO LIGHT BEAM

(4) BOLTS TO
ATTACH COPPER
TO WALL

6'-0"

③ SECTION@ WOOD BRACKET
1" = 3'-0"

④ SECTION@ LIGHT BEAM
1" = 3'-0"

⑤ COPPER BRACK.
1" = 1'-0' APPROX.

⑥

2

3

allows track lighting to have a safe harbor, but it also utilizes dyed bird's eye maple veneers to mimic the green oxidation of the aforementioned church spire. This project would not be memorable if it simply consumed a lot of money, made a fussy detail, and then walked away. The reality of this particular project which makes this construction so compelling is that it uses stock materials (veneer plywood), celebrates expressed fasteners (black painted bolts), and accommodates the most prosaic of flexible lighting forms (simple track lighting). When combined with field-determined curvilinear lines, integrating adjacent fixed lighting into its rhythmic pattern, and celebrating the distinctions between curvilinear brackets mounted on the side and the independently supported troughs which are dropped and connected to these brackets via a variety of copper details, the overall effect is somewhat fantastic and overtly kinetic. Simultaneously billowing and architectonic, these "light beams" effectively compete with the church spire, the view beyond, and even the large format television which is set within its context. Most detailing is gapped and cross-referentially interrelated by alignment (versus tight and complex joinery) thus allowing for a "loose fit," once again helping to ensure affordability and easy on-site adjustment. Joints are effected using stock copper elements, tubes, wires, and sheet stock. Although this is not an inexpensive detail, it is built with one eye toward cost and ease of installation. Given the extraordinary impact it has on the space, one can easily assert that Wisniewski definitely maximizes the "bang for the buck" for the work employed.

"The Light Beams are reminiscent of arched, beamed, and vaulted spaces in churches or other buildings that have a sense of being very old and grounded. The form, materials, and color give a sense of standing under a pagoda covered with vines. Standing in the space and looking out of the window at the view feels peaceful and centered, so we think this space is a success as a direct result of the Light Beam detail."

4

5

6

Figure 4 Joint. *Bracket on right is visually linked but dissociated from light box (left), and copper linkages overlap and integrate.* (Courtesy of the architect.)

Figure 5 The view. *A copper-clad church spire (right) forms the basis for many of the moves of these trim pieces, while the view beyond also serves to necessitate some fairly aggressive architectural expression to maintain interest within the apartment itself.* (Courtesy of the architect.)

Figure 6 Overall view. *Elements acting in concert and coordination—lighting, trim work, glass block, etc.—provide for a "pumped up" ambience of activity and articulation.*
(Courtesy of the architect.)

BED CANOPY

George Ranalli, Architect

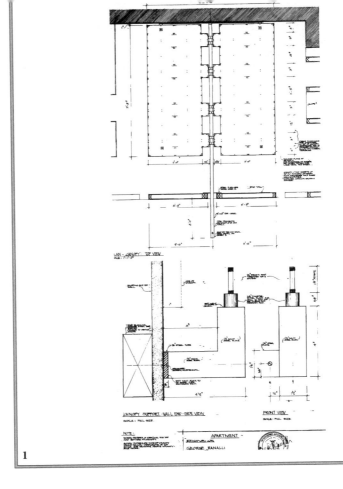

The inhabitants of large urban centers often find it necessary to convert spaces that once harbored large machines into what an architect once called "machines for living" (homes). The domestication of such "universal" space is not something to be taken lightly. Rejecting the notion that urban living is inherently transitory, virtually a lifestyle on the lam due to uncontrollable societal change, many city residents reinhabit one-time factory spaces with a definitive postindustrial mind-set. Rather than industrialize their home life, rendering it scaleless, randomly changing, and perhaps even dehumanized, it is a natural human desire to domesticate the spaces they inhabit, creating homes that meet their functional idiosyncrasies while providing an ambience which is aesthetically personalized and thus often detail conscious. So it was the desire of clients who wanted to remake a New York City loft with architect George Ranalli. The existing bedroom space of an earlier renovation had to be moved and thus a new space for sleeping had to be created. Rather than think of the space as something which would be decorated only at eye level, Ranalli saw the opportunity for the bed-bound prospect to determine a new way of thinking of bedroom ambience. This approach has some antique precedents. For a long time, many beds themselves were designed to function as the smallest room in the house. Whether curtained off and built into the wall of a Dutch home or set inside of a four-poster bed complete with canopy in Colonial America, the space where we slept often had a sense of intimacy that bespoke the desire to mitigate the impersonal quarters that our ancestors

Figure 1 *An extraordinary complete drawing which has full-sized details below and relatively large scale overall drawing above. Every bolt is rendered and almost every dimension indicated. There is a level of precision here that is more often associated with machine design than with architectural detailing.*

Figure 2 *Overall view. A two-part bed canopy with every joint articulated, with every surface caressed by technological detail, with its own support blissfully articulated, this is a marker to create a room and a space that is disconnected from the outside world.*
(Courtesy of the architect.)

Figure 3 *Every bolting condition is called out and every dimension indicated, right down to elements which are excruciatingly finite. The precision of the drawing ensures the precision of the final product. Involving meticulous attention to detail, this ultimate affectation is intended to be something which is more technological than human.*

2

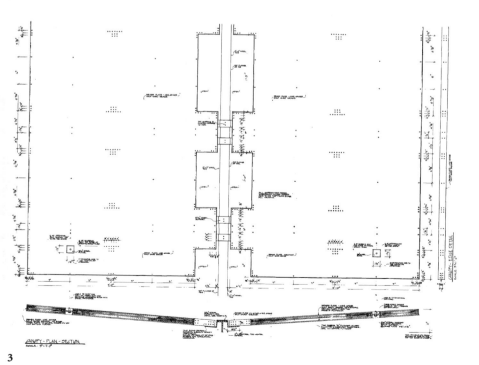

3

often dwelled within. Beyond nocturnal privacy, these accommodations of our most intimate moments were islands of separation from a chaotic world of multi-generational living.

In the present day chaotic world of loft living in New York, George Ranalli has opted to define a sleeping space via the ceiling plane—not with a gesture which expresses quietude, but rather with the ironic manipulation of industrial aesthetic to create space via the vertical alignment of two horizontal conditions, the necessary bed and its canopy. In this particular case, Ranalli has opted for a bilateral approach to his canopy design implicitly recognizing the two bed inhabitants.

To transform the cool light of the loft, Ranalli used brass to reflect the sense of sunlight's warmth that is absent from this once-harsh accommodation. And although it is nice to have a place to rest your eyes when lying horizontally, it might not always be the most comforting vision to have your own face and form directly reflected above you—hovering over you in a way which might preempt a quiet dissociation from the reality of the day-to-day world. So Ranalli canted the twin panels employed and verified that the mix of metals forming the brass used would have a minimum reflective quality.

The components and detailing employed are all straight distillations of a Machine Age aesthetic. Bolt patterns are mysteriously mutated and yet visually interconnected, and the joinery between pieces is at once overarticulated for purely prosaic design and yet, somehow, thoroughly antiornamental in ambience. Yet every joint and every piece has a marvelously conspired presence where reflectance, materiality, and craftsmanship are all choreographed to form a piece which is overtly human despite its industrial allusions. Fabricated with a plywood substraight and applied brass and steel components, this piece is a combination of the ambience of microarticulated machine tooling and an object which serves as the interpolator between the humanity of the dwellers and their potentially tough environment. In that sense, this functionally superfluous element, ornamental in its fundamental application, serves a poignant purpose—to provide an island of humanity within the ever-changing impersonal world of the urban context. In this way, it is not unlike the oasis its ancestors represented.

Figure 4 *Wall side detail. Parts that are seemingly created with a machinelike precision convey a sense of careful articulation and integration. Note the effective misty reflectance of the brass used, preempting a potentially embarrassing reflectance for the bed bound but effecting a depth and luster which are both alluring and evocative.* (Courtesy of the architect.)

"In the bedroom, natural light that enters is blue and cool in color. To help enhance the quality of light, a set of forms span over the bed. A golden canopy constructed of sheets of brass creates the yellow light absent without sun. The two planes are tightly inclined to spaces not too tightly enclosed, and any direct reflection is distorted. The brass is dull matte finished, high in zinc content to reduce undesirable reflective quality."

HARDWARE

George Ranalli, Architect

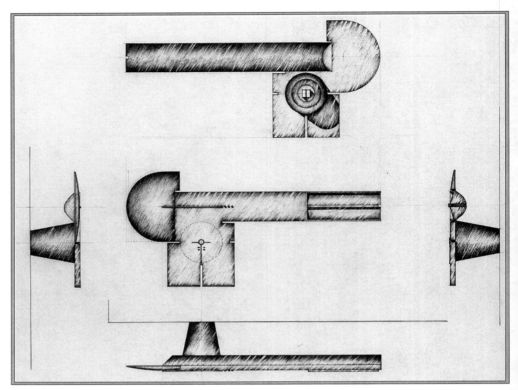

1

Doorknobs. No word evokes a more pat, almost iconic image in the mind of the listener. But when a Japanese hardware manufacturer approached George Ranalli (a New York architect known for intricate interiors and effervescent detailing), he leapt at the chance to reinvent the mind-set so many people have when confronted with the simple act of envisioning how a door might be pulled or pushed and a door lever or handle twisted or turned. The simple act of grasping and turning has its own set of ergonomic determinates, but prior to the actual physical encounter, doorknobs focus our eyes and ultimately our bodies, a demi-art piece not unlike earrings, buttons on a jacket, or cutlery surrounding a dish of spaghetti. To enhance this anticipatory act of long-range focus, Ranalli opted to invest a sense of inspired industrialism into his work.

Using shapes and techniques that are overtly Machine Age, these thoroughly custom-fabricated and craftsmanly art pieces are at once familiar and enigmatic. They combine a hint of arbitrarily industrialized detailing with an almost poetic sense of abstracting distillation. Every joint is articulated by plates, pins, or materials (stainless steel and brass). Almost all the geometric properties that might be ascribed to cylinders, planes, circles, octagons, and virtually every secondary and tertiary geometrically determinant influence is

Figure 1 Door lever handle. Line, shape, and materiality all conspire to create a miniature Machine Age sculpture—one that is somehow both architectural and sculptural.

Figure 2 Three-dimensional representation of a door pull-push plate. The flat plate to push, a projected bar to grab. The attachments seem tooled rather than cast, and the manipulations of the surface are at once carefully crafted and slightly rough hewn in sensibility. Note the back side of the push plate has a rounded finger- tip gripper.

Figure 3 Elevation of push plate grab bar. A variety of geometrical influences can be seen, and elements appear to be heavily machined in an aesthetically rich conspiracy.

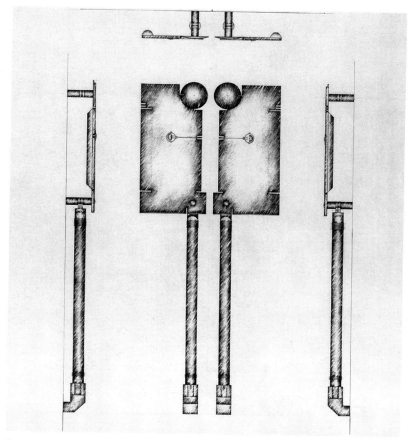

3

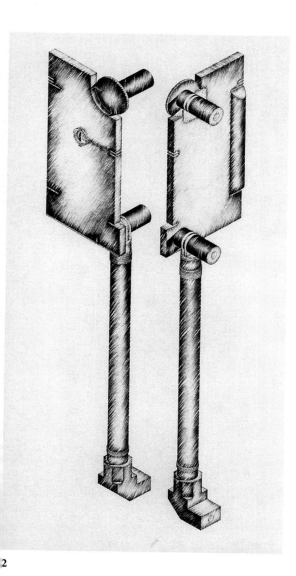

2

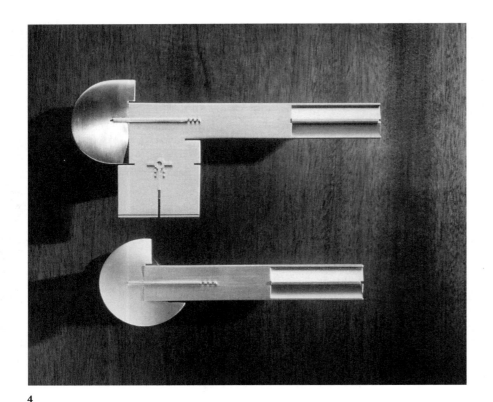

4

Figure 4 Lever handle. *The variety of materials and shapes from something which is both craftsmanly and somehow evocative of a Machine Age enigma.* (Courtesy of the architect.)

Figure 5 Push plate pull bar. *A sculptural techno-curiosity, this construction both beckons and implicitly asks a multitude of questions about its history, future, and origins.* (Courtesy of the architect.)

lightly articulated and enhanced. The form and outline of these pieces have great presence for long-distance apprehension, but the follow-through of extraordinarily precise and yet lightly lyric detailing sustains interest and even evokes a sense of curiosity. Are these recycled pieces of some fantastic disassembled machine? Or are they complete fabrications of a sculptor's mind? As such, they are metaphors for the architect's craft—utilizing a craftsmanly technology applied to enhance the sense of materiality while conspiring those hard-edged, antiaesthetic aspects into realized forms that are inherently idiosyncratic, expressive, and ultimately delightful.

CABINET HARDWARE

Kimo Griggs, Architect

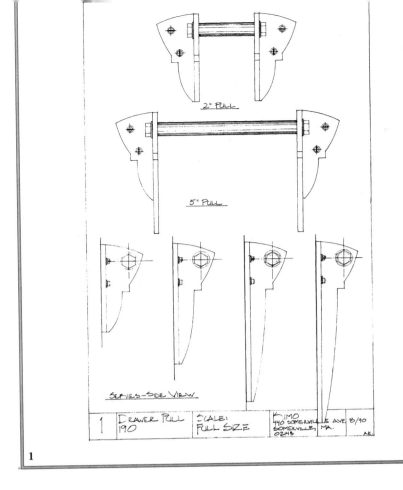

Trying to make something that is mass produced and yet expressive and innovative is a daunting task. With the overlying mantle of profitability always present, it takes an extraordinary knowledge of materials and construction techniques to "reign in" (or hopefully to inspire) any design while maintaining an eye for innovation and expression, whether it be for a spec house or, in this case, a prototype for production furniture. Designed by Kimo Griggs, the overall cabinetry employed uses solid and veneered cherry wood in a very straightforward manner, essentially as unornamented infill/between-metal appointments which are truly the "spice" of the piece itself. As such, metal elements employ a very simple technique of contrast to create something which has lightly industrial overtones via unapologetic use of standardized elements that allow for affordability while evidencing the overt and even celebratory embrace of custom-crafted design. This combination of the redundant/generic and the handcrafted/unique is most boldly present in the pulls employed which are conspired in concert with the corner brackets-cum-feet that dominate the cabinet's exterior form. Essentially, these pieces can use two pull widths (2 in and 5 in) and four pull bracket lengths ranging in size from 3 in to 7 in. Rather than simply attenuate a preconceived shape into something which is either completely customized or completely redundant, Griggs opted to make redundant that which could most effectively save cost while customizing those elements that could accept hand crafting with minimal cost. The redundant elements to each pull are stock compo-

2

Figure 1 Pull drawing. Considered redundancies of attachment patterning, pull detailing and base material specification are contrasted by the single act of attenuating the bottom line of the bracketed support for the pulls themselves. Note the specificity of screw head and hexagonal bolt head orientations.

Figure 2 Vaguely butterflied, overtly craftsmanly, these pulls have a sense of hand-hewn elegance, despite the prosaic parts of which they are made.
(Courtesy of the architect.)

nents—standard screws, bolts, tubular sections, and $1/8$-in aluminum angle for the custom-cut bracket which supports the prefabricated pull composed of a sleeved bolt. In addition, the spacing of the screws employed to attach the pull to the cabinet front and for the pull itself, involving the templated predrilling, are identical for all brackets employed (potentially eight different styles and sizes). Lastly, in a literally interesting twist, Griggs uses the consistent orientation of the screw head slots and hex head bolt heads themselves to underscore the latently ornamental lines of the aluminum brackets employed while the cut employed at the top of each bracket has a redundant shape. The idiosyncratic element for each pull is in the line and length of the attenuation of the bracket responding directly to the depth of the drawers or doors that the pull is mounted upon. This one customized element in an otherwise standardized detail is extraordinarily effective simply because it responds to the overall context (drawer or door front size) and provides maximal contrast to the context (the natural figuring of the horizontal cherry wood grain versus the stark aluminum). Overtly symmetric and vaguely botanic, while retaining a graphic sensibility, these pulls are ultimately the direct expression of the marriage between custom craftsmanship and industrial redundancy. The small elements employed for fastening are virtually icons in most people's consciousness (screw heads, hex head bolts, and tubing), and the final form of the bracket employed remains vaguely allusive to the graceful sensibilities of a crafts tradition. All these design criteria and built manifestations are, in fact, part of the "hook" which a potential purchaser might find irresistibly seductive on a stock piece of furniture. The rigorous overview of the profit motive imposed reality-based aesthetics on that which is often frivolously detailed architect-designed furniture.

Figure 3(a) As drawers grow, so does the ornamental bottom edge bracketing of the individual pulls, creating a sense of controlled animation. Note the coincidence between the cherry wood grain figuring and the crisp edge of the applied pulls. (Courtesy of the architect.)

Figure 3(b) The cabinets themselves utilize the spirit of the pull detailing to form the corners and legs of the overall tested drawers. Note that these legs become corner brackets that stabilize the entire cabinet and have, as part of their construction, a rod set to allow either ease of movement or belt, tie, or towel storage. (Courtesy of the architect.)

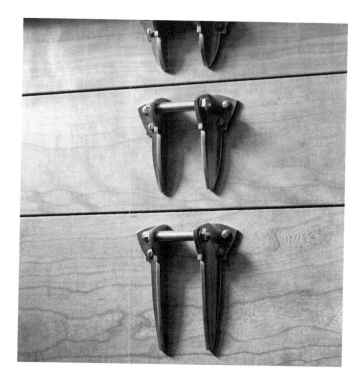

3(a)

> "Standardized components cut from
> standard shapes."

3(b)

TABLE

Arne Bystrom, Architect

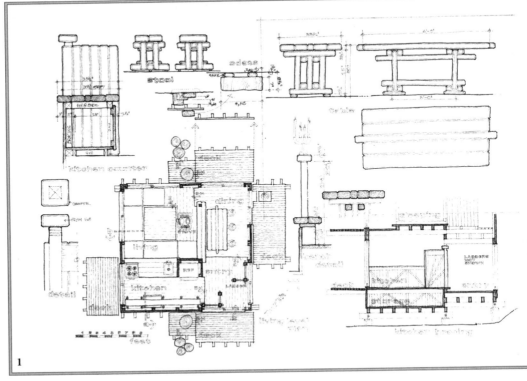

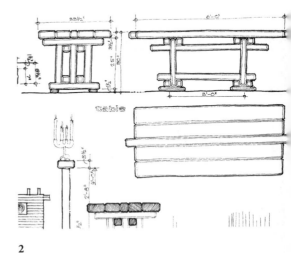

As part and parcel of the same vacation cottage depicted in the "Movement" part of this book (see section entitled "Ladders" on page 142), this table is architectural, carpenterly, craftsmanly, and fun. Using a redundant 3-1/2-in-thick module derived from available planking, the table evidences the consistent chamfering of all corners (making the alignment of all pieces less critical and field assembly practical) and overlapping joinery which facilitates "quick and dirty" screw and/or bolt fastening with a lack of fussiness. The working drawings are all softline, done to scale. Though all the drawings are a bit "wavy," the overall dimensions all work, and given that this is a field-built construction, the lack of anality is very appropriate. Bystrom adds artfulness to his ingenuity via the simple method of uneven extensions of the various components used. Trestle tables are often supported by triangulated wood assemblies of interweaving broad boards or poignantly minimal steel frames, involving intricate joinery and dimensional precision. This level of care is avoided in this construction by simply layering the elements up in a Lincoln Log fashion and by extending some of the horizontal lines a bit further than necessary. Implicit in all the extensions employed is the inherent 3-1/2-in module derived when 16/4 raw wood is planed into something approaching straight and true status. The inherent modularity employed has more to do

3

Figure 1 *The integration of this table into its architectural context is plainly evident in this drawing. Not only is the table aesthetically compatible with all the other elements depicted, but the actual graphics employed, softline tracing using aggressive line length, seem somehow perfectly fit to the controlled but expressive and rough hewn vacation home that is represented. Note that the ladders in the lower right corner of the floor plan can also be seen in Fig. 3 with the table in question set directly above it. Note that one side of this relatively fixed table has a built-in bench that serves to provide a barrier to a level change that in turn has a post that supports a candelabra. The seating for the other side is effected via the use of stumps, an element used elsewhere in construction as well. The interweaving plans, sections, elevations, orientations, scales, and so on show a drawing that was delightfully produced and executed with an extraordinary amount of conceptual integration and masterful control.*

Figure 2 *Table details. Minimal dimensions and maximum graphic communication.*

Figure 3 *Table in context. Amid a sea of raw but controlled wood, this table holds its own and, via its very massive presence, draws attention to itself.*
(Courtesy of the architect.)

with convenience than conviction, belying many architects' latent predilection for overwrought detailing derived from an abstract rather than a practical sensibility. Evident in all Bystrom's work is a knowledge of the way wood shrinks and grows as humidity changes. Considered discontinuities are present throughout the construction, accommodating unequal movements of cross-grain and parallel-grain wood shrinkage. The net aesthetics of all this casually careful design is a "soft" ambience which conveys the hand-hewn nature of the work.

"This whole exercise is intended to show "how to build functional elements out of stock pieces making them decorative elements."

Mechanical Systems

The literal building blocks of architectural design have few moving parts and simply respond to human occupancy. Structure, skin, and stairs are static, and doors, windows, and cabinetry only move to provide access. But the "working" parts of any construction are most often mechanical—we rely on them to make our day-to-day lives either viable or enjoyable. In simple terms, these systems allow us to be comfortably warm or cool, to provide light to see, to breathe fresh air, or to cleanse ourselves. We rely on mechanical systems every day. The simple common denominators of these systems is that they are often conduits for water, air, electricity, or their by-products. They are often luxuriant, but more often, they are fundamentally essential to the complete use of any building. The projects that follow evidence some tangible ingenuity, despite their need to integrate directly with thoroughly engineered environments and hard-edged technological design criteria. As such, they represent some of the more intense efforts at meshing the art and craft of detailing with the science and complexities of technology.

CHIMNEY

Michael Eckerman, Artisan

1

This project is unique for several reasons. Unlike most of the designers presented in this book, Michael Eckerman is not an architect, but he is a craftsman, and his design/build approach became absolutely imperative when a good friend of his asked him to create a fireplace for his new home. His client, Mathew Leeds, is a ceramist who makes very large pots, often 6 to 8 ft tall.

Since a new studio was being built at the same time, there were lots of pottery "rejects" lying about the site. As with much of the detailing presented in this book, there was a serendipitous coincidence between what Michael Eckerman normally does and what his client needed. Beyond the simple safe accommodation of combustion, this fireplace needed to be imbued with the sensibility of the person it was intended to serve, namely, someone whose whole life was centered around the creation of sinuous, often erotic, forms of fired clay. Fortunately, Michael Eckerman's masonry designs tend to be sinuous, curvilinear, and one might even say sensual, always using water-washed stones with deeply relieved grout lines in swirling, fluid patterns, literally representational of the movement of water. Eckerman picked up on the fact that he could create a chimney where the lines of the stonework and the lines of the owner's product (the gigantic pots) could be intertwined in a way which was both literal and figurative. Often using a humorous perspective of stones flowing in and out of the pots as well as the pots themselves serving as focal points and transition pieces in his fabrication, Eckerman created something

Figure 1 Exterior view. A classic California contemporary in the woods has its simple lines counterpointed by sinuous, bulbous, exquisitely intertwining stone work. Note the use of the stone both to serve as plinths for the owner's product (right) and the integration of the owner's product into the fireplace itself. (Courtesy of the architect.)

Figure 2 Detail. A stock louver and hatch for air access into the firebox is accommodated by a void created by manipulating the sinuous flow of water-washed stones. (Courtesy of the architect.)

which is both fresh and functional utilizing techniques that are hundreds, if not thousands, of years old. The final result is overtly idiosyncratic and, some might say, anti-intellectual in its design. It is a clever construction, right down to the incidental insinuation of a cast bust—its form and detailing grab attention and sustain it with Eckerman's extraordinary craftsmanship.

Avoiding the potential that this construction might be a simple gimmick, the subtlety and precision of Eckerman's workmanship bleeds down into every aspect of the design, even into the progressive spacing of the stone work and the inherent stability of the interlocking joints that are formed. As any mason will tell you, working with water-washed stone can be a difficult task to begin with, but in this case, the result is effervescent and delightful.

Figure 3 Interior view. The swirling patterns of the outside are brought inside complete with stones set for sitting beside the firebox, inglenook style. Note how the arch of the firebox itself is nicely transitioned into the fireplace face while a hand wrought and heavily decorated mantel is of a scale appropriate to the owner's handiwork (above).
(Courtesy of the architect.)

"In April of 1991, an old friend approached me on the subject of building a fireplace for his new house, under construction at the time. The house was being built at the same location as his studio, so there were many pots lying about…rejects, seconds, etc. I suggested we mix the pots in with the river rock to create not only a more interesting fireplace, but also a monument to his 25 years of pottery making. And that's what we did. I put extra reinforcing in where necessary to make sure the pots were secure. We even created a few bird houses in the process. We included the different styles and stages, from Zen to classical to abstract contemporary, that he's experienced through his career."

3

FIREPLACE
TREATMENT

Paul Lukez,
Architect

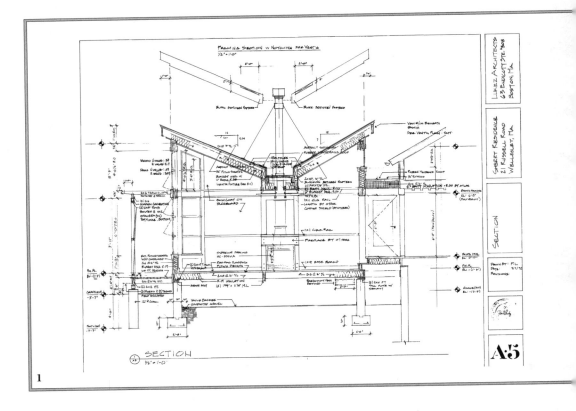

1

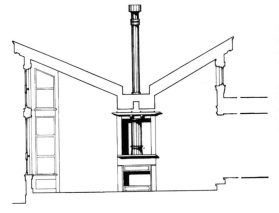

2

Prefab fireplaces are rapidly infesting our homes. Built of sheet metal and cement fiberboard, these "appliances" effectively shield any structure (almost universally wood) from the heat generated by our culture's version of an organic television set—the open-hearth fire. While preventing combustion of nearby building components, these fireboxes also convey, to one degree or another, desirable BTUs to the rooms within which they sit. Most often, these fireboxes are made to "fit" into the acknowledged sensibilities that most residences have, namely, that of a traditional masonry fireplace with massive mantle and stolid countenance. In this particular case, architect Paul Lukez has opted not only to isolate his firebox as a venerated appliance but to integrate this isolated object as a spacial fulcrum for the room it serves (a traditional role), and yet he orients it to mesh with the axial aspects of the overall context of the roofscape above it. The fireplace serves as large-scale ornament and even integrates with the lighting of the room. Using a copper cladding about its galvanized steel triple-wall sheet metal flue, and an attenuated subordinate rooflet-cum-light-fixture made of mahogany and copper, this fireplace ceases to be simply an isolated event but forms the linear crossroad for the entire space which it serves (a 14-ft x 22-ft addition to a traditional saltbox).

Figure 1 *Working drawing. Although relatively blank when it comes to the fine points of shrouding the flue in copper or displaying the level of detail needed to effect the ceiling treatment above the fireplace, this drawing does give a good sense of the context and of the three-dimensional integration between the fireplace, roof, and the original house (right).*

Figure 2 *The presentation drawing gives a good sense of the architect's intention to provide for a rooted centering element in his double-saw-toothed roof form.*

Figure 3 *A stock, zero set-back firebox is shrouded by a fairly normative hardwood mantel, and has its flue pipe framed by wood, sidelit by windows, and shrouded in copper, creating an almost worshipful recognition of the flue pipe itself. The copper shrouding is carried across this axial construction with a dropped copper sheet element which is, in turn, supported by hardwood ribbing whose dimensions are keyed directly to the flue pipe. Natural light is allowed to play all about these spaces, and the reflectance on the copper is enhanced by a clear coating. A stock component is thus aggrandized and custom fit into a dynamic context.*
(Courtesy of Greg Premru.)

"*The fireplace flue, clad as a copper 'column,' figuratively supports the low butterfly roof's trough. The compressed space above the fireplace axis is lightened by a reflector over a copper panel assembly concealing light fixtures.*"

3

In this way, invention is served within a familiar context. A radically expressive *tour de force* is brought down to earth via its traditional function and by its relatively simple hearth—a quasi-traditional demi-mantel of mahogany. In reality, the architect uses copper on the inside to reflect light and shroud the aforementioned triple wall flue and to relate to the roofscape which is highly visible from the outside, which uses copper to shed water from its collection point set axially above the fireplace as well. Thus, although the fireplace is not centered in its construction (the roof and space below defer to an outdoor exposure with a larger bay set away from the "parent building"), the entire assembly itself has a sense of architectonic conspiracy evidencing the best spirit of reinvention. Not only does the fireplace serve as an architectural fulcrum, but its abiding monolithic presence serves to meter the progression of sunlight through a single south-facing window as it approaches, glints upon, and leaves the copper-clad flue-sentinel.

FIREPLACE

House + House, Architects

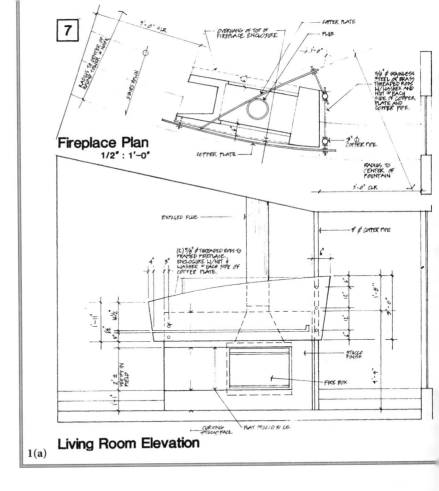

Fireplace Plan
1/2" : 1'-0"

Living Room Elevation

1(a)

Architectural detailing can often be said to overcome the inherent imprecisions and awkwardnesses of new technological innovations being fused into buildings. So it is with this fireplace done by the architecture firm of House + House in San Francisco.

One of the great dilemmas in late-twentieth-century custom residential architecture is how to take a wonderful innovation—the zero setback firebox—and make it something which is at once wholly familiar (a place to observe flames and fire) and yet somewhat unprecedented (a place which harbors fire that is made out of sheet metal and pressed cementitious board). The vast majority of fireplaces using fireboxes such as this are amalgamated and fused into the context of preconceived notions of architectural style, utilizing detailing dating from the seventeenth or eighteenth century. Essentially, these high-tech, mass-produced elements, often shrouded in the most traditional of materials, become a late-twentieth-century wolf in antique clothing. Rather than follow this somewhat disingenuous line of reasoning, House + House has opted to *celebrate* the fireplace's inherent components, sheet metal and cement board, with a shroud that hyperattenuates the features of both materials. The shroud utilizes copper pipe and heavy gauge copper-plated steel along with steel nuts and rods for metallurgical expression and conveys the more stolid qualities of safely harboring fire with a slightly animated stucco shroud around the prefab firebox. Both elements (stringy/flimsy metal and stolid/boxy stucco) are exaggerated and attenuated

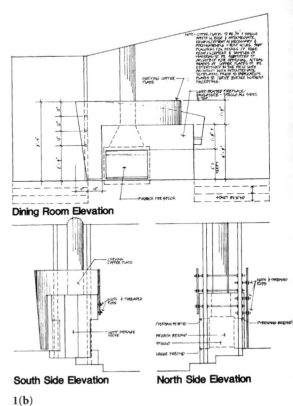

Dining Room Elevation

South Side Elevation   **North Side Elevation**

1(b)

2

Figure 1(a) and (b) Simple and direct drawings provide the opening salvo for some interesting in-the-field manipulations. Ultimately, the dining room manipulation allowed the applied steel plating to slightly inflect and be cast closer to the prefabricated firebox in question. Note that, in a variety of ways, the most standard of parts (the two-sided firebox) has been aggrandized and articulated to be the focal point of a large living area.

Figure 2 Dining room side. (Courtesy of Alan Weintraub.)

to effect the kind of sculptural distillation of both materials that grabs attention and sustains it. Zesty detailing can reinforce latent sensibilities as well. This particular firebox location has the most traditional of roles—center of the household.

In this way, expressively animated components enhance a thoroughly familiar function. Throw in the fact that the firebox occurs at a level change and that a variety of aesthetic "influences" allow for the shroud sculpture to have some angular, lightly curvilinear, eroding, and intersecting forms, and you virtually have materials dancing about a now-classic prefab icon. As always, it is the considered alignments (or misalignments) that make a construction like this a success or failure. The floor plane sets the front side base of the firebox (versus having the preset firebox sit up above it), and at the back side of this two-way firebox the in-and-out stucco work is allowed to create a plinth/hearth. The sculptural qualities of this firebox are enhanced by the fact that the chosen floor material (a limestone tile) is fireproof. Often, hearths set within the context of flammable materials (wood or carpet) add an element (the inflammable hearth) that can detract from the ability of the architect to create such a distilled and powerful sculpture.

It is not only that materials are set in blissful coincidence, House + House has opted to take their copper work and treat it with acid washes and dyes to enhance the sense of materiality and eliminate the potential for a purely Machine Age countenance. It is also important to realize that such a powerful construction might be out of place in any but the most passive of environments. In this particular case, a blissfully abstracted set of wholly unornamented walls, ceiling, and floor provides the appropriate datum and contrast for this powerful piece. As with all good sculpture, the character of each side of this piece (upper-level dining room front, lower-level living room front, copper-posted major access side, and noncopper minor access side) are all rendered to effect different results. Responding to the scales and the role-playing of the spaces it addresses, a larger "mantel" copper piece faces the larger living area, a smaller more aggressively canted piece addresses the dining room table, and the copper posts set to stabilize the planes of copper employed are set to the major passage between the two spaces involved. Beyond a modest alignment of the copper columns, the only other overt alignment is the copper-shrouded flue which is set above the prefab firebox itself.

Architectural detailing is a study in contrast and coincidence.

3

Figure 3 Living room side. What is three-dimensional and sculptural to the dining room side becomes enfronting and ceremonial on the living room side.
(Courtesy of Alan Weintraub.)

Figure 4 Simple components have direct applications of standard fasteners (threaded rod, copper washers, and hexagonal nuts) as well as a variety of oxidizing treatments applied to the heavy gauge copper utilized.
(Courtesy of Alan Weintraub.)

"The overlapping copper-plated screens trace arcs in the floor plan and are intended as permanently installed art pieces in a house designed to be minimally decorated. The copper columns, chimney, and threaded rods are intended to provide warmth and delicacy in contrast to the mass of the surrounding walls. The form of the fireplace, though grand, is appropriate to the scale of the house and a fire reflected in a natural copper finish creates an unforgettable memory of the home."

FLUE BRACKET

Donlyn Lyndon, Architect

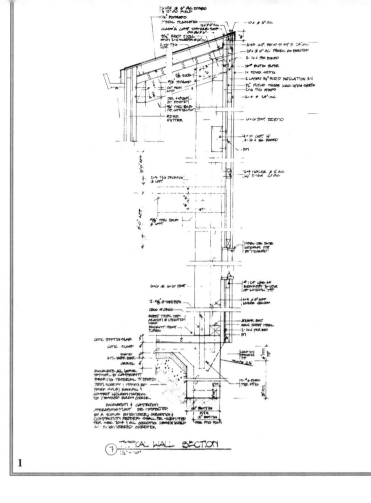

1

Sometimes a detail simply cannot be drawn. An undrawable detail might be more readily associated with flights of fine arts fancy, but in this case, an undrawable detail is absolutely essential to the use (and safety) of a heat-generating wood stove set within the context of a house in coastal California. Designed by the house's occupant, Donlyn Lyndon, of Lyndon/Buchanan Associates, this bracket celebrates some classic design criteria when it comes to architectural detailing:

1. *Materiality.* Made of the most prosaic of sheet metal materials (16-gauge galvanized steel), the bracket stands in stark contrast to the unfinished interior wood sheathing, and starkly counterpoints the jet black flue.

2. *Shape.* The most undrawable aspect of this particular piece is that it has a shape that was directly derived from on-site mock-ups. Not only is it graphic in its outline (its wall attachment side is lightly arced and its stand-off arms are canted and its attachment to the flue pipe is bent to fit the flue pipe's radius), but sculptural in its realized form.

3. *Context.* The pattern of the bracket is locked into the joints of the vertical board of the aforementioned sheathing via the location of the bend that launches the angled support from the wall.

4. *Economy.* As mentioned, the material itself is quite inexpensive, the pattern is redundant for the four brackets created, and the attachment (sheet-metal screws) is also as simple as one could imagine for such a condition.

Figure 1 Even though the detail dealt with in this section was never drawn, the context was heavily rendered by the architect, namely, an expressive wood construction, beautifully rendered and highly flammable, thus providing the necessity for an aggressive stand off of a naked flue pipe to a woodstove.

Figure 2 Bracket and flue. The ascendance of the flue pipe is recognized not only in the spacial manipulation of the house itself, creating a clear story light well, but in the ascendant gripping forms of the galvanized steel brackets shown here. Note the contrast between the blackened flue pipe, the shiny zinc coating of the galvanized steel, and the latent connection between the vertical fold and the orientation of the tongue-and-groove interior wall sheathing. The light radius present at the side of this bracket is perhaps the only arced element in the entire house. Note that the bottom brackets have been flipped in orientation, allowing for an implicit relationship between the two pairs of brackets used. (Courtesy of James Alinder.)

2

5. *Expressiveness.* Given items 1 and 2 above, the resultant subconstruction announces itself with stoic boldness while allowing for a clear functional purpose, namely, holding a very hot flue pipe away from a very flammable house.

The stock option for this particular condition (metal rods screwed into the wall) are almost invisible. The resulting detail is exquisitely simple, very affordable, practical, functional, and, most important, expressive.

GLASS SHOWER END

Duo Dickinson, Architect

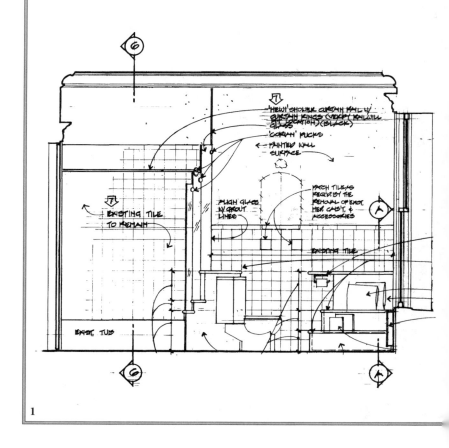

Figure 1 Plate glass is set upon a solid but stepping low wall that backs up a relocated toilet. Note the insinuation of a stock shower rod into the overall assembly.

Figure 2 The end wall, seen behind the toilet, steps up and has its corners fused with Corian pucks. Note that in the final realization of this stepping glass wall, the top piece of glass was held far below that indicated in this rendering.

(Courtesy of the architect.)

Stock prefabricated glass shower doors set upon tubs present two problems. First, there is almost always a track or some bizarre gasket detail to keep the water from coming out over the edge. Second, units that have less framework are quite expensive. The disadvantage with shower curtains is simple. Typically they require a solid wall at both sides of the shower enclosure to provide support for the shower curtain rod. This is not a problem if the shower stall is isolated, but if you want to lie in a tub and look out a window, an opaque wall doesn't help much. If, in addition, you are dealing with a 1920s tub with a curved end, it is hard to make a wall that will in some way rest comfortably upon the cast iron, porcelain glazed surface. In this particular project, the tub had to remain in a linear bathroom, and its tight confines would not accept an opaque wall, nor did the clients want to have the traditional looping shower rod which would provide a huge wad of mildew-infested shower curtain. So a hybrid was born.

A stock prefinished shower pole was procured from Hewi, and solid Corian was used as the material for the custom-crafted receiver for this rod and as the joinery for tempered glass panels that served to follow the curve of the existing tub while allowing light to flood the tub and allowing the tub's occupant to look out the window. Obviously, an intermediary plane was needed between the floor, the finished tub side, and the glass, so a stepping tiled low wall facilitated a water-tight joint and allowed for a full 6 in of overlap

2

Figure 3 Plan. *A renovated bathroom allowed for the existing tub to be maintained and a glazed end to be set behind a relocated toilet, thus providing a manageable shower curtain and a full view of the window (right).*

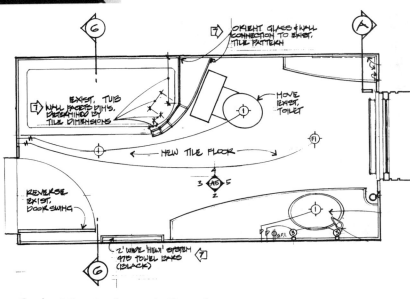

3

PLAN - SECOND FLOOR BATHROOM

between the new glass and the shower curtain. The inherent strength of silicone when applied to clean, impervious surfaces is evidenced here as well as the extraordinary flexibility of Corian—a product which can be shaped rather like wood and yet has a stability and density more akin to concrete. The frameless glass wall also gains tremendous stiffness from its shape—each pane reinforced by its canted neighbor.

Details often span conceptual gaps that are present when confronting functional problems. If standardized parts are used and simple customization can be effected, something that is both affordable and useful can result. And if art can be thrown into the mix, so much the better.

Figure 4 (a) and (b) Tempered glass is butt jointed and let into a Corian cap of a shop-fabricated low wall that is tiled at its inside face and lacquered on its outside face. The beveling geometry provides inherent stiffness, and the Corian pucks provide the final "lock" that holds it together. Note the expressed end of the prefabricated shower rod. (Courtesy of the architect.)

Figure 5 Context. The renovated bathroom saw the salvaging of existing tile and tub and relocating of existing toilet. The glazed end of the tub facilitates a shower enclosure that avoids visual obstruction of the overall ambience of the room. (Photo by Justin van Soest.)

4(a)

4(b)

DUCK BILL RANGE HOOD

Duo Dickinson,
Architect

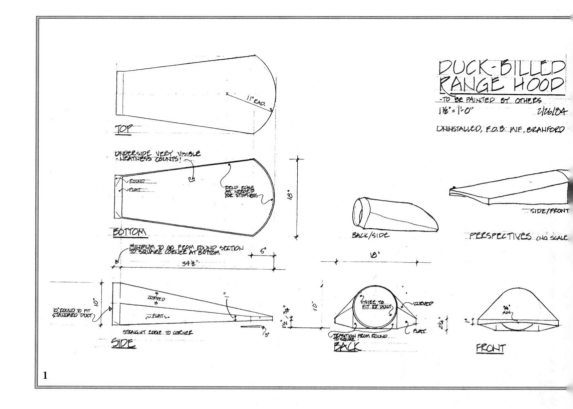

Range hoods are often a sorry marriage of practical need and industrial design that somehow has been aesthetically manifested in a 1950s take on what constitutes acceptable domestic ambience. Somehow akin to the worst of American automotive design, the standard range hood is not box, nor ornament, nor machine. It is but an awkwardly angled combination of distracting elements that projects forth at a level which is often best left clear for a comfortable encounter with the process of cooking. These oddly projecting, clumsily detailed stock components exist in their present form simply because the fans used are quite small and thus the area needed for grabbing vapors and smoke needs to be quite large and relatively low. In areas where the act of cooking is viewed as the dominant concern (versus the desire for ease of installation and mass-produced economy) large-scale, through-wall fans are utilized with larger hoods set at a higher level facilitating open space above the stove.

The growing trend is to purchase industrial-sized components for domestic-scaled cooking simply because there is a latent, intuitive realization by those who can afford honesty in their appliances that the standard range hood is at best a compromise and at worst an aesthetic insult to anyone spending time in the kitchen.

Figure 1 *In a simple attempt to communicate the ultimate shape of a project, what can be drawn hardline and what should be drawn in three dimensions is attempted. The result is remarkably like that which is drawn.*

Figure 2 *Utilizing a high air volume exterior mounted fan, this range hood serves to gather unwanted fumes and smoke (as well as attention). Note the exterior is spray painted with epoxy appliance paint and the interior galvanized area has been coated with a clear coating.* (Courtesy of Mick Hales.)

2

The hood evidenced here, utilizes an industrial fan (set through the wall) with a completely customized secondary system of two parts—a wood collar-gasket and a galvanized steel scoop. The fan's venting capacity is approximately four to six times that of a standard range hood, and the area covered by the scoop (named the "duck bill" range hood for its shape) is perhaps 50 percent larger than the standard unit. Thus this solution mimics the principles of the industrial range hood without its ungainly scale and somewhat roughshod ambience. Rather than high-tech, this is a craftsmanly solution where inherent properties of bent metal are combined with turned wood. The exterior is spray painted with epoxy-based paint (after a thorough washing of the galvanized surface), and the underside is left raw galvanized for ease of scrubbing. Unfortunately, there is no opportunity for a cheap "in line" damper, so a custom-fabricated stuffed vinyl stopper is set within the hole in the wall that accommodates the exterior mounted fan. The benefits of this design are many. First, an outdoor mounted fan is far quieter than a fan mounted inside at head height. Second, the height of the range hood allows for complete appreciation of what is being cooked. Third, the expressive shape of the fan is viewed upon entry to the house, and thus a potential eyesore is made into a welcoming sculptural gesture. Finally, the exterior flue shroud allows a springtime nesting place for transient aviary occupants.

There are down sides as well. Although not as expensive as "state of the art" industrial hoods, this hood is perhaps four times more expensive than a standard unit. To mitigate this cost, lighting was not integrated into its form and thus ambient light from other sources is required.

As with many cost-conscious details, there is often the need for trade-offs. In this particular instance, the trade-offs have more to do with the value judgments of the particular user. It is not problematic to pop in and pop out the aforementioned stuffed vinyl plug, and the lighting has never been a problem for this particular owner. And besides, the birds just love it.

Figure 3 Context. *As seen from entry into the kitchen, the enigmatic form of the duck bill range hood is neither predictable nor offensive but responds to the linear influence of the tongue-and-groove ceiling above and the teak counter below.* (Courtesy of Mick Hales.)

3

ADIRONDACK HOUSE LIGHTS

Peter Bohlin,
Architect

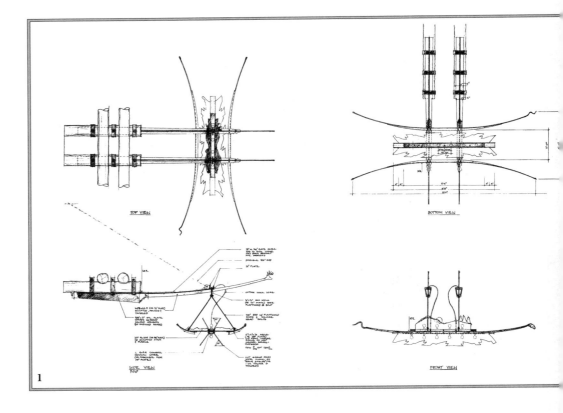

It is rare when an architect gets complete control over every aspect of a house design. It is even rarer when, given this control, the architect does not create a "Johnny One Note" design where a singular mental approach simply washes away all potential for delight and diversity within the context of a single dwelling. Architectural detailing often becomes enslaved by the architectural context to the point that the inhabitants of such a completely designed building feel smothered by its unrelenting presence, and any iconic or personal elements that are desired in the home become unwanted intruders into an event which has more to do with the workings of a machine than the natural choreography of dancers who maintain their own free will. In direct contradistinction to the machine ethic, Peter Bohlin of Bohlin Cywinski Jackson, Architects has stepped in and designed virtually every light fixture in a house he designed in the Adirondacks several years ago. This house has been thoroughly celebrated in the press and in the profession, but the design of the lighting fixtures in the house represent a veritable catalogue of possibilities rendered by one architecture office and some of the best craftsmanship available. It seems most fitting to simply show, portfolio style, each one of these fixtures with some basic descriptions provided by this author and the architect. In truth, when seen as a consistently articulated array of distinct art pieces, the power of these elements is absolutely extraordinary and unique in this book.

Figure 1 Note how in a simple set of four drawings, virtually every component can be thoroughly defined and completely expressed. Obviously a great deal of the field micromanipulation review is needed, but when a knowing hand draws something with a clear head, much can be described with a small graphic influence, especially when full-size templates are also provided.

Figure 2 Ornament iron chandelier. Overall view. Note the backlighting dominance of this feature.
(Courtesy of Karl A. Backus.)

3

"The design of a metal chandelier for the dining area proved to be another interesting opportunity. A 1-in = 1-ft scale drawing is shown, but full size templates (drawn by principal Peter Bohlin, his wife Sally, his son Nat and Robert McLaughlin, the project architect) were given to the local steelworker who made the piecve in the house's garage.

The chandelier provides both up and down light. The upper lamp shield alludes to the moon rising over the mountains across the lake; the lower shield is a negative abstraction of leaping trout. The inner surfaces have been sandblasted and clear coated to reflect light, while outer surfaces were allowed to rust. Porcelain socketsand clear bulbs are recessed into a pair of nested steel channels, which are then attached along the shields to a series of arms which end in dream-like beast heads, feet and tails. The remaining surfaces are sandblasted and allowed to rust.

Since the entire assemblage could not be supported from the roof alone, I-beams were cantilevered from the building's log structure. The beams were sculpted with a plasma torch, curved and then tapered into deer heads. Steel tie rods are anchored to the snouts of the metal beasts"

Ornamental Iron Chandelier

This design incorporates exquisite cantilevered metal work cut in figurative patterns and built with wrought linear motifs. It serves as an air-borne focal point for the entire dining wing of the house and provides an extraordinary synthesis of material expression and overall form. The detailing is simple yet unrelentingly articulate—note the iconographic use of the stag's head at the end of the primary cantilever and the marvelous interface between the lightly bowed/curved shapes and the fairly rigid/stiff structure which surrounds the fixture. The blending of both abstract and iconographic motifs creates an object evidencing whimsy, craft, subtlety, and complete control by the designer.

Stretched Rawhide Light Fixture

In a simple gable space set to one side of the main living space of the house, this project, virtually a craftsmanly frieze, evidences the power of stretched leather planes and laminated wood pieces, all set to a lightly curving ambience that blissfully counterpoints its context.

Figure 3 Dining room. *Note the potency of the arced cantilevered supports as they catch the upshine light of the lighting fixtures employed.* (Courtesy of Karl A. Backus.)

Figure 4(a) and (b) Conceptual sketch and final detail. *Note how raw materials are used in subtle and sophisticated ways to sustain visual interest once the initial impact has been realized. Note also the use of ordinary light fixtures behind this thoroughly crafted screen.*

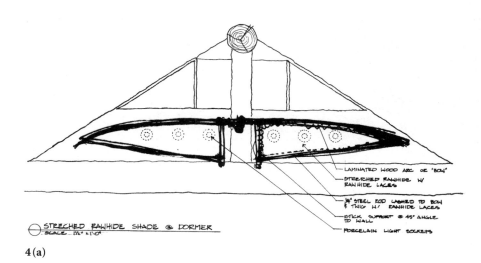

STRECHED RAWHIDE SHADE @ DORMER
SCALE = 1½" = 1'-0"

LAMINATED WOOD ARC OR 'BOW'
STRETCHED RAWHIDE W/ RAWHIDE LACES
¼" STEEL ROD LASHED TO BOW & TWIG W/ RAWHIDE LACES
STICK SUPPORT @ 45° ANGLE TO WALL
PORCELAIN LIGHT SOCKETS

4(a)

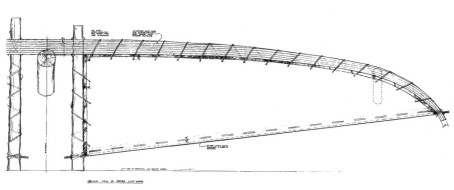

4(b)

6

Figure 5 *Overall view. A winged presence above a potent fireplace maintains its integrity (note in the upper right the cantilevered chandelier described earlier).*

(Courtesy of Karl A. Backus.)

Figure 6 *Close-up shot. Lightly touching and yet thoroughly integrated, this light fixture provides indirect lighting and articulation via illumination of the simple and yet sophisticated structure of Bohlin's house.*

(Courtesy of Karl A. Backus.)

"Another light fixture in a dormer over the living room is an evocative assemblage of wood, steel- and stretched rawhide. The rawhide is pulled over an iron rod and a curved laminated wood arm with rawhide laces. The rawhide is submerged in water and allowed to shrink in the local craft tradition of snow- shoe making. The resulting patterns are subjective, suggesting canoes, boat spars, the wings of birds or insects, archery or Native American images. Each observer forms his own interpretations."

7

Figure 7 *Interior shot. Note the almost mystical quality of the simple materials employed where glass is the "straight" piece counterposing the "organic" supports.*
(Courtesy of Karl A. Backus.)

Figure 8 *Hallway. Note the direct visual interaction between the structural components and the light fixtures employed.*
(Courtesy of Karl A. Backus.)

Figure 9(a) and (b) *Twig fixtures. The simplest sort of light fixture is set behind the interface of three twig-branch dowels in one sequence and four in another. Note the seemingly arbitrary but thoroughly controlled orientations of both glass and twigs.*

Twig and Glass Light Fixtures

Sometimes the best approach is simply to let the materials speak for themselves. In this case, individually cut pieces of glass, ends of branches and twigs, and a bare-bulb, keyless porcelain light fixture are coordinated to facilitate diffused lighting without glare and for the fixtures to be points of attraction themselves that are thoroughly conspired to marry with the architecture employed. As one can see from the drawings, these fixtures are dead simple and yet thoroughly controlled.

Steel Plate Light Fixtures

Not unlike the glass and twig fixtures shown, these fixtures use cantilevered struts of debarked branch pieces to support simple steel plates that have organic motifs cut out of their opaque presences. Used more for mood lighting than direct illumination, these pieces have some traditional background but are, in

8

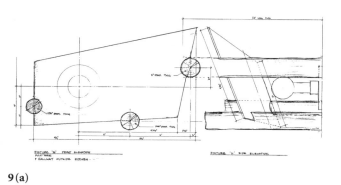

9(a)

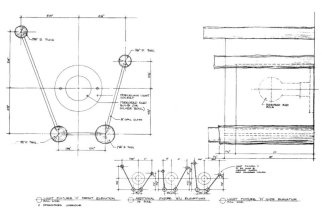

9(b)

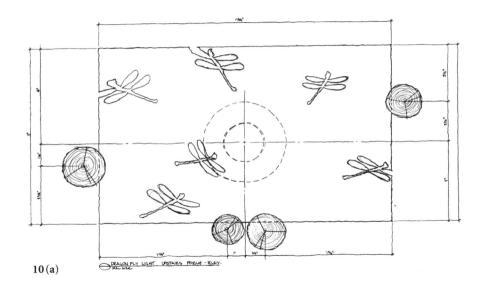

10(a)

Figure 10(a) and (b) With all dimensions completely controlled and yet all artistry left up to the craftspeople employed, these fixtures offer up the best evidence of the interface between those who design a building and those who elaborate upon its form.

Figure 11 Utilizing the opacity of the metal plates set as screens to obscure the light source and thus completely backwash the rough surface of the bark of the logs employed in this particular room, this fixture offers a direct view of the original source of most of the materials in the house—the heavily forested, ragged countryside of the Adirondacks.

(Courtesy of Karl A. Backus.)

truth, completely inventive in their use by Bohlin in this context. Combining both figurative and diagrammatic, even comedic, ambiences, these fixtures represent a marriage of technology, craft, and architecture that is simple, subtle, and yet powerful.

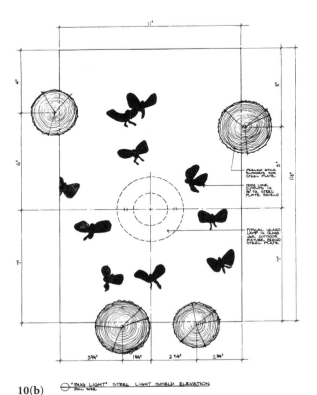

10(b) "BUG LIGHT" STEEL LIGHT SHIELD ELEVATION
FULL SIZE

"These light fixtures look to the historic craft of rustic stick work indigenous to the Adirondack Mountains. Local tradition is combined with glass and simple off-the-shelf incandescent electric lighting. The carpenters worked from complete full-size templates which could be transferred directly to the glass and walls.

The first fixture design is a single plane of opal glass held in place before a simple porcelain socket and bulb with three slotted twig dowels. This vocabulary is developed in twelve individual fixtures. In a hallway, for instance where the light is usually viewed from the side, places three planes of opal glass are placed perpendicular to the wall below and to either side of a silver bowl bulb."

11

12

"Here is a relaxed series of baffled steel light fixtures with back lit silhouettes. Moths and dragonflies swarm around lights, reversing the normal conditions of light and dark, substantial and airy. Another of the light shields is clipped between flying rafters and reflects the view through the forest to the lake which it faces. Consideration was given to engaging craftspeople to design and make the fixtures. Ultimately a local steelworker fabricated the pieces from templates designed by the architects, who enjoyed the challenge and found their process swifter and more economical. A common plasma arc torch to cut the details out of steel."

Figure 12 In contrast to many of the other fixtures in the home, the cut steel elements of these light fixtures reflect light and celebrate their cutouts via direct contrast with illumination (versus backlighting). Obviously, here the view is out over the lake, and thus the water edge and the jumping fish employed have a deliciously humorous undertone, as the author describes them.
(Courtesy of Karl A. Backus.)

Figure 13 Backlit, this simple metal plate with extraordinarily articulate cutouts is both craftsmanly and graphic while at the same time maintaining a quality of distinction from its harboring architecture. Held off its rustic context and given clarity with its crisp, rectilinear form, this light fixture is a study in contrast and integration. (Courtesy of Karl A. Backus.)

13

CANOPY LIGHTS

Louis Māckall, Architect

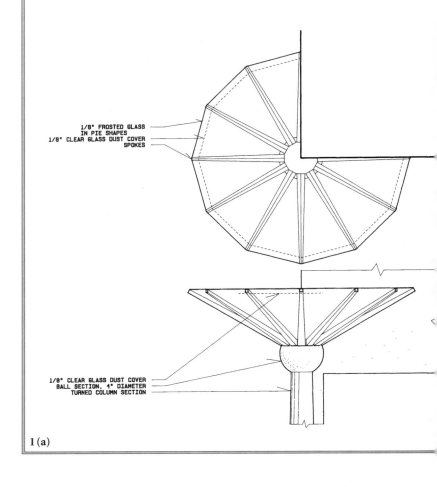

1/8" FROSTED GLASS
IN PIE SHAPES
1/8" CLEAR GLASS DUST COVER
SPOKES

1/8" CLEAR GLASS DUST COVER
BALL SECTION, 4" DIAMETER
TURNED COLUMN SECTION

1 (a)

For most people, it is often one detail that remains memorable even in a sea of otherwise proficient architecture. It is these glints of aesthetic light that somehow stick in the corners of our minds and, most often, these glints reflect the inspired detail design that architects can bring to bear within the larger context of a project. In designing a fairly large kitchen in New York, Louis Māckall "took care of business" with a wide variety of custom-crafted cabinetry involving many turned, shaped, molded, and hand-hewn elements which were truly gifts to the overall design. Despite the many delightful elements evidenced in this millwork, the one area that seems both to focus attention and to release the spirit within are light sconces which project forth from the corners of a suspended upper cabinet as well as at the corners of other floor-to-ceiling elements. Not only do they possess the inherently focusing aspect of artificial illumination, but their radial shape, angular articulations, and translucent material create an effervescent focal point. Such focal posturing would be almost impossible with "normal" detailing that kow-towed to the cabinetry. The means and methods of this expression are extraordinarily simple. Turned balls are set upon turned columns set to the corners of the cabinetry, and radial octagonal struts are let into these spheres, with frosted glass set in silicone between the struts. A $2.50 porcelain socket is set on top of the sphere and behind the glass, and a 75-watt bulb is screwed in. Hardwiring is effected within the body of the cabinetry, and a flick of a switch creates memorable art out of simple components. This seemingly sponta-

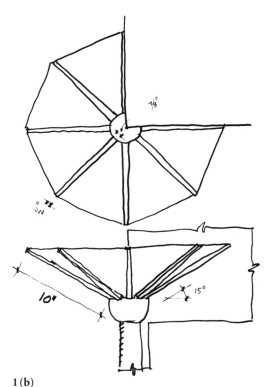

1 (b)

3

Figure 1(a) and (b) Mackall's articulate softline sketch (b) is transformed via his computer into the more dimensionally precise realization (a). Note that the radial pattern went from an octagon into a 12-sided shape. All the materials are easy for custom shops such as the one Mackall owns to effect.

Figure 2(a) and (b) Pieces and parts. Along with his precise computer drawings, Mackall utilizes these freehand sketches to bridge the gap between hard-edged ideas and built reality. Given that his office is in the same space as his millwork shop, this form of direct communication, right down to the narrative notes, is both appropriate to the project and delightful to see.

Figure 3 Set at corner points and now, finally realized in an octagonal format (versus the twelve-sided figure interpolated by Mackall's computer drawing), these forms have had their shape fine tuned in full size, providing more lift in the balled receptors of the spokes and a slightly grander imposition of the intermediate shelving. Note the use of these fixtures as wraparound corner sconces to the left and right of the photograph. (Courtesy of the architect.)

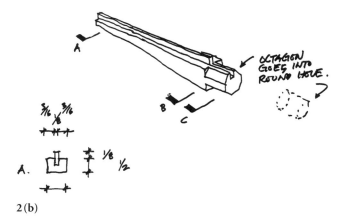

2(a)

2(b)

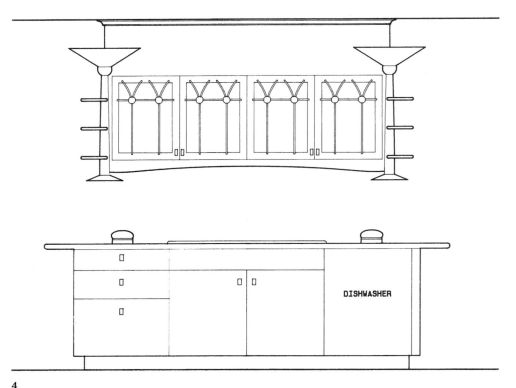

Figure 4 *The predominate presence of these light fixtures is the end points of a cabinet suspended over the sink area of a kitchen. Note the detailing of the muntin patterns of the cabinet doors which, in some way, seem to set up the final expression of the light fixtures themselves.*

Figure 5 *The wraparound corner sconce depicted is the full height articulation of the truncated version to the right and provides a full corner tapering pilaster transition between the flanking full height storage wall to the left and the main informal eating area to the right. Note that all openings are treated similarly in Mãckall's designs, whether they be for interior cabinet work (left, over the desk) or to a window and sink centering element (center).* (Courtesy of the architect.)

DISHWASHER

4

neous event is borne of careful three-dimensional sketches and even more careful computer-aided drafting that resulted in full-sized details. Ultimately, it is the careful on-site scrutiny of Mãckall that fertilizes and reality-checks all his detailing, as his own shop, Breakfast Woodworks, built this kitchen. Over the years, Mãckall has gained a remarkable knowledge base. If everything is expressive, nothing will be noticed. If nothing is expressive, then why bother custom crafting anything? In the selective use of light, geometry, and material set to crucial transition points within an overall room design, Mãckall has shown a combination of ingenuity and perspective that is seldom realized by those with less experience.

"Basically, the idea is to integrate lighting and the objects (cabinets, whatever) in any job so that you are sort of pulling energy off of the significant parts—corners, bottoms, insides, whatever—so that you get a certain sense of oomph out of the cabinet as a whole. Looking beyond the rest of the kitchen, you can see that there are lights inside the cabinets and there are also lights that surround the windows over the sink on the left, etc."

5

STEEL TIE ROD LIGHTS

Louis Mäckall,
Architect

1

For most architects, pro bono work means providing drawings for organizations that simply cannot afford architects. This often involves groups that serve special populations such as the homeless, those who provide subsidized medical care, or third-world countries in need of expertise that can be given free of charge. Pro bono work is often provided for those who serve our spirits as well. When the Shoreline Unitarian Universalist Society asked Louis Mäckall to help them create a church wing to spring from a single-family residence in Madison, Connecticut, he enthusiastically embraced the work at hand. Rather than simply provide free services that solved functional problems and responded to fiscal limitation, Mäckall also gave of his own special gifts as a master craftsman to create the one detail which is unforgettable in the simple space.

In structural terms, steel tie rods perform a very simple function. They hold the side walls of a gable-framed roof together, resisting their natural predilection for splaying, given the lateral thrust of the roof rafters. The tie rods are seldom held taught, as their passive presence is often enough to deal with the limited loading applied, so they often sag under their own weight given the lack of an adequate post-tensioning to keep them taught and horizontal. This sagging presence can be quite depressing to those who view it,

2

Figure 1 *These light fixtures were truly sculpted, hence no drawings exist to help define their origin. Suffice it to say, a cast composite bocci ball was sliced to wrap around a 1-in steel tie rod and its lightly triangulated steel conduit stay. This almost vertical piece both held the tie rod up from sagging and facilitated the insinuation of a wire from the ceiling into this intersection where a stock socket and light bulb could be attached. The rice paper ribbing and tethering cord are all in the best craftsmanly tradition, providing a sense of hand-hewn articulation of very simple materials.*

(Courtesy of the architect.)

Figure 2 *Context. A semistark space gains presence via the imposition of these large-scale structural illuminatory objects, their rakish angle somehow resonant in the diagonal skylight while seen above, all standing in contradistinction to the highly normative muntin divided Colonial style double hung windows that relate to the parent building, an early twentieth-century Garrison Colonial suburban home.*

(Courtesy of the architect.)

appearing not only limp but somehow structurally incompetent. Mäckall picked up on this and realized that in this spiritually evocative space, this sag needed to be preempted by complimentary steel stays that would allow the tie rods in this simple church wing to have a positive versus, quite literally, depressing ambience. It would be one thing to simply lift the rods, paint them a bright color, and walk away. But Mäckall realized that in a public space, general area lighting is a requirement, not a nicety. Dropping some stock pendant ceiling cans to provide the adequate foot candles per square foot would have been a simple solution, easily spec'ed for a "freebie" job such as this, but Mäckall, never one to miss an opportunity for expression, utilized stock components to effect an extraordinary product that is at once structural, sculptural, and overtly spiritual.

There was no money available in the construction budget to effect this artwork. Therefore, donatable stock components were a must. Bocci balls were purchased from the local Caldor's, routed and cut in half to accommodate the two tie rods involved. Wiring was effected through the vertically supportive stays made of pipe, and a standard lamp socket was used to support the light bulb. The actual diaphanous screening for this naked bulb was effected using small spines of wood let directly into the bocci ball, with rice paper glued and stitched together with twine to create a segmented, diagonally effusive fan shape. There are no drawings available for this piece. In fact, the entire construction was fabricated in the field, full sized, mostly by Mäckall himself, with a little assistance from his shop, Breakfast Woodworks. It is a wonderfully crafted, poignantly realized piece of focal integration between a mechanical system (lighting), a structural system (the tie rods), and the unique ambience of a worship space. These lights are in the best tradition of affordable and effective detailing and evidence the special genius that is the hallmark of Mäckall's career.

"*The procedure was to put the tie rods up first, jack them up with 2 x 4's to the arc I wanted, then attach the pipes coming down from the ceiling to hold them up to an arc, then take a few measurements, go back to the shop (after a trip to Caldor's to get the bocci balls), then essentially drill out each of the bocci balls in the drill press for the various elements going through or into it (the tie rods, the electrical pipe, the stays for the rice paper). After all the holes were drilled, I sawed the bocci balls in half on the band saw so that I could put them back together around the tie rod and, subsequently, stick the ribs for the lights in. What I like about it is that, again, there is a total integration of the structure and the lighting, but also the lights themselves are a cross between a butterfly, which is symbolism very appropriate for a Unitarian Church (i.e., transformation in the every-day), and also cobwebs which also, somehow, are appropriate (at least during long sermons).*"

TRANSOM LIGHTS

Louis Māckall,
Architect

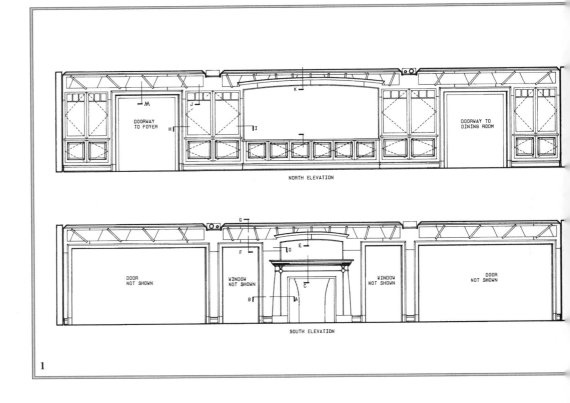

Even when architectural details are expressive, they can sometimes serve to unify the overall ambience of a room, rather than preemptively assert their own individual character. Such is the case with this system of valance transom lights. In a renovation in New York, Louis Māckall was confronted with a now-typical scenario. In renovating a large, open space, he was challenged by the extraordinary quantity of openings present, linking the inside to the outside and different interior spaces to each other. Given all the openings, what was left was more trim than wall. Thus, the standard 6-ft, 8-in door height, when combined with the standard 8-ft ceiling height, left a gap at the head of all the various openings employed. Additionally, there was a sense by Māckall that the desire for curtains, lighting, cabinetry, fireplace surround, and so on would present the opportunity for visual chaos without some sort of innovative, coalescing detail—a detail that could both be large scale in its application and deliciously eye catching it its realization. What results is a combination of trim, lighting, fenestration, and cabinet work which demonstrates Māckall's great skill—the visionary conquest of elements that often defeat architects—the nuts and bolts of materiality, trim, and excruciatingly specific and intolerant dimensioning. What Māckall set out to do was to unify all the disparate elements with a layer of trim, inset approximately 10 in from

Figure 1 A large-scale interior space created by the removal of a series of interior partitions, set above the replicative and unifying cabinetry that serves to link a variety of newly created openings to the outside as well as the inside of other spaces, is a subtle but unrelenting series of artificially illuminated light trough-transoms seen above all the elements employed. Note the respect for center lines evidenced by the diagonally applied trim pieces and the orientation of diagonal joints between the glazing.

Figure 2 Cabinet and trim detail. Note the considered coordinated misalignment between the lines of cabinetry, trim, openings, and the light troughs seen just below the crown above. These interrelated, and coordinated, but lightly dissociative, elements are all fused by the commonality of white paint and the rigorous application of center lines that can be seen in the large-scale elevation.

Figure 3 Cross section. Fixed lighting, draperies, trim, windows, and doors are all set proud of or within the perimeter walls of the space (left). Simple bull-nosed and radius trim elements provide softened edges for all elements, allowing for a relaxed fit amid all the interrelationships. Note the twin frosted glass that is allowed to slide to provide access to the fluorescent light fixture.

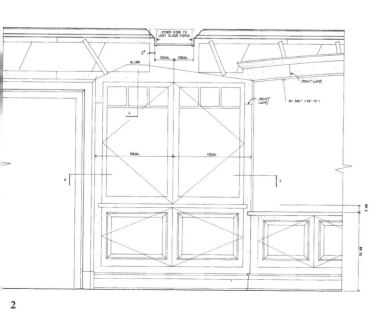

4

Figure 4 Exterior wall. This photo does not adequately express the delicate interrelationships of muntins, glass spacing, and so on, but the quiet, unrelenting lightened line can be seen as an intermediate presence to the windows and the point lighting of the low voltage system above, creating a variety of natural and artificial illumination which enriches a potentially scaleless space. (Courtesy of the architect.)

2

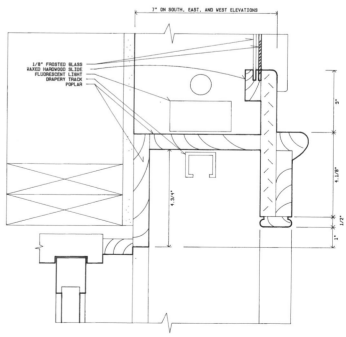

1/8" FROSTED GLASS
WAXED HARDWOOD SLIDE
FLUORESCENT LIGHT
DRAPERY TRACK
POPLAR

7" ON SOUTH, EAST, AND WEST ELEVATIONS

3

the outside wall and almost 2 ft from the inside wall, facilitating wiring, the accommodation of curtains and cabinetry, and lastly, but most visually important, the inclusion of transoms with artificial lighting which wraps around the perimeter of the entire room. This transom lighting facilitates a "connect-the-dots" gesture among windows, doors, fireplace, cabinetry, and even some faux dropped-beam trim elements in the ceiling which accommodate the rerouting of pipes from the bathroom spaces above. Local symmetries could be recognized by the gaps in the linear light trough and celebrated by the particular trim and muntin elements employed. The resulting construction is neither trim nor light nor wall but somehow all three simultaneously occurring via the careful hand of a master craftsman. Essentially, three elements are used—the painted wood frame, the light itself (using frosted glass diffused with applied painted wood chevrons) and bowed applied trim that relates to the fireplace on one side and an opening directly opposite. The bowed trim and the chevrons are all set to radiate from the aforementioned twin focal points of the room, and these centering elements are enhanced by the dropped ceiling trim items mentioned earlier, and are all crucial to the local symmetries present at each wall connection. Built-in cabinetry worships these center lines as well and follows the metering influences of the aforementioned trim work. The subtle brilliance of this particular detail comes in the varying angles of the applied chevrons, relating to a radial recognition of the center line, and in the unrelenting diagonal lapped joints between the pieces of glass which form the diffuser for the lighting and which also lightly recognize the centers employed by reversing their angle at the center points of each long wall. The coincidence between the applied chevrons and the diagonals of the lapped joints appears to be happenstance and yet is thoroughly conspired. Its loose-fit lightness stands in contrast to the stolid woodwork detailing employing traditional raised panel detailing and divided light-glazed cabinet fronts. All this detailing focuses on an element which is often not adequately treated in most interior spaces, namely, that awkward space between the heads of standard height windows and doors and the ceiling itself. In celebrating that which is often ignored, Māckall reinvents the room and allows a relatively large scale space to be simultaneously unified and expressive of its constituent parts. Māckall thus adds a sense of depth and richness to a space which could have been simply awash in light and space—inarticulate but accommodating, large but lifeless. In the considered application of standard elements (such as painted flat stock wood, butt joint glazing, and a stock light system) and conspiring the micro detailing to dovetail with the macro intentions, Māckall evidences the best potentials present in detail design.

Figure 5 End view. The wraparound quality of the artificial transoms are evidenced here as flooring lines, baseboard trim, ceiling crown, all of which work to wrap the space and, when combined with the rigorously consistent rendering of all trim around the openings provided, make the quiet and consistent illumination provided by this banding light a large-scale context upon which to present itself.
(Courtesy of the architect.)

5

"When I got there, there was a fairly large room with a bunch of sliding doors on one side and entry to other rooms in the house on the other. The client wanted some cabinets along one wall. I was reluctant to simply glom them on like cankers, so essentially, I created a whole new wall inside the existing walls. The new wall out by the doors, was only 8 in or 10 in in from the existing wall. At the cabinet side, it was more like cabinet depth (18 in or 20 in, something like that). Above, all around, is a clear story which is sand blasted glass with, as I remember, a couple of runs of Bend-o-lite inside just to provide a glow in the evening through the clear story. The glass is simply slid in a wooden track cut into the trim, so there is no particular framing for it, just grooves along the bottom and top edges so you could lift it up high and slide it down into the lower crack and it would stay. The glass slides so that if you need to get at the lighting, you can slide it and get behind. The joints between the glass are simple overlaps, but done on an angle to keep the whole thing moving."

ZOO LIGHTING

Bohlin Cywinski Jackson, Architects

1

It is pretty obvious that public areas that are occupied at various times of the day require the application of artificial illumination. But rude support of stock fixtures begs the question of enrichment. In creating lighting for the Philadelphia Zoological Garden, Bohlin Cywinski Jackson, Architects realized the need to "take care of business" but, at the same time, given the inherent spontaneity and celebratory nature of a zoo, felt compelled to apply a certain level of architectural ornamentalism to the elements conspired. The ornament used is figurative—cutouts of animal motifs set at the "crotch" between a vertical stanchion and cantilevered supports for the stock light fixtures. These literally crucial elements are not simply ornamental, they serve as the structural reinforcement for an assemblage of stock parts that would not normally be able to sustain their own weight without some form of stiffening element. Thus, the necessity for a "moment connection" provides an interesting bit of spontaneity and artfulness within the context of some fairly prosaic parts.

Stock lighting fixtures are directly attached to standard tubular steel sections which, in turn, arc back to a multiple pieced vertical stanchion formed using a central octagonal tube with flanking rectilinear channels which, in turn, have a welded channel connection to the light stanchion and the ornamental brace itself.

This assembly of stock elements is the modern equivalent of the cast iron sculptural fixtures seen in many nineteenth-and early-twentieth-century civic architecture lighting elements. Recognizing that cast pieces are costly, the

Figure 1 *Elevations. Stock light fixtures are suspended from bent tubing, which, in turn, is supported by a stock octagonal column. The joint between these two elements is stiffened via the use of ornamental brackets formed by cut pieces of flat stock steel.*

Figure 2(a), (b), and (c) *Typical bracket condition. Simple forms gain presence via their stock bracket quality and by the capacity to occasionally break the boundaries circumscribed by the image's frame.* (Courtesy of the architects.)

2(a)

2(b)

architects compensate via stock materials that have been manipulated to create the animated, craftsmanly ambience desired. In terms of the pictorial rendering of the animals employed, full-sized templates were used, and the cutouts were effected in a direct graphic style framed by thicker-gauge steel plate with a bent plate wrapped around its perimeter, also attached with welded connections. These images gain some zest via the rendered animals breaking their circular frame. Flanking the circular framed image are two arcing brackets which, in turn, are formed by two pieces of flat stock steel that have been cut and bent and welded into place. In addition, a prefabricated washer is used at the topmost connection

2(c)

between the bracket and the light supporting tubing, creating a level of detail which is not normally associated with this type of construction. On the pole itself, the capital is formed in a similar fashion by using cut pieces of steel creating a "ball" formed by two circles of sheet steel that intersect at 90 degrees. In short, this is an assemblage of stock items that utilize the focal element of surprise to compensate for the lack of fiscal capability to create the three-dimensional sculpture which was so prevalent in the previous century.

The detail of the paving that these lights illuminate can be seen on page 76 of Zoo Paving of this book, and additional zoo railings can be seen on page 160.

DIRECTORY OF ARCHITECTS AND DESIGNERS

Ofer Barpal
27445 Berkshire
Southfield, MI 48076

Robert S. Bast
307 Silver Street
Hinesburg, VT 05461

Kent Bloomer
988 Leetes Island Road
Guilford, CT 06437

Peter Q. Bohlin
Bohlin Cywinski Jackson, Architects
182 N. Franklin Street
Wilkes-Barre, PA 18701-1499

Brian Brand
Baylis, Brand, & Wagner, Architects
10801 Main Street
Bellevue, WA 98004

Arne Bystrom
1617 Post Alley
Seattle, WA 98101

Cheng Design
2806 San Pablo Avenue
Berkely, CA 94702

James Cutler Architects
135 Parfitt Way, S.W.
Bainbridge Island, WA 98110

Michael deStefano
Art & Metal Ltd.
232 Jupiter Street
Jupiter, FL 33458

Alfredo De Vido
1044 Madison Avenue
New York, NY 10021

Duo Dickinson
94 Bradley Road
Madison, CT 06443-2644

Duncan Wisniewski Architecture
207 King Street
Burlington, VT 05401

Michael Eckerman
P.O. Box 143
Freeland, WA 98249

Anne Fougeron
3537 21st Street
San Francisco, CA 94114

Kimo Griggs
Somerville Avenue
Somerville, MA 02143

Herman Hassenger Architects
P.O. Box 594
282 Chester Avenue
Moorestown, NJ 08057

Nagel Hartray
Architects Planners, Ltd.
One IBM Plaza
Chicago, IL 60611

House + House
1499 Washington Street
San Francisco, CA 94109

Laura Kaehler
Kaehler/Moore Architects
One Fawcett Place
Greenwich, CT 06830

Paul Lukez Architecture
63 Endicott Street, Studio 308
Boston, MA 02113

Donlyn Lyndon
Lyndon/Buchanan Associates
2604 Ninth Street
Berkeley, CA 94710

Kevin Mason
2101 Maple View Court
Westfield, NJ 07090

George Ranalli
150 W. 28th Street
New York, NY 10001

Louis Mackall
135 Leetes Island Road
Guilford, CT 06437

Robert Orr & Associates
441 Chapel Street
New Haven, CT 06511

Bart Prince
3501 Monte Vista NE
Albuquerque, NM 87106

Alex Varga Design
67 Mill Rock Road
Hamden, CT 06517

Tigerman McCurry, Architects
444 North Wells Street
Chicago, IL 60610

INDEX

About the Author

Duo Dickinson, a registered architect, has a practice in residential and light construction design. In 1985 he won a Record House Award from Architectural Record, and his work has been featured in Better Homes and Gardens and The New York Times. He is the author of Small Houses for the Next Century and Adding On, both available from McGraw-Hill.